LIBERATION PRACTICES

Liberation psychology is an approach that aims to understand wellbeing within the context of relationships of power and oppression, and the sociopolitical structure in which these relationships exist. *Liberation Practices: Towards emotional wellbeing through dialogue* explores how wellbeing can be enhanced through dialogue which challenges oppressive social, relational and cultural conditions and which can lead to individual and collective liberation.

Taiwo Afuape and Gillian Hughes have brought together a variety of contributors, from a range of mental health professions and related disciplines, working in different settings, with diverse client groups. *Liberation Practices* is a product of multiple dialogues about liberation practices, and how this connects to personal and professional life experience. Contributors offer an overview of liberation theories and approaches, and through dialogue they examine liberatory practices to enhance emotional wellbeing, drawing on examples from a range of creative and innovative projects in the UK and USA.

This book clearly outlines what liberation practices might look like, in the context of the historical development of liberation theory, and the current political and cultural context of working in the mental health and psychology field. *Liberation Practices* will have a broad readership, spanning clinical psychology, psychotherapy and social work.

Taiwo Afuape is a Clinical Psychologist and Systemic Psychotherapist who has worked with transitional populations, torture survivors in a human rights charity and adults in a mental health systemic service. Currently she works for CNWL in adult mental health and for Tavistock and Portman NHS Foundation Trust in a CAMHS. She published *Power, Resistance and Liberation in Therapy with Survivors of Trauma* in July 2011.

Gillian Hughes is a Consultant Clinical Psychologist and Systemic Psychotherapist who currently leads the Child and Family Refugee Service at the Tavistock and Portman NHS Foundation Trust. Throughout her career she has worked in the state sector in inner-city locations with marginalised communities as a practitioner and trainer, where she has developed innovative community, systemic and narrative approaches.

LIBERATION PRACTICES

Towards emotional wellbeing through dialogue

Edited by Taiwo Afuape and Gillian Hughes

LONDON AND NEW YORK

First published 2016
by Routledge
2 Park Square, Milton Park, Abingdon, Oxon OX14 4RN

and by Routledge
711 Third Avenue, New York, NY 10017

Routledge is an imprint of the Taylor & Francis Group, an informa business

© 2016 selection and editorial matter, Taiwo Afuape and Gillian Hughes; individual chapters, the contributors

The right of Taiwo Afuape and Gillian Hughes to be identified as the authors of the editorial material, and of the authors for their individual chapters, has been asserted in accordance with sections 77 and 78 of the Copyright, Designs and Patents Act 1988.

All rights reserved. No part of this book may be reprinted or reproduced or utilised in any form or by any electronic, mechanical, or other means, now known or hereafter invented, including photocopying and recording, or in any information storage or retrieval system, without permission in writing from the publishers.

Trademark notice: Product or corporate names may be trademarks or registered trademarks, and are used only for identification and explanation without intent to infringe.

British Library Cataloguing in Publication Data
A catalogue record for this book is available from the British Library

Library of Congress Cataloging in Publication Data
Liberation practices : towards emotional wellbeing through dialogue / edited by Taiwo Afuape and Gillian Hughes. – First Edition.
  pages cm
  1. Social psychology. 2. Well-being. 3. Dialogue. I. Afuape, Taiwo, 1975– editor. II. Hughes, Gillian (Clinical psychologist)
  HM1025.L53 2016
  302–dc23   2015023434

ISBN: 978-1-138-79112-1 (hbk)
ISBN: 978-1-138-79113-8 (pbk)
ISBN: 978-1-315-75824-4 (ebk)

Typeset in Bembo
by Wearset Ltd, Boldon, Tyne and Wear

*For our children, Adam, Esther and Zaida Hughes and Abiade Afuape,
and all the next generation in whose hands our future lies.*

CONTENTS

Notes on contributors   x
Preface   xvii
Acknowledgements   xix

An introduction to the book   1

PART I
Introductory chapters   7

1   Introducing ourselves   9
    Gillian Hughes and Taiwo Afuape

2   Historical development of liberation practices   27
    Taiwo Afuape and Gillian Hughes

3   Looking further at 'liberation'; a critical perspective   37
    Taiwo Afuape and Gillian Hughes, with commentary by Nimisha Patel

PART II
Working with young people   49

4   'Holdin' on': using music technology as a tool of cultural liberation with respect to performing masculinities at a young offenders' institution   51
    Ornette Clennon

5 'What's our story?': centralising young people's experiences of 'gangs', crews and collectives to promote wellbeing 64
Gillian Hughes and Taiwo Afuape

6 A clinical service for gender non-conforming young people: what can a liberation psychology perspective contribute? 78
Bernadette Wren

7 The use of film and creative media to liberate young refugee and asylum-seeking people from disempowering identities: a dialogical approach 89
Sue Clayton and Gillian Hughes

PART III
Working with adults 101

8 'Keeping it real': oppression, liberation, creativity and resistance 103
Ornette Clennon, Elisha Bradley, Taiwo Afuape and Amelia Horgan

9 'Women can build a nation. Our disease, HIV, cannot stop us to be mothers because we are the mothers of the nations': a liberation approach 114
Angela Byrne, Jane Tungana, Upenyu, Monika, Devota, Janet, Fay, Rose, Rukia, Wonderful, Patience, Becky, Mary, Hope, Lizzy, Linda, Barbie and Uwamaria of Re:Assure Women's Project at Positive East

10 Liberatory praxis alongside elders 127
Maria Castro Romero

11 Breaking out of the gender binary: liberating transgender prisoners 140
David Nylund and Heather Waddle

PART IV
Teaching and practice within wider systems 149

12 Hard to reach services? Liberating ourselves from the constraints of our practice 151
Gillian Hughes and Nsimire Aimee Bisimwa

13	Teaching liberation psychology *Maria Castro Romero and Taiwo Afuape*	162
14	A story of political consciousness and struggle across time and place *Cristian Peña and Leopoldo Garcia*	174

PART V
Issues and dilemmas — 185

15	Is it possible to take a liberation approach as a clinical psychology trainee? *Dzifa Afonu, Katarina Kovacova and Abbie Unwin*	187
16	Is psychoanalysis a liberation approach? African sisters in dialogue *Taiwo Afuape and Tayo Afuape*	199
17	Towards and beyond liberation psychology *Carolyn Kagan and Mark H. Burton*	211

PART VI
Reflections on practice — 223

18	A passion for change: liberation practices and psychology *Geraldine Moane, with final reflections by Gillian Hughes and Taiwo Afuape*	225

Index — 240

CONTRIBUTORS

Dzifa Afonu, at the time of writing, was a trainee clinical psychologist. She has over ten years' experience of working in youth participation projects in the voluntary sector with a range of marginalised young people. Before her clinical training she co-founded an organisation called Heya, which aimed to support youth participation and engagement with social justice issues. She worked for a project called Voice Collective that supports young people who hear voices, which promotes non-pathologising approaches to understanding young people's emotional and mental distress. She is currently particularly interested in participatory action research approaches in academic and community work. She is passionate about community organising, creativity, resistance, and draws from postcolonial and queer theory in her work.

Taiwo Afuape is a Lead Clinical Psychologist and Systemic Psychotherapist at the Tavistock and Portman NHS Foundation Trust, working in South Camden Community CAMHS, and Lead Systemic Psychotherapist at Central and North West London Foundation Trust Psychology and Psychotherapy Adult Mental Health Department. Prior to this, she helped to set up community psychology services in primary care for transitional populations (women escaping domestic violence, homeless people, people misusing substances, travelling communities of Roma and Irish heritage and refugee people), worked in a human rights charity for survivors of torture and as a manager of an adult mental health systemic consultation service.

Tayo Afuape is an Associate Fellow of the BPS, a child and adolescent psychoanalytic psychotherapist and chartered educational and child psychologist. She has worked as a senior specialist psychologist on domestic violence projects, clinical child senior psychologist and lead psychotherapist. Her specialist knowledge and skills are in the area of race and culture, looked-after children, kinship care, domestic violence and 'pervasive development disorders'. In addition, she has an interest in transgender identity.

Nsimire Aimee Bisimwa is a qualified Systemic Practitioner working as a Community Mental Health Practitioner at the Tavistock Centre in the Child & Family Refugee Service. She trained as a doctor at the University of Kinshasa and at the University of Bujumbura. She also qualified as a Health Promotion Specialist at North London University and worked for the Migrant and Refugee Forum as a Health Promotion Practitioner. Furthermore, she works as a Freelance Health Promotion Specialist in various communities, including working with refugee and migrant communities and other vulnerable families. She is also a qualified community advocate and interpreter with a longstanding experience of working with survivors of torture at the human rights organisation Freedom From Torture. Moreover, she worked for Camden Children Schools and Families Directorate to support Congolese families and improve the achievement of their children in Camden schools for several years. Her work has always involved a great deal of community engagement.

Elisha Bradley is currently a student of archaeology at the University of Manchester. She also volunteers with the Manchester Museum Youth Board, a group of young volunteers who plan and participate in creative projects at the museum. She hopes to continue working with young people after graduating from her degree, either in museum work or as a secondary school history teacher.

Mark H. Burton lives with Carolyn Kagan in Manchester, where they have worked since the late 1970s. Mark worked in community intellectual disability services and in various professional and management roles and has emphasised the linkage of practice with the social conditions within which people live, using a variety of frameworks from the critical social sciences to inform this. He has qualifications in clinical psychology and management. Since retirement he describes himself as a scholar-activist, working on a variety of environmental, economic and political issues. He is Visiting Professor at Manchester Metropolitan University. Mark and Carolyn have also collaborated on a variety of practical and intellectual projects including the text *Critical Community Psychology* (Wiley, 2011) and many articles about liberation psychology.

Angela Byrne is a Clinical Psychologist. Together with Jane Tungana (African communities worker), she initiated the Re:Assure Women's Project for refugee, asylum-seeking and migrant women living with HIV at Positive East. Angela also works for the East London NHS Trust in a service to improve access to psychological therapy for Black and minority ethnic communities in Hackney. Angela's work is influenced by community and liberation psychology approaches and narrative therapy.

Maria Castro Romero has been a Senior Lecturer and Academic Tutor in the Professional Doctorate in Clinical Psychology at the University of East London for the last five years. Before this she was a Principal Clinical Psychologist in NHS Older People Services. In previous publications she used only her first surname; in this book she is reclaiming her Spanish heritage and is for the first time using the two surnames given to her at birth (the first her father's the second her mother's). Maria has an interest in teaching-learning and researching as dialogical and innovative processes; a psychology for social inclusion and equality; and creative and collaborative praxis with older people, women, minorities and other historically and still today largely marginalised groups. She is working alongside oppressed peoples, people who seek help or use mental health services, their families and communities, to construct humanising alternatives reflective and respectful of the pluralist societies in which we live.

Sue Clayton is a feature and documentary film writer and director (www.sueclaytonfilm.com) who has filmed with young asylum-seekers for over ten years, and in 2014 received a commission from BBC Current Affairs on this topic. Participatory arts projects include the Project Phakama theatre show 'Strange Familiars' (www.liftfest.com/about-us/lift-learning/project-phakama), the play 'Mazloom' (www.mazloom.org.uk) and the award-winning documentary film *Hamedullah: The Road Home* (UK, 2012; www.hamedullahtheroadhome.com), which has been screened in the House of Lords and was the focus of a conference 'Facing the Abyss' held at the Tavistock, which was attended by over 120 senior figures in law, policy, therapy and social work. *Hamedullah* has been submitted as evidence to the Parliamentary Select Committee on the Human Rights of Migrant Children (2012). Sue has created an online story archive of her work with young people – www.bigjourneys.org – and collaborates on asylum research at www.uncertainjourneys.org.uk. She is Professor of Film and Television at Goldsmiths, University of London, and Director of the innovative Screen School.

Ornette Clennon is a composer, researcher, cultural theorist and Visiting Enterprise Fellow at Manchester Metropolitan University, UK. Ornette's research combines his work as a composer and social entrepreneur, as he facilitates arts-led community social enterprises with various communities across Greater Manchester, Cheshire and beyond. He also writes for Media Diversified and Open Democracy. Ornette's published books and articles explore the complex relationships between youth culture, the market, education and community engagement. Ornette is also a Public Engagement Ambassador for the National Co-ordinating Centre for Public Engagement (NCCPE) and his enterprise work has been nationally recognised with a NCCPE Beacons New Partnerships Award.

Leopoldo Garcia was politically active in the Socialist party before and during the democratically elected government of President Allende in Chile. Mr Garcia was also a high functionary at the hippodrome in Santiago de Chile. Following the coup d'état led by General Pinochet in 1973, Mr Garcia was imprisoned and tortured and in 1975 he was expelled to the UK, where he now resides with his wife and family.

Amelia Horgan is a feminist and anarchist activist and is currently working as the full-time women's officer for Cambridge University Students' Union. Next year she hopes to complete a Masters and continue her work in feminist theory. She is from London but currently lives in Cambridge.

Gillian Hughes is a Consultant Clinical Psychologist and Systemic Psychotherapist who currently leads the Child and Family Refugee Service at the Tavistock and Portman NHS Foundation Trust. She has brought community psychology approaches into her work throughout her twenty-year career in the NHS in inner-city boroughs of London, working with adults, children and families. She set up the systemic consultation service for couples in adult mental health services in Newham. She is an honorary lecturer at the University of East London, where she contributes to the clinical psychology doctorate programme. She also offers training in systemic and narrative practice, work with refugee and BME communities, and liberation and community psychology.

Carolyn Kagan is a community activist and Emerita Professor of Community Social Psychology. Carolyn Kagan and Mark Burton live together in Manchester, where they have worked since the late 1970s. Carolyn has been based at Manchester Metropolitan University as Professor of Community Social Psychology and until semi-retirement in 2012 was Director of the Research Institute for Health and Social Change. She has worked in a variety of arenas including disability, poverty, urban regeneration and migration. She is also qualified as a social worker and counselling psychologist and is involved with a variety of community projects and organisations as trustee, board member or advisor.

Katarina Kovacova completed her Master's degree in Psychology in the Czech Republic, after which she moved to the UK to study for a Doctorate in Clinical Psychology at University of East London. Katarina is passionate about supporting vulnerable children, young people and their families in creative and alternative ways that both recognise and address the socioeconomic, political and practical challenges impacting on their lives. At present Katarina is a clinical psychologist working at Kids Company in London and visiting lecturer at the University of East London, where she delivers lectures for MSc Clinical and Community Psychology. Katarina is particularly interested in critical approaches to the psy-disciplines, ethical issues in therapy and human, animal and nature rights (conservation/environmentalism).

Geraldine Moane is a Senior Lecturer in the School of Psychology and an Affiliate with the School of Social Justice in University College Dublin. Gender and colonialism have been a key focus of her scholarship and activism. She has applied feminist and liberation psychology in her work with women in disadvantaged communities and with lesbian, gay, bisexual and transgender (LGBT) communities. She also has extensive experience as an activist in the feminist and LGBT movements. She has played a central role in creating dialogue and synthesis between feminist and liberation psychologies. Her publications include *Gender and Colonialism, a Psychological Analysis of Oppression and Liberation* (Palgrave Macmillan, 1999; 2011), and, with M. Brinton Lykes, a special issue of *Feminism & Psychology* on 'feminist liberation psychology' (2009), which received the 2010 AWP Distinguished Publication Award.

David Nylund, LCSW, PhD, is a Professor of Social Work at Sacramento State University and the Clinical Director of the Gender Health Center. He also serves as a Clinical Supervisor at Empower Yolo and La Familia Counseling Center. Dr Nylund is on the board of the Restorative Schools Vision Project and a faculty member of the Vancouver School for Narrative Therapy. He is an expert on transgender mental health care and a widely known scholar in queer theory and critical sport studies. David earned his PhD in Cultural Studies at University of California, Davis and his MSW from Sacramento State. He is the author of several books and articles on narrative therapy, family therapy and gender theory.

Nimisha Patel is a Consultant Clinical Psychologist, Reader in Clinical Psychology at the University of East London and Director of the International Centre for Health and Human Rights. She has worked for many years in the NHS in the UK and in human rights organisations in the UK and internationally. In 2011 she was given an Award for Distinguished Contributions to Professional Psychology after the Psychology of Women Section (POWS) of the BPS committee proposed her for her work around cultural and 'race' equality and human rights. Nimisha Patel has written extensively on the hugely important interface between clinical psychology and human rights and critiqued clinical psychology's complicity in oppression, discrimination and human rights abuses.

Cristian Peña is a Clinical Psychologist working with adolescents and young adults with cancer and their families at University College London Hospitals. Cristian is also the founding director of the multilingual Londres Psychology Practice. In 2013 Cristian worked as a consultant for Redress, a human rights organisation in London. Previously, he worked with terminally ill children and adolescents at Life Force (Camden & Islington, NHS); in a Specialist CAMHS team with adolescents presenting with psychosis, self-harm and complex needs in Greenwich (Oxleas, NHS); adults with neurodevelopmental disorders in Hertfordshire, NHS; and has more than two years' experience with marginalised young people at Kids Company. In addition, Cristian worked for nearly three years at the Medical Foundation for the Care of Victims of Torture in London. Prior to that, he conducted a one-year placement at the International Rehabilitation Centre for Victims of Torture, IRCT, in Copenhagen, Denmark.

Jane Tungana works in her present capacity at Positive East, a London community-based HIV charity, with communities, advocating for better access to medical, social support and care. She also runs the Re:Assure Women's Project – a community-focused mental health programme supporting refugees, asylum-seeking and migrant women living with HIV on their journey in overcoming traumatic experiences – with Angela Byrne, a clinical psychologist. Jane shares openly with the women attending the project her positive HIV status, providing peer emotional and practical support. She describes the disclosure of her HIV status as opening a magical relationship with the women because of the trust and the feeling resulting in hearing information from someone they feel understand what they are going through because she went through it. Jane loves the fact that she learns a lot from the women she meets daily and feels that it contributes a lot to her professional and personal growth.

Abbie Unwin, at the time of writing, was a Trainee Clinical Psychologist in her final year of training at the University of East London. She has an interest in community psychology, liberation and green care approaches, and narrative and systemic therapy. At present Abbie is working as a clinical psychologist for the Brandon Centre, a North London-based charity that provides support to young people. Her main role involves working with a colleague on the Brandon Reach project which provides flexible outreach support to young people who have had a child removed from their care by social services. Brandon Reach is a responsive and evolving service, developing in line with the needs of the young people while working alongside them to meet their hopes for the service, such as creatively challenging the stigma they often face within society.

Heather Waddle, LCSW, is currently employed as a Clinical Social Worker at California State Prison, Sacramento. Heather has provided training at the prison to the organised medical staff on working with transgender inmates in the correctional setting. She has also provided mental health custody collaboration training in order to effect change in the environment and treatment under which mentally ill offenders are subjected. Heather received her Master's in Social Work at California State University, with a mental health focus, and facilitated a transgender support group at the Sacramento Gay & Lesbian Center. Heather's thesis, 'Barriers to Healthcare in the Transgender Population' was chosen for presentation at the university. Heather is currently working to create a streamlined policy to ensure ethical mental health treatment and medical care for the transgender inmate population. In addition, she is committed to implementing a victim–offender reconciliation programme, working with marginalised populations and utilising practices such as narrative and liberation psychology.

Bernadette Wren trained as a Clinical Psychologist and Systemic Psychotherapist, and is now trust-wide Head of Psychology at the Tavistock and Portman NHS Foundation Trust. She has degrees in philosophy and psychology and a continuing interest in the relevance of each discipline to the other. She works clinically with transgendered young people and their families in the trust's Gender Identity Development Service. She teaches clinical research methods across a number of Tavistock courses and is an Honorary Senior Research Associate in the Department of Clinical, Educational and Health Psychology at University College London.

PREFACE

A dialogical approach

Todd (2011) points out that 'Methodologically, liberation theologies are constructed *contextually*, using experience as the starting place for theological reflection' (p. 201; italics in original). Our aim was to demonstrate the variety of practices that constitute 'liberation practices' which emerge from dialogue in the real world with people who come to us for help, when we punctuate *liberation* as our central aim. Freire (1973) explained that dialogue represents an encounter between people in the act of describing the world, in which reality is transformed and new possibilities for action emerge. Dialogue is 'an existential necessity' (Freire, 1973; p. 69), not only because it connects us to what it is to be human, but because it prevents stagnation in our theories, so that we do not apply ideas in ever-changing contexts that have ceased to be useful. Dialogue is therefore essential to any liberation practice.

This book is the product of dialogues: between contributors; between contributors and their colleagues, families, friends, those using services and those in chance encounters; in recent conversations and in those going back over many years. The chapters we (the editors) wrote together were based on conversations with each other, interviewing each other and reading and reflecting on each other's written text. Part of the process involved writing together and being stimulated by each other's ideas, and part of it involved writing on our own and then getting each other to reflect on what the other had written.

We started by inviting contributors to meet and dialogue together in a series of meetings that were audio taped, about their own connections with liberation ideas and how these emerged in their practice. At the end of the meetings, contributors were encouraged to keep dialoguing with people who come to them for help, colleagues and significant others about these ideas. Contributors were thus invited to hold a particular lens about oppression and liberation that both shaped and was being shaped by their life experiences. Not everyone who took part in these conversations was able to provide a chapter for the book (including Emilios Lemoniatis and Vikki Lee), but their ideas have nevertheless influenced what others wrote.

Some contributors were concerned that they could not 'write well'; that writing a book or a book chapter was something that *other people did*. We disclosed that we had also felt this in the past, and had come to the conclusion that feeling like a minority voice should be *a reason* to write rather than a reason not to. If we reflect on who gets to write, who feels worthy and whose voices tend to get heard, it is the subjugated voices which often contribute the most original and important insights. This is particularly true given that there are certain forms of writing, speaking and knowledges that are considered more valid than others, at least certainly among 'academic' literature.

The multiplicity of dialogues shaped, shifted, deepened and at times changed our ideas. Sharing our personal stories with each other not only helped expand our understanding of liberation theory, but enabled us to embed our approach in real life experiences; which posed more questions.

As well as developing dialogue, our aim was to create a 'collaborative writing community' in the spirit of African-American feminist activist and author bell hooks, who writes about teaching and learning in a community (2003), and social constructionist systemic therapist Harlene Anderson (2000), who describes 'collaborative learning communities'. Contributors who felt stuck in their writing were encouraged to contact other contributors as well as the editors to get support and feedback. Many contributors continued meeting and dialoguing throughout the writing of this book, and will continue into the future. It is hoped that the dialogical nature of the book, far from excluding or alienating the reader, will include them; essentially making them part of the text and the dialogical experience.

This book represents an evolving set of ideas which are open to influence and challenge through further dialogue. It draws not just from psychology, but also from therapeutic models rooted in systemic and narrative therapy, and psychoanalysis, as well as the creative and expressive arts. It also seeks to critically explore the different ways of conceptualising what liberation is. Multiple dialogues are essential if we are to allow liberation theory to be responsive to multiple voices and experiences related to what it means to be oppressed. As McCarthy (1994) suggests, 'an uncritical acceptance of theories and practices which do not speak of those they theorise about creates situations of injustice' (McCarthy, 1994; p. 234).

References

Anderson, H. (2000). Supervision as a collaborative learning community. *American Association for Marriage and Family Therapy Supervision Bulletin*, Fall, 7–10.

Freire, P. (1973). *The pedagogy of the oppressed*. New York: Seabury Press.

McCarthy, I.C. (1994). Abusing norms: Welfare families and a fifth province stance. *Human Systems*, 5, 229–39.

Todd, N.R. (2011). Community psychology and liberation theologies: Commonalities, collaboration, dilemmas. *Journal of Psychology and Theology*, 39 (3), 200–10

ACKNOWLEDGEMENTS

We would like to thank our wonderful families, our friends, and our colleagues at the Tavistock Centre who have all helped to support this project in invaluable ways and made it possible. I (GH) want to particularly acknowledge the support from Jim Boddington in this. Special thanks also go to Angela Hughes who was instrumental in shaping the design of the cover (cycling around East London to take photographs of graffiti), and Aisling Kelly and Eric Rindal who commented on chapter drafts.

Most importantly we wholeheartedly acknowledge all those people who struggle with and resist social abuse, and who are not afraid to take a stand in pursuit of liberation.

AN INTRODUCTION TO THE BOOK

Where we refer to 'liberation practices', we are describing practices that go beyond the role and tasks of psychology. We use the term 'liberation psychology' to describe the relevance of liberation praxis (theory and practice combined) to psychology specifically. Chapter 1 explicitly links the editors' personal experience to the development of their ideas about liberation practices. This chapter situates the editors in their personal contexts and histories in order to enable readers to make sense of the positions they each take. Chapter 2 takes the reader through an introduction to the historical development of liberation practices, and introduces some of the key players, namely W.E.B Du Bois, Frantz Fanon, Paulo Freire and Ignacio Martín Baró. Chapter 3 reflects on the relevance of liberation practices today and briefly outlines current liberation theory from writers and clinicians in the UK and Ireland. Nimisha Patel then offers a critical commentary in which she explores the complexity and shortcomings of the term 'liberation' further, as well as some important considerations with respect to challenges for the future.

Working with young people

In Chapter 4 Ornette Clennon describes how his music technology project engaged young male offenders in critical examination of popular culture, looking at the racist, misogynistic and homophobic attitudes in the rap lyrics they were writing, and how this related to the impact of hegemonic masculine identities on their lives. Ornette explores culture as a series of signs that can lock people into believing they must perform their identities in a certain way. Underlying this work was the tension between cultural identity and personal identity which might be morphed into one. This can be unhelpful when cultural identity becomes commodified and used as a tool of dominance – which is often the case with urban culture. In describing ways of decoupling these forms of identity, Ornette demonstrates that when engaging in a creative activity, power relationships which are notoriously difficult to articulate can be laid bare, in ways that can be explored in the young offenders' unique way and from their unique perspective.

In Chapter 5 Gillian Hughes and Taiwo Afuape describe the 'What's Our Story?' (WOS) project which provided a platform for young people to share their experiences of 'gangs', crews and collectives, and create opportunities for dialogue with adults about their lives. The project aimed to inform mental health service providers, commissioners and policy makers about ways services could more effectively meet the needs of young people to improve their wellbeing, social capital and life chances. WOS used film, music, performance and social media as a means to facilitate young people to express themselves and facilitate dialogue with carers, teachers and other adults working in statutory services and the voluntary sector. It enabled young people to build on their creativity, ethics and resistance to oppression, discrimination and adversity.

In Chapter 6 Bernadette Wren explores the complexity of liberation and how the values and practices of liberation psychology might be applicable in a state-funded clinical service with gender non-conforming children and adolescents. The Gender Identity Service espouses affirmative aims and practices, while acknowledging the impact of living in a social world where negative and fearful attitudes towards gender variance are widespread. A liberation psychology perspective, directed towards principled social change, may generate fresh insights into how stigmatising and shaming practices work and how psychological difficulties for these young people become 'privatised'. Bernadette discusses how power wielded by professionals and other experts may narrow options for these young people; as well as how these forces may be contested. She considers how different aspects of the social context might be seen to constitute 'oppression' for this marginalised group, with different consequences for intervention and activism.

In Chapter 7 Sue Clayton and Gillian Hughes, who have both worked with young refugees and separated young people seeking asylum, describe their use of film and theatre to liberate young people from disempowering identities. Gillian, as a clinical psychologist and family therapist, and Sue as a documentary and feature/fiction film maker, have developed projects that enable young people to explore issues they face around trauma, loss and discrimination, and build an enabling identity. These authors reflect on the importance of young refugee and asylum-seeking people accessing *and themselves creating* discourses of survival and resistance in order to support their recovery and the development of positive futures.

Working with adults

In Chapter 8 Ornette Clennon, Elisha Bradley, Taiwo Afuape and Amelia Horgan use the concept of a 'rapper tag' to reflect on liberation, oppression creativity and resistance. A rapper tag is a non-interrupted, consecutive and cyclical battle rap. The chapter starts with a quote from 'Fender' from an interview with Radio Stoke in 2007 about his work with Ornette using music technology to reflect on the limitations of hegemonic masculinity. Ornette then writes his reply as though responding in a rapper tag. Ornette and Taiwo tag into the evolving text young adults they have worked with. Rather than Ornette and Taiwo speaking for the young people or presenting their interventions in ways that centralise them as professionals, the young adults speak for themselves; not in relation to either Taiwo or Ornette, but with respect to their own creative responses to, and reflections on, oppression; as well as some solutions towards liberation.

In Chapter 9 Angela Byrne, Jane Tungana and participants of the Re:Assure Women's Project describe the history, principles and practices of the project, which aims to support refugee, asylum-seeking and migrant women who are living with HIV/AIDS. This chapter centralises the voices of the women who are involved in the development, delivery and promotion of their group. Together they aim to create community, bringing women together to share their stories, skills and expertise, as well as campaign for improved rights for asylum-seekers, refugees and migrants and people living with HIV. This chapter is based on dialogue between seventeen participants, in which they describe how creating an 'HIV family' sustained them in the face of multiple oppressions, and enabled them to take action against stigma and discrimination. Transforming the stigma of HIV and creating an 'HIV family' meant that their shared experience became a source of liberation. The principles underlying this work, of solidarity, empowerment and 'Ubuntu' shine through the dialogues presented.

In Chapter 10 Maria Castro Romero argues that liberatory praxis is often associated with high levels of activity and activism, and often seen as the preserve of younger generations; the underlying, and mistaken, assumption being that elders do not have the energy or level of activity necessary to make social changes. Maria draws on her work with elders, and dialogues with a woman she has worked with as a clinical psychologist, to challenge this view. Maria argues that, in the UK, a liberatory praxis has not been focused on older generations; either in terms of any analysis of their increasing marginalisation and disenfranchisement, or in terms of an examination of the ways that older generations *engage with* liberatory discourses and activities. Highlighting this is of particular importance given the oppressive impact the rise of industrialism and capitalism has on elders, often leading to gross inequalities.

In Chapter 11 David Nylund and Heather Waddle describe how they take a liberation psychology approach in their work with transgender prisoners in the USA. They explain the oppressive context of the prison system, where the well-being of transgender inmates is severely compromised by the common experience of abuse from other inmates and staff, the lack of medical policies and treatment of hormone regimes (with devastating consequences for identity), and the use of crude biological markers to define gender leading to placement with others of a different gender. David and Heather draw on liberation psychology and narrative practices in their work and see their role as re-orienting the focus from an individualistic lens to one of a social-relational one. They describe how their work is at the level of both individual relationships and the whole institutional prison system.

Teaching and working with wider systems

In Chapter 12 Gillian Hughes and Nsimire Bisimwa examine the limitations of current practices within mental health services in the UK and why they are failing to meet the needs of communities who are often described as 'hard to reach'. For many people, particularly from Black and minority ethnic (BME) and refugee communities, mental health services are stigmatising, oppressive and too culturally different to be considered helpful. Gillian and Nsimire describe how they have drawn on liberation principles in their work with the Congolese community in the Tavistock Child and Family Refugee Service in an attempt to address these issues. They describe the practices they have developed to bring them alongside families, in order to bridge the gap between their professional ideas and the values shaped by the community. They discuss how, through their practices, they attempt to liberate themselves from unhelpful professional doctrines so they are able to respond to issues of power that arise in relationship with the families that consult them.

In Chapter 13 Maria Castro Romero and Taiwo Afuape reflect on how they have brought liberation psychology into clinical psychology training. The chapter is based on a number of dialogues between them over the course of several months, which have helped them reflect on the link between wellbeing and liberation, both in terms of expanding how wellbeing comes to be understood by trainee clinical psychologists and in terms of using liberation praxis to inform an understanding of wellbeing in the context of education and training. Maria and Taiwo share some ideas about how liberation psychology fundamentally challenges the essence of mainstream psychology both in its academic and clinical sense, and how such a fundamental challenge is potentially threatening as well as liberating. In this discussion, they explore key ideas from mainstream psychology, such as neutrality, boundaries, expertise and the mind–heart divide.

Chapter 14 describes how in 2012 Cristian Peña worked for Redress, a London-based human rights charity, supporting a seventy-nine-year-old Chilean survivor of torture, Mr Garcia, who was taking the state of Chile to the Interamerican Human Rights Court. Cristian, a Chilean exile himself, describes how he came face to face with the same state that forced his family into exile, tortured a member of his family as well as thousands of other Chileans, and killed more than 3,000 people during Pinochet's bloody dictatorship. Cristian reflects on the relationship between distress and social injustice; the importance of *conscietización*; and the principles practitioners should embrace in the face of social injustice. Cristian and Mr Garcia describe liberation praxis as a living activity. In particular this chapter is an example of the ways clinicians can learn from the people they work with and the power of a dialogical heartfelt relationship in contributing to activism which has a far-reaching and global impact.

Issues and dilemmas

In Chapter 15 Dzifa Afonu, Katarina Kovacova and Abbie Unwin explore the additional barriers facing trainees, in comparison to qualified psychologists, of trying to adopt liberation praxis, with respect to: inclusion or exclusion in the course curriculum; the tensions between liberation praxis and academia; and the power differentials within the supervisory relationship. Dfiza, Katarina and Abbie highlight the impact on trainees' emotional and professional wellbeing of using methods that feel disconnected from their everyday realities and the lives of the people they work with. More hopefully, they give examples of how they have been able to centralise liberation praxis in their clinical work and research, despite these barriers.

In Chapter 16 Tayo Afuape and Taiwo Afuape (who are sisters) engage in dialogue about the extent to which psychoanalysis can be regarded as a liberation approach. As Black African women they both feel passionately about challenging oppression, but approach the notion of liberation differently. Tayo is a child-and-adolescent psychoanalytic psychotherapist who originally trained as a teacher and educational psychologist, and she believes that *liberation comes from the soul*: a fortified and integrated ego facilitates progressive rather than regressive thinking, proaction rather than re-action and the desire to tackle challenges. Despite its origin in sexism, Tayo feels that psychoanalysis has always been about challenging conformity. Taiwo is a clinical psychologist and systemic psychotherapist and her position is that *liberation is inherently social*: therapy that focuses on what is wrong with the individual has the potential to uphold oppression by influencing people to fit into pre-existing norms and adjust to that which is unjust. It might also obscure the ways in which people do not submit to their experiences but resist them. The dialogue between Tayo and Taiwo highlights not just their distinct views, but also the ways in which dialogue shifts them both towards an expanded view of this question. By including snippets of their conversation, they do not just describe the results of their thinking, but show real pieces of the dialogical process.

In Chapter 17 Carolyn Kagan and Mark Burton reflect on their two distinct but linked journeys in relation to the theme of social liberation; this includes their engagements with disability, poverty and urban life; their encounters with other cultures and locations and with intellectuals from those cultures, and with frameworks outside psychology, namely feminism, Marxism, ecology and Latin American decolonial and liberation praxis. In conversations over several sessions, they articulate what they call 'a really social psychology' in transdisciplinary and anti-disciplinary terms, thereby questioning the boundaries of psychology and the other disciplines constructed by dominant social, academic, political and economic systems. This chapter breaks away from their usual mode of writing, exploring a more personal, bi-vocal and narrative style, based on their dialogue, as well as enabling the reader to locate the historical and intellectual references that they make.

In the concluding reflections of Chapter 18, Geraldine Moane, Gillian Hughes and Taiwo Afuape reflect on the preceding chapters – what the book as a whole says about liberation practices, as well as reflections on the different positions contributors take about the complexity of liberation. Geraldine describes how her own history has shaped her understanding of liberation practices, before she highlights important themes running through the book. She then poses further questions for readers to consider in their ongoing dialogues about liberation practice. Gillian and Taiwo summarise what they believe the key elements of liberation practices are, based on reflecting on the chapters of this book, and offer suggestions for what a health service based on these principles might look like. They talk about the role of creativity in this, and the centrality of solidarity and community in any form of liberation practice.

PART I
Introductory chapters

1
INTRODUCING OURSELVES

Gillian Hughes and Taiwo Afuape

We felt it was important to begin by introducing ourselves, in order that you, the reader, can understand some of the contexts in which our ideas developed. Liberation theory is interested in how our relationships are shaped by our present experiences *and* by our pasts, including what we have inherited from our ancestors about who we are and our position in the world (historical memory). For example, historical relationships of domination and oppression developed during the transatlantic slave trade continue to impact on our interactions with each other, the ideas held in society and the nature of our institutional structures, as the Stephen Lawrence inquiry highlighted.[1] McCarthy (1994) suggests that professional narratives can serve to colonise and silence local wisdom (knowledge and expertise gained from our own personal and cultural experiences) for practitioners and clients alike.

Given that everyone has a different relationship to theories of liberation depending on their own contexts, we would like to invite you as readers to consider the following questions as you read on:

- How has your own life story influenced your understanding of liberation?
- How have the different relationships you have had over time influenced your views about what liberation might mean?
- How has your professional life supported or suppressed the development of your ideas in relation to liberation over time?

Part 1: snapshots of Taiwo's journey in relation to liberation approaches

I have described elsewhere ways in which the people who have come to me for help have shaped my commitment to liberation psychology ideas and how these ideas in turn inform my practice (Afuape, 2004, 2006, 2010, 2011, 2014). Here, I share snapshots of my personal journey with respect to this commitment.

Early memory

My family life growing up was largely characterised by warmth, humour, affection and love. The news was always on TV and there was political debate and reflection. My parents and siblings are some of the most thoughtful and socially caring people I know. Creativity was an especially important part of how we expressed ourselves, celebrated life and felt connected to others. As a Nigerian British-born woman of working-class origin, I cannot think of a time when the idea that social liberation was key to emotional wellbeing, *did not* fit. Much of the distress I experienced or witnessed growing up was linked not to the normal vicissitudes of life, but to experiences of prejudice and oppression based on skin colour, ethnicity, gender and class.

I would have been very young, and yet I remember watching the TV drama *Roots* with my family and being both haunted by the sheer horror of what I saw, and inspired by acts of resistance. *Roots* was a novel by African-American writer Alex Haley, based on his family history, and became a TV series charting the history of his family, from a young Gambian man called Kunte Kinte being captured by slavers and taken to the USA, to his descendants' emancipation in the aftermath of the Civil War; it then focused on these descendants, all the way down to Alex Haley himself.

At that time it was not cool to be African. I spent much of my primary school dodging racist remarks about being 'an African'. Despite the painful realisation that I, and people from the African diaspora, were viewed as inherently inferior and deserving of derision, by what seemed to be the majority of people I came into contact with, I came from a proud, vibrant and creative family who celebrated who we were and where we come from. Interestingly, my clearest memory of *Roots* is not the deeply harrowing scenes of brutality (enslavement, transportation in the Middle Passage, punishment on plantations, rape and lynching), but one small act of resistance, where an elderly Kizzy, Kunte's daughter, spits into her former slaver Miss Anne's tin cup when told to fetch her water. At that young age I must have been struck by this story of resistance. It struck me that even in the face of the worst of humanity, there are ways of resisting that are never trivial, because they uphold something of ourselves, even when they have no discernible impact on gross injustice. Kizzy spat in this cup without Miss Anne being aware. Kizzy's action was a rejection of Miss Anne's view of her, and it seemed to me, a defiant act of knowing oneself in the face of not being known. Miss Anne could never really know Kizzy, her beauty and her wisdom, because the vehement savagery of racism and slavery prevented such knowing. We cannot truly see each other when we believe on any level that there is not much to see. This act of resistance also seemed to me to disrupt any tendency to feel pity, at the expense of respect, for those tortured and enslaved. This story of resistance was as important to me growing up as the story of oppression.

I was nine or ten when I heard my dad's verbal support of the miners as they scuffled with the police during the UK miners' strike in 1984/1985. My dad, who normally took a non-violent stance on social issues and political affairs, was supporting their resistance and protest. I understood that there was something very important and essential about collective power and resistance; that liberation itself was the key to emotional, spiritual and collective wellbeing. More recently, I was on my way to the British Library to meet Gillian when we were on sabbatical writing this book, and a tall White man shoved aggressively into me as he went past. As is my tendency when someone pushes into me, I responded by saying 'sorry' for getting in his way and as I did heard him call me a 'stupid Black c★★t'. I could have carried on walking and absorbed his racist sexist attack, but I chose instead to turn around and challenge him to repeat what he had said directly to me. Instead he kept walking. I reflected on my way to the library how common those sorts of experiences are for me and other Black people. It felt important for me in that moment to give back what he had tried to leave me with. Despite feeling angry and distressed, it was also important for me not to spread hate with another hateful remark back. This mini protest enabled me to both *give it back* and *let it go*.

My parents

My mother is my ultimate heroine when it comes to being a courageous woman, but I did not always appreciate what I now appreciate about her. Growing up, my mother's commitments to others, to community and to action, were at times experienced by me as absence, and I wanted more of her presence. My mother worked hard and was always tired. Bullies in my primary school made fun of how she dressed and her tendency to fall asleep in public places. I now hugely admire my mother's dedication, strength and fearlessness. In particular, she embodies a different way of being a woman than is popularised by the media. I remember telling my nursery teacher that my mum could chop apples in half with her hand and open bottle tops with her teeth. Of course my imagination was running away with me, but I believed my mother was strong, at a time when feminine beauty was supposed to be weak, soft and subordinate. Despite tiredness, my mother is not enervated. My mother takes pride in her appearance but not based on narrow Western definitions of beauty, as she prioritises comfort and warmth. My mother speaks her mind and takes up space in a world where women are supposed to be silent objects of an authoritarian gaze. She is deeply loving and warm, but not vapid. She challenges the tyranny of *the Beauty Myth*[2] without wasting time getting to know it from the inside. Every time I act from what feels true to my nature, my body and my authentic sense of myself, I am embodying her. I was told by my parents that I was capable; that being female, Black and working class were not limits. To this day I will attempt at least once to carry or lift something that most people around me think is beyond my small frame and nine times out of ten I will manage it!

I would describe my father as pro-woman, and he told us that he vowed at a young age to make sure his daughters (in particular) would not only be educated but would contribute to making the world kinder and more just. This is not to say that, both my parents, do not in some ways uphold traditional views about gender, but both embody ways of doing their gender that is opposite to dominant discourses about what is 'natural'. My mother is strong physically, emotionally and mentally; she is practical, hardworking, business-minded, fearless, savvy and outspoken. My father is gentle, spiritual, intuitive, sensitive, romantic and loves flowers (of course these are not fixed positions and both also exhibit the qualities I've assigned the other). As a result, I respect men who similarly connect to and love the feminine inside of them.

Experiences of prejudice

I have three sisters and one brother, who I experience as existing beyond traditional ideas about what it means to be men and women. As a result I have always questioned dichotomous and fixed understandings about gender that exclude the possibility that there are as many different genders and sexualities as there are people. The type of Black progressive masculinity prevalent in my upbringing is often treated in mainstream society as an oxymoron. Despite the fact that there are alternative and progressive masculinities emerging within mainstream society all the time, the persistent image in mainstream society of Black masculinity does not mirror this diversity. I have been acutely aware of the mostly denigrating way African-Caribbean men are viewed in British society (and globally) and have deep admiration for Black men surviving in this context of White male supremacy. In fact I would say that I love and embrace the African man in me, the way my father seems to love and embrace the African woman in him.

As someone who identifies as working class, I am also sensitive to the ways in which mainstream society and media seem to scrutinise, ridicule and demonise the working class (see, for example, UK TV programmes such as *Benefit Street* on Channel 4 and *Illegal Immigrants and Proud* on Channel 5) and refer to White working-class culture as 'chavy' and unsophisticated. My experience of racism is that it is not the sole property of uneducated, reactionary people, or confined to the past, but operates in many different ways in the present, that I often do not have the opportunity to talk about, given the anxieties this raises in others. I often feel shut down by a change in conversation or focus on some other form of discrimination when talking about racism.

Creativity and community

Growing up, I was also surrounded by examples of the links between resistance to oppression and creativity. On one hand, we were encouraged to respect authority – for example, to behave in school and listen to teachers – while on the other hand my parents communicated a respect for subjugated discourses and mistrust of dominant discourses such as the medical model. We were taught about ancient wisdoms from Africa and Asia, such as Ayuveda, yoga, meditation, shamanism, Chinese medicine and African herbalism.

Creativity, and in particular music, was a big part of my life and I tended to listen to music that had a social and political message.[3] My mother would often burst into song, filling the air with a joyful energy imbued with wisdom and surrender; the type of surrender that lets go, rather than gives in; that lifts you up not pushes you down; that promotes peace, not passivity. The power of creativity, much more than merely an escape, was a means of simultaneously digging deeper into ourselves and connecting to an infinite resource beyond ourselves.

I started to write because I could not always speak; in fact I was an elective mute as a child and struggled to have confidence in my own voice. Being socially awkward and shy, I would hide in the library at school break-time and read books, as reading connected me to others and helped me listen to myself. I loved poetry and Irish literature and from a young age was drawn to books about social justice and celebrating subjugated cultures. The more I read the more I developed a sense of myself and each book led me to another voice that gave dimension to mine. My secondary school English teacher gave me *Beloved* by Toni Morrison, which blew me away. I re-read *Beloved* four times and each time it led me to other books that expanded the edges of my understanding of liberation: *Ain't I a Woman?* by bell hooks (1982), *Refusing to be a Man* by John Stoltenberg (1990) and *Sister Outsider* by Audre Lorde (1984). What began as reading in response to feeling lonely at school resulted in finding community and consciousness in books; much like the hand in Alan Bennett's play *The History Boys*, coming out of history, and the consciousness and experiences of others, to make links with mine (Bennett, 2004).

The books I read mirrored the strong affinity I felt with other oppressed people, and my family's emphasis on being part of a global community. I was in awe of the special qualities you acquire as a result of surviving oppression. The world of reading opened me up to different forms of resistance throughout history and the dialogue that took place between activists in different parts of the world; for example:

- In 1964 Ernesto Che Guevara (14 June 1928–9 October 1967) spoke before the UN in favour of Paul Leroy Robeson (9 April 1898–23 January 1976), an African-American singer and actor who became involved with the Civil Rights Movement; in support of murdered (by the American and Belgian government) Patrice Lumumba (2 July 1925–11 February 1961), the first legally elected prime minister of the Democratic Republic of Congo (DRC); against racist segregation in the Southern USA and against the South African apartheid regime. Ernesto Guevara fought with a Cuban force of 100 Afro-Cubans and Congolese fighters in the DRC, against a force composed partly of White South African mercenaries. Guevara offered assistance to fight alongside the Mozambique Liberation Front (FRELIMO) for their independence from the Portuguese. As a result, he was heralded by Malcolm X (19 May 1925–21 February 1965), Nelson Mandela and the Black Panther's Stokely Carmichael (Anderson, 1997).
- Leo Tolsoy (9 September 1828–20 November 1910), Russian writer, philosopher and political thinker and Mohandas Karamchand (Mahatma) Gandhi,

leader of Indian nationalism in British-occupied India and civil rights and liberation campaigner, were in regular correspondence with each other (Leo Tolstoy wrote a letter to Mahatma Gandhi about non-violent resistance and love as a weapon). Tolstoy's ideas on non-violent resistance are said to have heavily influenced Gandhi (Anand, 2010).

- Bayard Rustin (17 March 1912–24 August 1987) an African-American civil rights and gay activist, brought Gandhi's protest techniques to the African-American civil rights movement from India, which helped Martin Luther King Jr. become an international symbol of peace and non-violence (Rustin, Carbado & Weise, 2003).
- Bayard Rustin supported human rights struggles worldwide and consulted with Kwame Nkrumah of Ghana and Nnamde Azikewe of Nigeria in the 1950s. In the USA he helped organise the Committee to Support South African Resistance, which later became the American Committee on Africa. In addition, Bayard Rustin supported the rights of refugee people and gay people (Rustin *et al.*, 2003).
- Nelson Mandela's 1997 speech in Durban, South Africa, described how he gained strength during his twenty-seven-year imprisonment on Robben Island by bringing to mind African-American abolitionists like Sojourner Truth, Harriet Tubman and Frederick Douglass, who helped him believe that social justice and transformation were possible in South Africa (Tibbles, 2005).

How my liberation approach developed

One of the first things I did when I arrived at Manchester University in 1993 to study psychology, was join the Socialist Worker Party (SWP). Within the first term I had already attended three marches and left the SWP to join the Revolutionary Communist Party (RCP). Like other members, I had definite opinions about world events and social issues that I regarded as 'right' over other opinions that were 'wrong'. I was obnoxiously self-righteous and would get into heated debates about how the world should be. A number of people challenged my approach to world affairs as 'rigid'. One of them was a Northern Irish man studying media production, who thrust a microphone in my face and asked me questions about what I knew about the situation in Northern Ireland, during a march calling for British troops to leave Northern Ireland. I felt a dissonance between my desire to show solidarity with my Irish comrades and my arrogant stance of knowing, in conversation with someone who had more factual and personal knowledge than me. Soon after this interview I left the RCP and realised that the grammar of liberation could take forms that, although more subtle than direct protest, were not indifferent. I started to re-think my belief that caring about the world always meant fighting it.

I trained to be a clinical psychologist, systemic therapist and narrative therapist, choosing training institutions that emphasised social context and social justice in their approach to enhancing wellbeing (namely the University of East London (UEL) and Kensington Consultation Centre (KCC)). I have been lucky enough to have had some incredible mentors, friends and inspiring people come into my life along the way (such as Glenda Fredman, Karen Partridge, Angela Byrne, Nimisha Patel and Sharon Bond). Each of them helped me connect to who I am and where I am coming from in relation to liberation approaches.

My dad taught me to meditate when I was a child and I began going on London Buddhist Centre retreats in 2006. In September 2010 I became a Mitra – which simply means someone who believes themselves to be a Buddhist and wants to study and live by those principles. As well as challenging me to be compassionate rather than judgemental, I have learnt through meditating and Buddhism how to make friends with myself and not grasp at thoughts and emotions as solid, unchanging things. In particular, meditating has become a significant way of connecting with others. I am learning that despite the intensity and power of the moment, reflective space is always open to me, and can help me see things very differently. Rather than my previous emphasis on being 'strong', I am learning how to tolerate being uncertain, disappointed or even vulnerable. Being political can encourage me to be certain of my position, and Buddhism is teaching me to question myself in ways I was not doing before. Now I regularly remind myself 'I could be wrong' in my view and am more aware of the limited ways I often construe my assessment of experience. Going on retreats confronts me with myself and the ways in which my ego (sense of *I* as separate from *others*) can get in the way of truly appreciating the complexity of humanity. Rather than only focusing on what 'other' psychologists do 'wrong', I am humbled by my growing appreciation of what *I* do that is unhelpful. Although challenging, I also find this deeply liberating.

Meeting Gillian

In 2009 Gillian Hughes and Karen Partridge started working at the Tavistock, where I also worked. It was exciting having three KCC-trained social constructionist systemic therapists and clinical psychologists in the same department and we began teaching and peer supervision together. We realised we had similar values and approaches to psychology and mutual passion for systemic practice, narrative therapy, community psychology and liberation psychology. I noticed that I shared a similar humour and silliness with Gillian (jumping up and down and dancing when excited) and a passion for developing true dialogue. Something useful got created when we came together in dialogue and possibilities emerged when we planned projects that were not previously present. Gillian's thoughtfulness meant that our dialoguing together was generative rather than restrictive, and we often felt *larger* afterwards; having *more ideas*, and ideas that were *more useful*.

All of my experiences have led me to believe that how we do conversation with people shapes experience, that it is important to honour the soul's desire for liberation, however quiet the voice, and that any meaningful anti-oppression movement has to challenge *all* systems of domination and reinforce the importance of solidarity across 'difference'. For me, this is an energising alternative to the tendency for oppressed groups to compete over who is more oppressed and whose issues have more public support. It highlights for me that it makes no sense for any one particular cause to claim centrality, given that all systems of domination create hardship and struggle. Although there are times we might concentrate our energies in one direction, it seems important that we not assume a focused effort constitutes liberation as a whole. Our everyday lives will always present us with multiple opportunities to challenge different forms of oppression and strengthen the cause towards the liberation of us all.

Nature, the essential interrelated wholeness of the universe, has always been for me a fitting symbol of liberation rather than a relic we need to modernise, outsmart or control; it is the highest context, describing the interrelationship between *everything* within it. This explains why its preservation is critical for our wellbeing and future survival. We exploit each other because we exploit nature and vice versa (Afuape, 2006).

Ignoring the mutuality and interconnection inherent in nature leaves us open to the allure of power over those we recast as 'inferior'. As I have suggested elsewhere, the idea that we can separate out those that matter to us and those that do not is as ridiculous as the idea that we can separate one part of ourselves from another. To train psychologists to listen to clients' life stories with heart and then find technical solutions to them could be viewed as equally nonsensical and even, at times, unethical.

Citta[4]

> The sour grapefruit, showy on the tongue,
> Reveals something of the joyous tang
> Of the sky-on-sea mute kiss of dawn.
>
> Sunset's translation of silence
> Versioning moments that pass,
> Eventually dissolves all separateness.
>
> Braiding together connote and denote
> A full moon says 'o' at night
> Before its month-long slow-wink.
>
> This is nature:
> fire–water, sound–sight
> Not the breaking apart of head and heart.
> *(Taiwo Afuape)*

Part 2: Gillian's journey to liberation ideas

I remember a friend of mine, a Black man, saying that every day of his life he has experiences where he is reminded of his colour and 'difference'. As a White British-born woman whose father had professional training and a good income, I didn't grow up feeling 'different' from the majority of those around me. At the age of eighteen, when I left school, I truly thought the world was mine to follow my dreams.

One of my first jobs was as a race relations officer for Sheffield City Council. When I was offered the job I thought 'why me?' However, I came to understand that White people have as much a role fighting racism as Black people. I realised that you don't need to be in an oppressed position yourself, but you do need to be good at listening and be prepared to understand and hear the pain of what this experience is like for others. I also learnt how important it was to manage my feelings about my position as a potential oppressor so that I didn't shut down conversation and silence others in my efforts to escape the discomfort of guilt. I remember sitting with a young woman in her kitchen, hearing her describe coming home one day to find a note in her letter box telling her 'go back to your own country', and feeling like crying with shame, sadness and anger. But I realised how important it was to just listen and hear. She didn't need to know in that moment what I was feeling, or have to deal with the discomfort that it left in me.

In this job, I heard many stories of the injustices people endured on a daily basis. It began to dawn on me what automatic privileges my position as an able-bodied, university-educated White woman bestowed on me. People I met talked about how they had to endure the pervasive assumptions of others that they would not make it to the top, and that what they had to say had less value. I noticed that sometimes when a Black colleague and I were talking to a White person, that person would make eye contact with me, but not my colleague. I began to understand that the world I lived in was not such a benign place as I had assumed, and that much of the social behaviour I was observing around me functioned to subtly undermine some people and elevate the positions of others (and often this process was not so subtle).

I had to work doubly hard to learn about and try to understand the position of those I was representing and advocating for. I came to realise that those in positions of power have a responsibility to acknowledge their privilege and use their position to challenge and address inequality, rather than leaving this job to others. As Michael White (2004) points out, people have a tendency to talk of those who are part of the dominant order as 'other', and routinely place themselves outside of positions of power, regardless of their privilege in relation to race, class and social advantage. However, until we realise that we are also contributing to the status quo unless we are actively questioning it, we too are participating in the disempowerment of many in society for the benefit of a few. In the words of bell hooks (2010)

> We are bombarded daily with a colonizing mentality ... one that not only shapes consciousness and actions, but also provides material rewards for submission and acquiescence that far exceed any material gains for resistance, so we must be constantly engaging new ways of thinking and being. We must be critically vigilant.
>
> *(p. 26)*

But what was it that made me want to engage with the pain of others? I think it is a mixture of several things: a sense of social responsibility, and conviction; a belief that a world which holds multiple voices and ways of being is a much richer and interesting place; my sense of (useful) guilt that I have been born into a position of privilege which others cannot access; my family and the Christian values which my parents instilled in me; and of course, the people I have met along the way, who I care deeply about. Speaking as a White person, we are not forced into a position of caring about these issues; we have to make a conscious decision.

What led me to liberation psychology?

Community was a central theme for me. The word 'community' derives from the Latin *communitas*, which combines *cum* meaning 'with/together', and *munus*, meaning 'gift'. Acceptance by, and immersion in community relationships is a life-affirming gift. We know from research that networks of social relationships protect us from distress (Tew *et al.*, 2012) but they can also enrich and expand our lives. As Moane (2011) describes, community can offer a source of identity and pride; it can be the locus of support and solidarity; it can provide an outlet for creative and cultural activity; it can nurture political activism, and it can support actions, through community traditions, that challenge dominant ways of being.

Community was core to the identity of my family. I grew up with both parents, in a family of four children and in a home where the door was always open, with visitors staying for anything from five minutes to many months. My mother was very active in our local community, which centred around the Protestant church near to my home. My childhood was full of memories of calling on people to collect old clothes for the latest jumble sale, ferrying elders between their homes and the local lunch club, singing Christmas carols in the nearby hospice, and stuffing leaflets through letterboxes to advertise the next community event. Although I now call myself an atheist, the community traditions rooted in my Christian upbringing and the ways of my family have remained central to who I am.

I decided to train as a clinical psychologist, thinking this role would fit with the traditions I had been raised with. Although I found some of the theories exciting, I was uneasy with the focus on individuals and the assumption that people's behaviour could be measured, described and explained. I did my training in Trent region in the early 1990s, during the second wave of mine closures, and worked with miners who had lost their jobs. Their depression seemed so connected with their loss of finances, role and community, and yet my psychology training was telling me to help individuals challenge 'unhelpful cognitions' and, in isolation, build their personal resources. I began to understand that if our work as psychologists is not connected to the social circumstances of people's lives, we are likely to reinforce the idea that distress is the fault of individuals, not a response to disempowerment. I had become active in the organisation 'Women Against Pit Closures', and as I stood at the gates of a mine one morning and witnessed the nods and smiles of miners going past our placards, I realised the power of solidarity to connect people and give strength in times of adversity.

These experiences led me to community psychology, which brought a social and political perspective into psychological practice. I read the work of David Smail, Sue Holland, Jim Orford, and Mohammed Seedat, who all offered ways of using psychology to work not just with individuals and families, but whole communities. Community psychology draws on preventative models so that we facilitate change before problems take a strong hold over people's lives. By working with whole communities, people are less likely to locate their problems within themselves and are more able to mobilise the resources of those around them.

When I qualified as a clinical psychologist, I sought out jobs where I could use these ideas. I met an enormous variety of people with life experiences that were very different from mine, and learnt what it was like for people to live with long-term unemployment, and to bring children up in poverty. I remember one poignant moment when I was a newly qualified clinical psychologist, offering a workshop on parenting skills for women attending a voluntary project in Hackney, London. As I talked through the behavioural management techniques for pre-school children that I had learnt in my training, one woman said to me 'You don't have children of your own, do you?' In this moment, I realised how far my world was from the lives of the women in the room, and how inadequate my theories and techniques, straight from a book, were. These did not fit with the reality the women faced – of overcrowded housing, with neighbours who banged on the ceiling if their children made too much noise, young children with no space to run around, or absent partners who offered no support. I learnt an important lesson about the importance of coming alongside people so that we do not impose our professional practices, and invite a sense of failure when our theories don't fit.

Shortly after this, I began working in Adult Mental Health services in Newham, East London, in a team where community psychology was practised. I was inspired by the ideas of a colleague and friend, Adrian Webster, who was interested in the ways that radio could be used to provide a platform for the voices of Black men who made up such a large proportion of those using mental health services. These men were viewed as damaged, ill, unable to cope, dangerous even, but our experience in the adult mental health team was that they all had their own stories to tell and that among these were stories of resilience, determination, hope and passion. I began to collaborate with two men, Alexis Kier and Tippa Naphtali, who were working in local voluntary organisations, and together we set up the Newham Making Waves project. We sought funding to employ a Black man who had used mental health services himself, in order that we had the experience of someone on the receiving end of services to guide us. We then set up training in radio production skills for a group of men who were using local services, who then produced a programme about their experiences of the mental health system. They interviewed a psychiatrist and the Trust director and described their personal experiences of the mental health system. They talked of disempowerment and loss of identity, as well as isolation and shame, and wrote beautiful and moving poetry. Their piece was broadcast on BBC Radio London, and was used in training events for mental health professionals and presented at the Fourth National Community Psychology Conference in Sheffield. They went on to get further funding to make a short film about their experiences. It was extraordinary to witness what was possible for these men, by simply offering a way for them to express their sense of injustice and to locate their disempowerment within the systems in which they lived, rather than within their personal pathology; it was deeply humbling for me.

I remember one man, Jeremiah,[5] did not feel able to attend our first meetings without his social worker. When asked for his thoughts, he struggled to connect with the group or articulate his views in a way that made sense to others. He seemed like a broken man. However, through talking with the other men, learning radio skills with them, and creating the programme together, he realised that his voice did matter. At the end of the project, he was able to stand up with the other men in front of 100 people at the Sheffield Community Psychology Conference, and gave the most moving and coherent account of his experiences. It hardly seemed possible this was the same man. Jeremiah showed me how strong the human spirit is, how there is always hope, and if people can work together and form relationships in contexts that sustain them, where their voice is listened to and their words validated, then so much is possible. By working together, the men helped each other to see that alternatives were possible, and their collective voice was loud enough to help them believe that the descriptions people had been using about them for years were not unalterable truth.

In the words of liberation psychologist Ignacio Martín Baró (1994):

> Consciousness is not simply the private, subjective knowledge and feelings of individuals. More than anything, it represents the confines within which each person encounters the reflexive impact of his or her being and actions in society, where people take on and work out a knowledge about the self and about reality that permits them to be somebody, to have a personal and social identity
>
> *(p. 38)*

Irreverence towards authority/the established order – questioning how we do things

My father, who I respected deeply, taught me to notice and question rules. He was an accountant who worked in a small city firm and rode a rattling old bicycle into work. He liked this bike because it was solid and reliable, he was never held up by public transport delays, and because it was so old, he didn't worry about it getting stolen. It didn't bother him that this was not the expected conduct of a city accountant.

Sadly, my father died in January 2012. At the time my siblings and I struggled to find a place that embodied his memory adequately where we could go to remember him. His ashes were scattered in the garden of our family church, but only my mother continues to feel connected to the church as an institution, and for the rest of us it has not become a place we visit. However, we have found ourselves gathering in a place we call 'the secret garden', which is a hidden away spot in some heathland, near to our family home. My father loved this place because undiscovered blackberry bushes grew in abundance, which could be plundered for my mother's pies and jams. As this area is a regulated part of London parkland, we could not plant a tree there in my father's honour, so we decided instead to enhance the beauty of this spot by encouraging the growth of indigenous flowers. This became our 'guerrilla gardening' project and now to join the bluebells are daffodils, snowdrops, primroses and cornflowers. My father would have approved.

Over the years, I have found this impulse that my father taught me, to question received wisdom and not accept unconditionally the way that things are normally done, incredibly valuable. It has given me the courage to question, and to speak out when the rules create inequality, and has also got me into trouble at times. It often feels very difficult to do, because we are so governed by the 'normalising gaze', or normative standards widely held in society that Foucault (1980) has described, putting constraints on ourselves for fear of social rejection. There are also institutional obstacles when we swim against the tide and try to do things differently to the norm, so we have to be strategic, work alongside others, and explain why and what we are doing in ways that people will understand.

If we are to be critically conscious of the contexts which are positioning us in the social order, and informing our actions, we also need to be aware of alternative ways of acting and being. If we are from majority groups, it can be particularly difficult to notice alternatives so I think we need to actively seek out 'subjugated voices' to discover other ways of doing things. This may be through direct association with others, or through literature, film, music, the arts.

Maxwell Mudarikiri, a Zimbabwean family therapist and a shaman, was a valued colleague and friend when I was working in the Adult Mental Health team in East London. When I asked him 'how are you?' he would always reply 'delightful!' Maxwell taught me many things about African ways of doing things, and one of them was his (different) relationship to time. He had a saying: 'I have got the time, and you have got the clock.' Although Maxwell was often late – in my Western view – he always did have the time. He showed me that rushing on to the next thing can mean we don't take enough care in attending to our interactions, and we can miss out on important moments of connection with others. In the UK, we are very driven by time, and the discourse of 'efficiency' rings ever louder for those providing public services. But what is the cost of this, and are there moments when it is important to take a different stance? What space is there for these other ways of being, and how can we ensure we hold onto the multiplicity of voices? Liberation psychology invites us to question the normative understandings embedded in our professional practices, and interrogate whose needs they serve. Are there times when it is more useful for a person we are working with to extend our conversation beyond the boundaries of the time we have planned?

Another of the cardinal rules of psychological practice that I began to question was that of personal disclosure. Amina Hassan, a Somali family therapist, was a close and important colleague when I was working in Tower Hamlets in East London, and together we developed a model of training therapists about working across race and culture. We realised that if we were to invite people to take risks in looking at their relationship to the sensitive issues of power and difference, we needed to join in this process too. We decided to have a conversation that trainees could listen in to, about some of the dilemmas and struggles we had encountered in our multicultural practice in which we had talked directly with clients about issues of race and power – from the perspectives of a Black and a White therapist. In the words of bell hooks (2010), 'by making ourselves vulnerable we show our students that they can take risks, that they can be vulnerable, that they can have confidence that their thoughts, their ideas will be given appropriate consideration and respect' (p. 57).

Amina and I found that having shared some of our personal stories in relation to this area, others felt more able to bring their experiences to the training session and the learning for everyone was very rich. Of course, it is important that we look after ourselves when we are working with people who are distressed. However, if we protect ourselves too tightly, I believe we lose something in our connection with others and become less useful to the people we are trying to help.

While I was working in East London, I was fortunate to meet two people who started me on an inspiring journey with systemic ideas – Sharon Bond and Isabelle Ekdawi, who both trained as systemic therapists at KCC in London. They invited me to start viewing problems as constructed within multiple relationships between people, and embedded in social contexts that constrain and shape these relationships. This was a welcome shift from an individualistic focus, and I noticed that when problems were seen as existing within wider contexts and patterns of relationships, there was more likely to be a communal and shared response to solving difficulties. This chimed with the community psychology work I had been involved in but offered specific techniques for working effectively with whole systems.

I went on to train at KCC myself, and was drawn to the social constructionist ideas of post-Milan systemic theory. It seemed to me that one difficulty with community psychology was that it did not offer an adequate critique of the positivist/scientific rationalist frameworks that underpin psychology. It appeared to be concerned with the ways that silenced voices could be given space within these frameworks – for example, in supporting the user movement in mental health networks. It did not seem to adequately question the forms of knowledge that are considered valid, such as societal ideas about what is normal, and what counts as 'mental illness' or 'dysfunction'. Postmodern systemic therapy offered a way of doing this through theories and practices related to deconstructing social narratives.

I was very fortunate to have Glenda Fredman, also a KCC-trained clinical psychologist, as my supervisor for many years and she became an invaluable mentor to me. Glenda nurtured my narrative practice, which gave me a language for talking with people about how their struggles were connected to the circumstances of their lives, and for examining the stories being told about who they were. Narrative practice fits well with liberation psychology, in that it offers technologies for working with discourses of power and oppression, and an approach that is congruent with liberation ideas.

In the early days of experimenting with narrative practices, I remember meeting Joseph,[6] a young Kenyan man, who was struggling with self-imposed isolation because of his fear of people finding out he was gay. Joseph had fled Kenya after he had been attacked by his father, and his boyfriend had been murdered by people in his village on account of his sexuality. We talked about how homosexuality was viewed in Kenya, and how whole families could be ostracised and excluded from their community if one member was gay. Joseph began to make sense of his father's behaviour within the context of this discourse, and he talked about his father's whole life depending on being an accepted member of their community. We looked at the different stories about homosexuality in the UK, and how these differences were reflected in our legal systems. Together, we searched for evidence of gay people in the UK who were open about their sexuality, and particularly Black men who had overcome barriers to speaking out. Joseph began to talk about his uncle in Kenya who had helped him to escape, and this connected him with other examples of times when people had helped him to resist oppressive practices. By exploring these 'subjugated' stories, Joseph showed me how it was possible to start living different stories, even when change had felt so impossible. He began seeking out safe relationships and started learning to trust.

Over time, narrative practices have become increasingly embedded in my work with marginalised communities. But my personal journey towards liberation practices has really been most significantly influenced by the people who have come to use the services I have worked in. Through many years of working in the NHS in inner London boroughs, I have listened to the stories, struggles and triumphs of numerous people. For me, this has been an amazing and enriching process in which I have grown both as a psychologist and as a person, and I see it as a great honour to have had this access to people's lives.

Meeting Taiwo

When I first met Taiwo, I saw someone who had the courage to question how things were being done, and who had a strong voice in spite of (at that time) her junior status at work. As I got to know her, I was surprised to learn that she considers herself a shy person, and that her courage to speak up came from a profound commitment to social justice. This made me think about our responsibilities to act when we observe practices that are oppressive, particularly if we are in positions of power. When I started working at the Tavistock Centre, which has a longstanding reputation as a powerful institution, I was excited to find myself in a meeting with Taiwo, who was challenging others to include social context in their thinking. I felt surprised to discover that these things could be openly voiced! I realised that at times the biggest barriers to change can be ourselves, and the way that we censure ourselves through fear of social rejection.

Since then, Taiwo and I have supported each other to develop ideas that reach out of the box and beyond, and have created an energy that has drawn others in. Our shared passion for social justice, and for developing creative ways of working with those using our services, has generated far more than would have been possible for either of us alone. Ideas have grown out of dialogue; energy and enthusiasm from laughter; and the strength to carry on through difficult times from knowing that we are not working alone. We also noticed that the more our enthusiasm grew for the ideas we were developing together, the more opportunities seemed to present to us for taking things further. We realised that dialogue and joint action were extraordinarily powerful for developing and maintaining momentum. We discovered the following quote which seemed to capture our experience:

> Until one is committed, there is hesitancy, the chance to draw back. Concerning all acts of initiative (and creation), there is one elementary truth, the ignorance of which kills countless ideas and splendid plans: that the moment one definitely commits oneself, then Providence moves too. All sorts of things occur to help one that would never otherwise have occurred. A whole stream of events issues from the decision, raising in one's favour all manner of unforeseen incidents and meetings and material assistance.... Boldness has genius, power, and magic in it.
>
> *(Murray, 1951)*

It is much easier to be bold and committed to an idea when you have others standing alongside you.

Taiwo and Gillian's final comment

As we walked out of a reading room of the British Library together on 13 May 2013, Maurice Roy-Macauley, a security officer, asked Taiwo why she wore red (which she had done a few times in the week). A conversation ensued about socialism in which Gillian told Maurice that the book he was checking did not belong to the British Library, but was her copy of Taiwo's book. Noticing Taiwo's shyness about the book in his hand he looked her in the eye and said 'You should celebrate that you wrote this book. You must write. Leave it with us, for our grandchildren; don't take it to the grave.' We were so moved by this statement and its wisdom we asked Maurice's permission to add it to our book. He articulated so beautifully that knowledge is not something that certain people hold at the expense of others, but something we do together in both a horizontal community – communing with significant others around us – and vertical community – communing with those who are no longer alive, and those who have not yet been born. Knowledge is passed down and shared, and spoken for the future. It is in our inter-actions; our oral history; our writing; our expressions; our embodiment; our lived experience; not in our heads.

Notes

1 Stephen Lawrence (13 September 1974–22 April 1993) was a young Black teenager from Eltham, South-east London, who was murdered in a racist attack while with his friend Duwayne Brooks (now a Lewisham Liberal Democrat Councillor). The case became one of the highest profile racist murders in UK history and led to an inquiry by Sir William Macpherson, which uncovered multiple examples of institutionalised racism in British institutions (BBC News, 2012).
2 *The Beauty Myth: How Images of Beauty are Used Against Women* (Wolf, 2002).
3 I listened to women who challenged dominant ideas about femininity and the feminine voice like Kate Bush, Janis Joplin, MC Lite; music that had a social message like The Christians, Tracy Chapman, PWEI, Afrika Bambaataa, Public Enemy, KRS1, Manic Street Preachers, Rage Against the Machine, as well as music that celebrated survival such as Afrobeat, gospel/soul and jazz/blues.
4 In Pāli, the language of the earliest Buddhist scriptures, there is no distinction between thinking and feeling and 'citta' (pronounced chitta) means 'heart-mind'.
5 Not his real name.
6 Not his real name.

References

Afuape, T. (2004). Challenge to obscuring difference: Being a Black woman psychologist using self in therapy. *Journal of Critical Psychology, Counselling and Psychotherapy, 4*(3), 164–76.
Afuape, T. (2006). Subjugating Nature and 'The Other': Deconstructing dominant themes in Minority world culture and their implications for Western psychology. *Journal of Critical Psychology, Counselling and Psychotherapy, 6*(4), 238–55.
Afuape, T. (2010). Community education: Progressive African/Caribbean masculinities as a challenge to domination. In: J. Guishard-Pine (Ed.), *Psychology, race equality and working with children* (pp. 115–33). London: Trentham Books.
Afuape, T. (2011). *Power, resistance and liberation in therapy with survivors of trauma: to have our hearts broken*. London: Routledge.
Afuape, T. (2014). The significance of dialogue to wellbeing: Learning from social constructionist couple therapy. In: K. Partridge & S. McNab (Eds), *Outside in/ inside out: Creative positions in adult mental health* (pp. 187–202). London: Karnac.
Anand, Y.P. (2010). The relationship between Leo Tolstoy and Mahatma Gandhi: A historical review. *Dialogue: A Quarterly Journal of Astha Bharati, 12*(2), 1–7.
Anderson, J.L. (1997). *Che Guevara: A revolutionary life*. New York: Grove Press.
BBC News (3 January 2012). Stephen Lawrence murder: Dobson and Norris found guilty. BBC News. Retrieved 2 March 2014 from www.bbc.co.uk/news/uk-16347953.
Bennett, A. (2004). *The History Boys*. (1st edn.) London: Faber & Faber.
Foucault, M. (1980). *Power/knowledge: Selected interviews and other writings 1971–1977*. New York: Harvester Wheatsheaf.
hooks, b. (2003). *Teaching community: A pedagogy of hope*. New York: Routledge.
hooks, b. (2010). *Teaching critical wisdom: Practical wisdom*. New York: Routledge.
Martín Baró, I. (1994). *Writings for a liberation psychology*. Cambridge, MA: Harvard University Press.
Murray, W.H. (1951). *The Scottish Himalayan expedition*. J.M. Dent & Sons: London.
McCarthy, I.C. (1994). Abusing norms: Welfare families and a fifth province stance. *Human Systems, 5*, 229–39.
Moane, G. (2011). *Gender and colonialism: A psychological analysis of oppression and liberation* (2nd ed.). London: MacMillan Press.

Rustin, B., Carbado, D.W., & Weise, D. (2003). *Time on two crosses: The collected writings of Bayard Rustin* (2003 edition). San Francisco, CA: Cleis Press.
Tew, J., Ramon, S., Slade, M., Bird, V., Melton, J. & Le Boutillier, C. (2012) Social factors and recovery from mental health difficulties: A review of the evidence. *British Journal of Social Work, 42*(3), 443–60.
Tibbles, A.H. (2005). *Transatlantic slavery, against human dignity*. 2nd ed. Liverpool: Liverpool University Press.
White, M. (2004). *Narrative practice and exotic lives: Resurrecting diversity in everyday life*. Adelaide: Dulwich Centre Publications.
Wolf, N. (2002). *The beauty myth: How images of beauty are used against women*. New York: Harper Perennial.

2

HISTORICAL DEVELOPMENT OF LIBERATION PRACTICES

Taiwo Afuape and Gillian Hughes

Introduction

There is not a single liberation theory or approach but rather a collection of *liberation practices*. However, the term *liberation psychology* is most often used in the literature describing liberation practices linked to emotional wellbeing. Liberation psychology is closely associated with the work of Ignacio Martín Baró, the Latin American psychologist who offered an eloquent critique of psychology and argued for a radical new approach. Liberation psychology developed out of liberation theologies in distinct cultural, historical and political contexts around the world with some common aims and assumptions. Liberation theology is based on the idea that God is a 'God of the oppressed', takes a stand with those who suffer injustices at the hands of the powerful, and joins them in their struggle for liberation. Liberation theologies are constructed 'by reflecting upon the common experience of oppression by virtue of membership of particular social groups' (Todd, 2011; p. 201). The Latin American liberation theologists the Boff brothers (Boff & Boff, 1986) and the Peruvian priest Gutiérrez (1971) confronted the wealthy and racist elite and highlighted the hugely oppressive conditions of the majority population living in poverty, warfare and under totalitarian regimes. They proposed that liberation could be achieved through dialogue and transformative action. It was this position that Martín Baró adopted in the development of his theories.

There are *Black (and 'Third World') liberation theologies* (for example, Dyrness, 1990; Cone, 1997; Ngewa, Shaw & Tienou, 1998; Hopkins, 2002) originating in the African-American social movements of 1950s and 1960s USA (Azibo, 1994), including the views espoused by Martin Luther King Jr. (for example, King, 1958) and in the context of the anti-apartheid movement in South Africa (for example, Biko, 1972; Tutu & Battle, 1997; Tutu, 2007). These theologies describe ways of liberating Black people from multiple forms of political, social, economic and religious oppression. In addition, there are *feminist liberation theologies* (for example, Ruether, 1993; Johnson, 2002) based on challenging intersecting oppression based on skin colour, class, and gender experienced by women (Williams, 1995). Liberation theologies thus focus on changing the position of oppressed people, and emphasise collective action in order to bring about social change.

The liberation theologies so far mentioned have been based on the Christian faith; however, it is not the only religious belief system from which liberation theories have sprung. *Socially engaged Buddhism* views social action as a form of spirituality expressed in acts of compassion, grassroots empowerment, and non-violent social action that humanises everyone (Sivaraksa, 1992; Nhat Hahn, 2003; King, 2009). *Islamic liberation theology* proposes that within the oppressive forces of global capitalism and postcolonial empire, liberation requires a movement which is cross-cultural and global in order to mount effective resistance to it (Dabashi, 2008; 2011). *Jewish liberation theology*, rooted in the historic and present-time suffering of Jewish people, advocates new forms of liberation in light of more recently acquired affluence and power (Ellis, 2004). *Hindu liberation theology* is credited to Mahatma Gandhi (Gandhi, 1993; 2001), who is widely known for his non-violent forms of resistance. All such liberation theologies borrow ideas from each other, but emphasise different contexts for liberation depending on the particular experiences and circumstances those theorists foreground.

It is disappointing that the emphasis on solidarity in the writings of theologists rarely mentions sexual-orientation equality with respect to 'liberation'. This begs the question of whether we can really view any movement as liberating if the personal freedoms and expressions of all people are not sanctioned. Of course, there are some notable exceptions, such as Archbishop Desmond Tutu (2004), who has said: 'A student once asked me if I could have one wish granted to reverse an injustice, what would it be? I had to ask for two. One is for the world leaders to forgive the debts of developing nations which hold them in such thrall. The other is for the world to end the persecution of people because of their sexual orientation, which is every bit as unjust as that crime against humanity, apartheid' (p. 5) and 'A parent who teaches a child that there is only one sexual orientation and that anything else is evil denies our humanity and their own too' (Tutu, 2004; p. 6). Writing in *The Lancet*, he says that in the future, the laws that criminalise love and commitment will look as obviously wrong as apartheid does to us now (Tutu, 2012).

Key liberation theorists

W.E.B. Du Bois

The origin of Black liberation theory is often traced to the writings of Martinque-born psychiatrist Frantz Fanon (1963; 1967), although W.E.B. (William Edward Burghardt) Du Bois (23 February 1868–27 August 1963) was a forerunner to Fanon in the development of liberation theory. A significant amount of Du Bois' work was produced in the early decades of the twentieth century, before the development of critical theory and liberation psychology. W.E.B. Du Bois was an African-American sociologist, historian, civil rights activist, Pan-Africanist, author, poet, researcher and editor. Born in Massachusetts in 1868, shortly after the legal emancipation of enslaved African-Americans, Du Bois was the first African-American to earn a doctorate (Green & Driver, 1978). Du Bois is often called the father of social science and pioneer anthropologist (Bay, 1998). At fifteen he became the local correspondent for the *New York Globe*, where he used his position as a writer, editor and speaker to challenge racism. He received a scholarship to attend Fisk College, obtained a PhD from Harvard University, studied at the University of Berlin and became a professor of history, sociology and economics at Atlanta University. He devoted himself to sociological investigations of the Black experience in America, publishing sixteen research papers between 1897 and 1914. At the age of twenty-six he wrote and published *The Philadelphia Negro: A Social Study*, the first US case study of a Black community, and the first time a qualitative approach to studying social phenomena was undertaken. Du Bois set the standard for emancipatory forms of research long before the term was used by critical research theorists. He published his famous book *The Souls of Black Folks* in 1903 and *The World and Africa: An Inquiry into the Part Which Africa has Played in World History* in 1947.

Du Bois critiqued the scientific view of an objective universal reality (positivism), arguing that human experience is not machine-like and research is always informed by values and therefore cannot be neutral. He shaped the thinking of critical education theorist Henry Giroux and African-American feminist, activist and author bell hooks, with respect to his belief that schooling should ground itself on a transformative vision of society rather than simply reinforce the status quo. He pointed out the existence of structural and institutional racism seventy years before these concepts were used in mainstream sociology.

Du Bois' work anticipated that of the French historian of ideas, social theorist and philosopher Michel Foucault (15 October 1926–25 June 1984) on subjugated knowledges. Du Bois understood dominant knowledges as stories or discourses (the spoken, written or behavioural expectations shared within a social or cultural group) that are dominant because they are accepted as 'truth', not questioned, and are maintained by social structures. 'Subjugated' knowledges, stories or discourses are those which are ignored or dismissed, such as the experiences, views and values of those who are marginalised. Du Bois argued that we are confined by our social, cultural and historical position in the world but potentially emancipated by our appreciation of the ways we are oppressed (Du Bois, 1906; 1994; 1996).

Frantz Fanon

Frantz Fanon (20 July 1925–6 December 1961) was a Martinique-born psychiatrist from a middle-class Black family, who practised in Algeria. Given his own exposure to violence – fighting in the French army against Germany, witnessing military and police brutality, as well as exposure to colonialism and racism – violence became central to his theories about the impact of oppression (Moane, 2011). Fanon argued that institutional violence divided the world into 'us' and 'them', 'good' and 'bad', 'Black' and 'White' and formed the basis of racist ideology. As a psychiatrist, Fanon was interested as much in the impact of this violence on the psyches of individuals as with its impact on everyday relationships and cultural practices (Moane, 2011). Black liberation was about the transformation of Africans out of 'wretchedness' into a dignified and free Black humanity (Fanon, 1963; Azibo, 1994).

Paulo Freire

Paulo Reglus Neves Freire, born on 19 September 1921 in Recife, north-east Brazil, became one of the most influential critical thinkers of the twentieth and twenty-first centuries, influencing the diverse fields of critical pedagogy, community activism, critical theory, feminism, Black liberation, community psychology, Theatre of the Oppressed, narrative therapy[1] and liberation psychology. Donald Macedo (professor of liberal arts and education at the University of Massachusetts), writing in the introduction to the 2004 thirtieth anniversary edition of Paulo Freire's classic text *Pedagogy of the Oppressed*, explained that 'Freire's denunciation of oppression was not merely the intellectual exercise that we often find among many facile liberals and pseudo-critical educators ... [it] was rooted in a very real and material experience' (Macedo, 2004; p. 12) – of hunger when his middle-class family lost their economic base in the 1929 Great Depression.

In his early twenties Freire joined the Faculty of Law at Recife University and worked at the Social Service for Industry as well as participating in the Movement for Popular Culture, all of which galvanised him to 'devote his energies to the area of adult literacy' (McLaren, 2000; p. 147). He received his law degree in 1943, and also studied philosophy and psychology of language. He gave up law soon after qualifying in order to study pupil–teacher–parent relationships in working-class Brazilian communities. Following an invitation from the mayor of Recife, Freire developed a literacy programme and became a life-long committed 'educator'. Influenced by *Catholic liberation theology* and based on living communally alongside those he was 'teaching', Freire's approach to literacy helped oppressed Brazilians to significantly transform their lives. In 1962, 300 sugarcane workers learnt to read and write in just over a month as a result of his approach, which was rolled out across the country (McLaren, 2000). This approach to education was based on the belief that learning to read and write involved 'a process of ideological struggle and revolutionary praxis – or *conscientização*' (*concientización*) (McLaren, 2000; p. 148); that is, supporting people to gain a critical understanding of their reality and their place in the world. *Concientización* promoted an awareness of strategies of oppression and social alienation and involved learning to write their own personal and collective history. He argued that this process of learning could not take place through the transfer of knowledge from one person to another, but would only happen through dialogue.

Freire (1973) explained dialogue as occurring when people critically reflect on their experience, and through a newly acquired critical consciousness, the mechanisms of oppression become visible and new possibilities for action emerge that are liberating for all participants. With new knowledge of the social world, people acquire new understanding of themselves and their identity. Freire (1973) felt strongly that knowledge was useless if it was not connected to possibilities for action and asserted that knowledge could only be termed 'true' if it was connected to the transformation of reality and human relationships. 'True' knowledge (or 'true word') only emerged in 'true' dialogue, where monologue and domination are broken down. For Freire, reflection and action have to go together for 'true dialogue' to take place. Without meaningful *action* words are 'idle chatter', 'verbalism' or 'blah blah blah' and without *reflection* actions are merely 'action for action sake' or 'activism' (Freire, 1993). *Praxis* was Freire's term for the inextricable interaction between reflection and action. In isolation both verbalism and activism make true dialogue impossible.

Friere became Secretary of Education and a professor at the Pontifical Catholic University in São Paulo and received honorary degrees from twenty-nine universities. Following a military coup supported by the USA on 31 March 1964, which culminated in the overthrow of President João Goulart, Freire was imprisoned as a traitor for seventy days. After a brief exile in Bolivia, he worked in Chile for five years. In 1967, Freire published his first book, *Education as the Practice of Freedom*, followed by the world-famous book *The Pedagogy of the Oppressed*, in which Freire outlined his critical pedagogy and liberation approach. He described the pedagogy of the oppressed as 'a pedagogy which must be forged *with*, not *for*, the oppressed (whether individuals or peoples) in the incessant struggle to regain their humanity' (Freire, 1970; p. 30; italics in original). He argued that the oppressor dehumanises the oppressed in the quest for power and control, but in dehumanising another, so too the oppressor becomes dehumanised. Liberation of the oppressed is, thus, also liberation of the oppressor and results in the total liberation of humanity.

Ignacio Martín Baró

Liberation psychology is widely associated with Jesuit priest Ignacio Martín Baró, who built on the work of Paulo Freire. Martín Baró (1994) did not see liberation psychology as a specific knowledge or approach to clinical work, but as the task of all psychologists concerned with improving the wellbeing of people (Montero, 2009). He offered a critique of psychology's tendency to focus on individuals in an attempt to ameliorate their distress, and proposed a new approach based on understanding experience from the point of view of the oppressed. He asked 'Have we ever thought of looking at educational psychology from where the illiterate stands, or industrial psychology from the place of the unemployed, or clinical psychology from the standpoint of the marginalized?' (Martín Baró, 1994; p. 28).

Martín Baró (1994) called for psychology to critically examine itself so that it could be a force for transformation rather than conformity and proposed three essential elements for the building of a liberation psychology that supported people towards emotional wellbeing: *a new horizon, a new epistemology* and *a new praxis*. A new horizon meant focusing on *conscientización*, so that the links between personal distress and social oppression were not obscured (Martín Baró, 1994). As Martín Baró (1994) argued, 'There is no person without family, no learning without culture, no madness without social order' (p. 41). Therefore psychology should have a *new approach* (epistemology) to alleviating distress based on 'a new way of seeking knowledge'. He saw the role of psychologists as supporting people in creating their own futures, rather than imposing a view about what wellbeing should look like. This did not mean throwing out our existing knowledges, but necessitated their revision through critiquing what we have come to 'know'. This new approach was underpinned by *a new praxis*, based on Paulo Freire's (1973) aforementioned concept of combining reflection with social action; this 'new praxis' involved taking a stand by placing ourselves alongside the marginalised and challenging oppression.

Martín Baró (1994) also described three tasks of psychology within his new vision:

1. *The recovery of historical memory* – facilitating people to recover an identity that is liberating rather than constraining through exploring their social history. Dominant discourses often present reality as though things are not influenced by history, which makes it more difficult to learn from past liberation struggles (Martín Baró, 1994). To recover historical memory means to discover through social, interpersonal and collective memory those elements of the past which have proved useful in challenging oppression and facilitating liberation.
2. *De-ideologising everyday experience* – deconstructing experiences so that individuals understand mechanisms of oppression and no longer view them as natural. As Martín Baró (1994) said, 'Our countries live burdened by the lie of a prevailing discourse that denies, ignores or disguises essential aspects of reality' (p. 31). He saw psychology as part of the establishment that supported this lie, focusing its efforts on getting individuals to change and adjust to an unjust social order rather than challenging that social order.
3. *Utilising the people's virtues* – supporting people to develop a new understanding of themselves which acknowledges their strengths, resources and values. By helping people to discover the roots of who they are, they might connect to their hopes for what they can become. In particular Martín Baró (1994) talked about the importance of bringing alive the virtues that enable people to survive oppression, as well as connecting them to what is life-affirming.

Unfortunately, Martín Baró's challenging ideas cost him his life. In November 1989 Martín Baró, along with six Jesuit scholar priests, their housekeeper Elba, and her fifteen-year-old daughter Celina, were massacred in their residence at the campus of Universidad Centroamericana (UCA) by the Salvadoran army. Although nine members of the Salvadoran military were put on trial in 1991, most were absolved or found guilty of lesser crimes. The two convicted (Colonel Guillermo Benavides and Lieutenant Yusshy René Mendoza) did not serve their sentence of thirty years in prison; instead they were freed on 1 April 1993 as a result of the Salvadoran Amnesty Law (Goodman, 2008).[2]

The relevance of liberation practices today

Liberation is a complex concept and as we examine it throughout this book, we would like to invite you, the reader, to consider the following questions:

- What does it mean to take a liberation approach in our work?
- Who is defining liberation and oppression?
- What and who are we trying to liberate?
- Who liberates who?

In considering these questions, we would argue that it is not possible or even desirable to come to any firm, fixed and universal conclusions as this would risk creating an orthodoxy which takes over from the one that we are trying to challenge (Afuape, 2011). However, there are some themes which may help us to orientate our reflections as we search for ways of understanding the significance of liberation to emotional wellbeing. In the next chapter, Nimisha Patel critically reflects in more detail on the above questions and argues that the term 'liberation psychology' itself needs challenging. Many of the chapters in the main body of the book explore aspects of the complexities and dilemmas surrounding the concept of liberation, examine a variety of liberation practices in different contexts and describe ways of making the intervention process towards liberation a collaborative one.

What is liberation?

The *Oxford English Dictionary* defines liberation as being set free 'from imprisonment, slavery, or oppression; release; freedom from limits on thought or behaviour'. In this definition liberation is action for a solitary person, which 'suggests fighting for one's own self-interest' (Watts, 2004; p. 864). As Watts (2004) points out, when men ally with women against sexism, they are engaged in social justice work, not liberation for their own self-interest. The American *Merriam-Webster Dictionary* definition – 'the seeking of equal status or just treatment for or on behalf of any group discriminated against' – better fits the idea of liberation as a social movement, in which the liberation of some leads to the liberation of us all. One such liberation movement, the *women's liberation movement* of the 1960s, campaigned for the removal of attitudes and practices that uphold the assumption that men are superior to women and invited us to think about the relationship between the personal and political. This led to recognition that experiences previously thought to be the domain of individuals were intricately shaped by social structures and attitudes. For example, women's 'depression' was linked to social conditions, and solutions were sought through political and social changes, not just through individual interventions such as building self-esteem. With an increasing focus on the impact of the political on the personal, there was also a growing interest in the idea that we could influence society more widely, through, for example, protest or collective social action (Moane, 2011).

Liberation can take place at multiple levels of influence, from individual actions and beliefs, to group and community interventions, to those that are targeted at society more widely. These ideas are reflected in the developing community psychology movement, as well as being embodied in liberation psychology. We will return to this idea of liberation through multiple levels of influence in the next chapter. However, liberation is not an uncomplicated concept. As Afuape (2011) points out, 'the politics of liberating others and bringing them what we think they need for their own sake is very often the politics of domination. Powerful nations have spent decades referring to liberating countries from themselves' (p. 70) in ways that have been imperialist and oppressive. So how do we join in solidarity with those seeking liberation, without imposing our views and acting as dominators? And why should we be focusing on liberation in the first place? These are questions we explore in the next chapter.

Notes

1 Theatre of the Oppressed and narrative therapy are described in more detail later in the book.
2 Given that five of the murdered scholars were originally Spanish citizens, in 2008 two Spanish human rights organisations filed lawsuits in a Spanish court against the former Salvadoran president Alfredo Cristiani and fourteen members of the Salvadoran military for direct responsibility of this mass murder. During the judicial process the fourteen members as well as members of the government and the CIA were implicated. On 30 May 2011 the court ruled against twenty Salvadoran members of the military, and ordered their immediate arrest internationally. President Cristiani was not included in the ruling, but all of the other accused were found guilty on the counts of murder, terrorism and crimes against humanity. The ruling of the Spanish court specified that the Jesuits were murdered for having made efforts to end the Salvadoran civil war peacefully (Goodman, 2008).

References

Afuape, T. (2011). *Power, resistance and liberation in therapy with survivors of trauma: To have our hearts broken*. London: Routledge.
Azibo, D. (1994). The kindred fields of Black Liberation Theology and Liberation Psychology: A critical essay on their conceptual base and destiny. *Journal of Black Psychology, 20*(3), 334–56.
Bay, M. (1998). 'The world was thinking wrong about race': The Philadelphia negro and nineteenth century science. In: M.B. Katz & T.J. Sugrue (Eds), *WEB Dubois, race, and the city: The Philadelphia negro and its legacy*. Philadelphia, PA: University of Pennsylvania Press.
Biko, B.S. (Ed.) (1972). *Black viewpoint*. Durban: Black Community Programmes.
Boff, I. & Boff, C. (1986). *Introducing liberation theology* (P. Burns Trans.). New York: Orbis Books.
Cone, J.H. (1997). *God of the oppressed*. Maryknoll, NY: Orbs Books.

Dabashi, H. (2008). *Islamic liberation theology: Resisting the empire*. London: Routledge.
Dabashi, H. (2011). *Brown skin, white masks: The Islamic Mediterranean*. London: Pluto Press.
Du Bois, W.E.B. (1906). *The souls of black folks*. New York: Dover.
Du Bois, W.E.B. (1947). *The World and Africa: An inquiry into the part which Africa has played in world history*. New York: Viking Press.
Du Bois, W.E.B. (1994). *The souls of black folks*. New York: Dover.
Du Bois, W.E.B. (1996). *The Philadelphia negro: A social study*. Philadelphia, PA/London: University of Pennsylvania Press.
Dyrness, W.A. (1990). *Learning about theology from the third world*. Grand Rapids, MI: Zondervan.
Fanon, F. (1963). *The wretched of the earth*. New York: Grove Press.
Fanon, F. (1967). *Black skin white masks*. New York: Grove Press.
Freire, P. (1973). *Pedagogy of the oppressed*. New York: Seabury Press.
Gandhi, M. (1993). *An autobiography: The story of my experiments with truth*. Boston, MA: Beacon Press (first published 1929).
Gandhi, M. (2001). *Non-violent resistance (Satyagraha)*. Mineola, NY: Dover Publications (first published 1961).
Goodman, A. (2008). Former El Salvador leader in war crimes case. CNN.com. 13 November. Retrieved 31 March 2010 from http://edition.cnn.com/2008/WORLD/americas/11/13/el.salvador.cristiani.
Green, D.S. & Driver, E.D. (Eds) (1978). *WEB Dubois on sociology and the black community*. Chicago, IL: University of Chicago Press.
Gutiérrez, G. (1971). *A theology of liberation: History, politics and salvation* (rev. ed., C. Inda & J. Eagleson, Trans.). New York: Orbis Books.
Hopkins, D.N. (2002). *Heart and head: Black theology – past, present, and future*. New York: Palgrave Macmillan.
Johnson, E.A. (2002). *She who is: The mystery of God in Feminist theological discourse* (rev. ed). New York: The Crossroad Publishing Company.
King, M.L.J. (1958). *Stride toward freedom: The Montgomery story*. New York: Ballantine.
King, S.B. (2009). *Socially engaged Buddhism*. Hawaii: University of Hawaii Press.
Macedo, D. (2004). Introduction. In: P. Freire, *Pedagogy of the oppressed*. 30th anniversary edition. London: Continuum International Publishing Group Ltd.
McLaren, P. (2000). *Che Guevara, Paulo Freire, and the pedagogy of revolution*. Oxford: Roman & Littlefield
Martín Baró, I. (1994). *Writings for a liberation psychology*. New York: Harvard University Press.
Moane, G. (2011). *Gender and colonialism: A psychological analysis of oppression and liberation*. (2nd ed.) London: Macmillan Press.
Montero, M. (2009). Methods for liberation: Critical consciousness in action. In: M. Montero & C.C Sonn (Eds), *Psychology of liberation: Theory and applications* (pp. 73–91). New York: Springer.
Ngewa, S., Shaw, M., & Tienou, T. (Eds) (1998). *Issues in African Christian theology*. Nairobi: East African Educational Publishers.
Nhat Hạhn, T. (2003). *Creating true peace: Ending conflict in yourself, your family, your community and the world*. London: Rider.
Ruether, R.R. (1993). *Sexism and God talk*. Boston, MA: Beacon Press.
Sivaraksa, S. (1992). *Seeds of peace: A Buddhist vision for renewing society*. Berkeley, CA: Parallax Press.
Todd, N. (2011). Community psychology and liberation theologies: Commonalities, collaboration, dilemmas. *Journal of Psychology and Theology, 39*(3), 200–10.

Tutu, D. (2004). Foreword. In: V. Baird, *Sex, love and homophobia: Lesbian, gay, bisexual and transgender lives (A–Z)*. London: Amnesty International.

Tutu, D. (2007). *Believe: The words and inspiration of Desmond Tutu*. Boulder, CO: Blue Mountain Arts Inc.

Tutu, D. (2012). Anti-gay laws 'as wrong as apartheid'. *Pink News*. Retrieved 15 March 2013 from www.pinknews.co.uk/2012/07/20/desmond-tutu-anti-gay-laws-as-wrong-as-apartheid.

Tutu, D. & Battle, M.J. (1997). *Reconciliation: The Ubuntu theology of Desmond Tutu*. Cleveland, OH: Pilgrim Press.

Watts, R.J. (2004). Integrating social justice and psychology. *The Counselling Psychologist, 32*, 855–65.

Williams, D.S. (1995). *Sisters in the wilderness: The challenge of womanist God-talk*. New York: Orbis books.

3

LOOKING FURTHER AT 'LIBERATION'

A critical perspective

Taiwo Afuape and Gillian Hughes, with commentary by Nimisha Patel

Introduction

In this chapter we attempt to critically reflect on the complex questions: *what is liberation? Why should clinicians interested in people's emotional wellbeing be concerned with it?* We briefly outline current liberation psychology theory from writers and clinicians in the UK and Ireland, to show how contemporary theorists have addressed these questions in their work, and then add our own reflections and critique.

Why care about liberation?

Wellbeing from a liberation perspective

Throughout this book the authors describe how they work alongside people who come to them for support in relation to varying ideas about the relationship between liberation and wellbeing, despite the complexity of these concepts. The core aim of psychology and psychotherapy is to increase wellbeing, but the stark reality of oppressive systems undermines this aim. Thus it is central to our role to integrate the aims of psychology and psychotherapy with both analysis and challenge of this structural reality (for example, Comas-Diaz, Brinton Lykes, & Alarcon, 1998). In the 1967 classic *The Colonizer and the Colonized*, the writer and essayist Albert Memmi described how the psychology of liberation is intimately linked to the psychology of colonisation. He emphasised the effects of political, economic and psychological domination on both the coloniser and the colonised. Whereas Freire's model of liberation was a process of humanisation – that is, becoming more authentic – for Memmi (1967) liberation was the process of decolonisation – breaking free from colonial oppression (Moane, 2011). However, it could be argued that colonialism is by no means entirely abolished, even once a nation becomes independent of foreign rule. In place of colonialism as the main instrument of imperialism is often neo-colonialism, a term coined by former Ghanaian president Kwame Nkrumah to describe the socioeconomic and political control that can be exercised economically, politically and culturally by promotion of neo-colonialist culture, using capitalism, business globalisation or direct military/political control. This promotion facilitates cultural assimilation of the colonised people and opens the national economy to the multinational corporations of the neo-colonial country (Nkrumah, 1965).

Beyond colonisation, Michel Foucault argued that in the modern age, power is supported by more than simply the social structures that serve the needs of dominant individuals or groups to coerce others (what he termed 'traditional power'). He argued that power is intricately linked to dominant forms of knowledge which become enacted in everyday, seemingly innocuous, social practices (what he termed 'modern power'). Power is pervasive in social ideas, stories and 'truths' (discourses) about how we should behave, and perpetuated by people in their social interactions (Foucault, 1980; 1982). Ideas that we come to accept as true can constrain our ability to live by our personal values, and thus be oppressive. Through oppressive social norms (what Foucault termed 'normalising judgment'), systems of social control are maintained. For example, women may be encouraged to believe that their worth ultimately lies in the quality of their appearance rather than their being. From this perspective, practices of power – traditional and modern – as well as unequal relationships of privilege and oppression, exist in *all* societies. This means that liberation practices have relevance in all contexts and not just within the revolutionary societies in which many liberation ideas were first developed.

Traditional psychology from a liberation perspective

As the root causes of oppression lie in social structures and discourses which create everyday experiences of violence, poverty and prejudice, a central tenet of liberation psychology is that the role of the psychologist is to facilitate social transformation (Martín Baró, 1994). Drawing on the work of French philosopher Dider Deleule, Martín Baró (1994) suggested that the problem for psychology is that the solutions it offers for socially produced problems often attempt to change individual behaviour, while the social order remains preserved. He suggested that this individualistic approach is unhelpful because individual attributes and behaviours only make sense when viewed in social and relational context. Liberation psychology is therefore concerned with interventions that involve the transformation of social relationships and structures to alleviate personal and collective distress (Martín Baró, 1994; Freire, 2006). As Martín Baró (1994) said, 'the concerns of the social scientist should not be so much to explain the world as to change it' (Martín Baró, 1994; p. 19). The chapters in the main body of this book explore what these ideas mean in practice, and how those interested in enhancing wellbeing can contribute to social transformation. We might see our role as creating dialogical spaces that challenge both modern and traditional power; where an understanding of the strategies for oppression can emerge and possibilities for resistance become visible. Although this process may begin with a personal journey, it inevitably connects people with others in the search for a more just society. The variety of work described in the different chapters that follow shows how interventions from this perspective are at multiple levels: individual conversations, in groups, with whole communities, and at the level of social policy. Liberation practices therefore expand the mainstream focus on individual approaches to include collective, community and social interventions (Martín Baró, 1994). Martín Baró argued that liberation practices constitute 'an orientation for psychological practice and reflection, a mode of doing psychology, a paradigm' (Montero & Sonn, 2009; p. 4) and clearly outlined his view that this should be the task of *all* psychologists if we are to remain true to our core aim of improving wellbeing. However, before looking at the writings of the book's contributors, it is important to mention some key people who have shaped liberation thinking and practice in the UK and Ireland. This brief mention of *some* key people in no way does justice to the importance and scope of this work.

Key players in the shaping of liberation practices in the UK and Ireland

Sue Holland

The *social action psychotherapy* model was developed by clinical psychologist, psychotherapist, Marxist and feminist Sue Holland in 1980, following her experience of working with women from a housing estate in West London who were coping with emotional distress (Holland, 1992). Sue had a background in community action and noticed that the difficulties the women presented with were fundamentally tied to the gendered, social, cultural, political and economic obstacles they encountered as working-class women. She felt that the 'treatment' approach (both medical and psychological), which was prevalent at that time, was not sufficiently addressing the women's experiences and needs.

Sue's work involved supporting women through a series of steps from individual counselling to talking in groups, and finally moving to social action. Through psychoanalytic counselling, she reflected with the women on the links between their past and present experiences, and their hopes for the future. The women moved from viewing their lives as a consequence of personal failure and 'break down' to seeing themselves with respect to personal histories and rich niches of resistance (Holland, 1992). For example, there was an African-Caribbean women's history group in which women explored their personal stories and discovered a collective strength in struggling with daily racism. As a result the women used their collective voice to take action in their community, such as running their own neighbourhood support advocacy and counselling service, which became the Women's Action for Mental Health (WAMH) group. Its aims were awareness-raising (drawing on Freire's idea of 'concientización') about the relationship between social issues and women's wellbeing, and finding solidarity around common forms of oppression.

From this perspective, liberation is a pathway from individual 'treatment' to sociopolitical action that addresses wellbeing both privately and socially. Sue Holland's model has influenced many psychologists in the UK interested in social action, justice, equality and human rights, such as: Angela Byrne in East London, working with Black and minority ethnic communities; Nimisha Patel in her work with torture survivors and her international human rights work; and Steve Melluish in Nottingham, who developed the Men's Advice Network (MAN) (Melluish & Bulmer, 1999).

Nimisha Patel

Nimisha Patel is a consultant clinical psychologist who has worked for many years within a human rights framework and in human rights organisations. In 2011 she was given an Award for Distinguished Contributions to Professional Psychology after the Psychology of Women Section (POWS) of the BPS committee nominated her for this award in recognition of her work around cultural and 'race' equality and her human rights work with torture survivors. Nimisha has written extensively about clinical psychology and inequality, the hugely important interface between clinical psychology and human rights, and clinical psychology's complicity in oppression, discrimination and human rights abuses. Her 2003 article published in *The International Journal of Human Rights*, 'Clinical psychology: reinforcing inequalities or facilitating empowerment?' (Patel, 2003), challenged clinical psychologists and trainee clinical psychologists to reflect on the type of psychologist they want to be with respect to either reinforcing the oppressive status quo of the profession or supporting the people we meet to move towards their liberation.

Geraldine Moane

Geraldine Moane is a senior lecturer in the School of Psychology and an affiliate with the School of Social Justice in University College Dublin, Ireland. In addition, Geraldine has extensive experience as an activist in feminist and LGBT movements. Her pioneering book *Gender and Colonialism*, first published in 1999, provided an outstanding contribution to the field of liberation psychology, particularly as applied to a feminist agenda and reflecting on the impact of colonialism, given the Irish context. Geraldine provides an analysis of oppression and liberation that recognises diversity and globalisation, and has played a central role in creating dialogue between feminist and liberation psychologies. She proposes models of practice at the level of individuals, groups and communities to transform people's lives. She espouses a liberation psychology that 'aims to facilitate social change by aiding in the development of a clear analysis [of oppressive situations], confronting the psychological difficulties associated with oppression and enhancing the capacities for organising and taking action' (Moane, 2011; p. 89).

Mark Burton and Carolyn Kagan

Few people have championed the liberation psychology agenda in the UK more than Mark Burton and Carolyn Kagan, whose commitment to promoting the epistemology and vision of liberation psychology within the UK has led to countless publications, including their most recent book (published in 2011) *Critical Community Psychology* (Kagan, Burton, Duckett, Lawthorn & Siddiquee, 2011); as well as devising the first ever UK-based English-language Liberation Psychology Network (libpsy) in order to 'disseminate, discuss and develop liberation psychology in English' (http://libpsy.org/welcome).

A proposed framework for liberation practices

We understand the core values of liberation practice to be:

- A belief that those working to support the emotional wellbeing of people should critically examine themselves and their discipline so that they can be a force for transformation rather than conformity.
- Mental health problems are understood in the context of social oppression enacted in social structures, relationships and discourses rather than psychopathologies residing within individuals.
- Emotional wellbeing results from social transformation which liberates people from these oppressive structures and relationships.
- Society's most disenfranchised members should take an active role in shaping and driving the interventions that professionals, interested in enhancing wellbeing, develop. Only from the oppressed can we understand fundamental truths about society.

What is of particular interest to us, the editors, is Martín Baró's assertion that liberation practices are necessary for any ethical psychological practice and should therefore be the task of *all* psychologists and those in related fields. There are multiple possibilities for how these ideas might be translated into practice. This book illustrates how liberation practices can incorporate different theoretical standpoints (for example, systemic, psychoanalytic and narrative approaches); draw on theory from fields as diverse as youth work, theatre and creative media; and operate on multiple levels ranging from interpersonal relationships to national policies. Consequently, we propose the framework Coordinated Management of Meaning (CMM), devised by Barnett Pearce and Vernon Cronen in the 1980s (for example, Cronen & Pearce, 1985; Pearce, 1994), as a useful way to understand how such diverse forms of liberation practice can all be understood as operating within the set of guiding principles described above.

CMM explores how meanings and actions emerge in context, and it considers how wider social forces shape individual experience, as well as how individuals shape their social world. As Afuape (2011) describes, 'Individuals neither stand outside of their social world nor are passive receivers of it' (p. 85). How we respond to our experience will be influenced by our beliefs about the situation, which have been shaped by a number of different contexts (Pearce, 2007). As a hypothetical example, when a child asks a mother to buy some sweets, her response may depend on: what she knows of that child's bodily responses (she has been told her child is 'hyperactive' and should avoid food with artificial colourings); the context of the speech act (they are in a supermarket and last time the mother refused her son had a screaming tantrum); the context of their relationship (this is her sole child and the mother dislikes refusing her son things he enjoys); the context of her family stories about mothers (mothers cannot control sons); cultural stories (e.g. when children have tantrums in public it is taken as a sign of the mother's poor parenting, ideas about 'good' and 'bad' parenting are rife in society, mothers are often 'blamed'); wider social/political context (there is an epidemic of childhood obesity; cuts to benefits puts financial strain on families on low income); and so on. How the mother responds is shaped by the particular contexts that have the most weight and power in the moment and the interaction between different contexts.

In Chapter 1 we demonstrated the relationship between context and our ideas about liberation, showing how liberation can be experienced at many different levels of context, from bodily sensations to the social and political context. In addition, Gillian Hughes and Nsimire Bisimwa in their chapter describe how interventions at any one level have the potential to influence change at other levels. Friere's *conscientización* may begin with just a conversation between two people, which enables connections to be made with others that in turn leads to social action (and change at a higher level of context). Ekdawi, Gibbons, Bennett and Hughes (2000) depicted Cronen and Pearce's model as shown in Figure 3.1, and Afuape (2011) later added to this by likening contextual forces to power and implicative forces to resistance (marked with an asterisk in Figure 3.1).

An understanding of multiple contexts and their impact on our lives is essential in any liberation practice. If we understand liberation approaches as an orientation or set of values rather than a fixed and universal model, our practice is likely to be more open to revision and adaptation in different theoretical, social, and cultural contexts.

In order that in the process of writing this book we did not fall into the trap of developing an alternative orthodoxy that risks becoming a force for conformity rather than transformation, we invited Nimisha Patel, with her critical perspective, to share her thoughts about these developing ideas. Her commentary further explores and critically reflects on the concept of liberation, which she argues, requires a social analysis leading to visible structural, legal and policy changes. It is our (the editors) hope that readers engage critically with the whole range of ideas and reflections presented in this book, coming to their own conclusions about what liberation practice is about. We also hope that, with the support of Nimisha's critique, this book's ideas are held lightly to allow opportunities for influence and challenge, so that liberation can be an emerging concept, rather than sliding into orthodoxy.

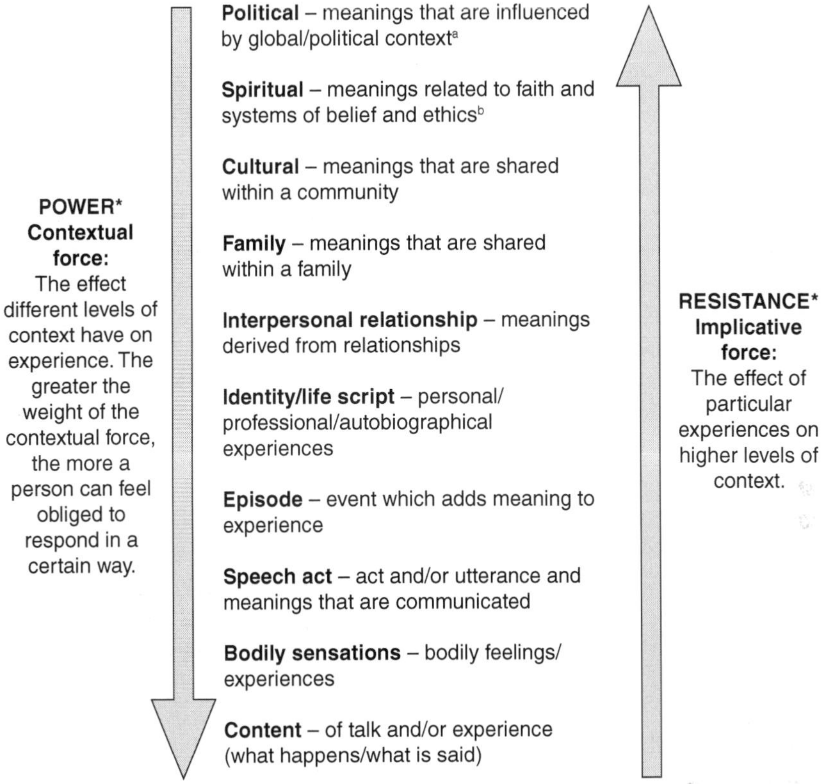

POWER*
Contextual force:
The effect different levels of context have on experience. The greater the weight of the contextual force, the more a person can feel obliged to respond in a certain way.

Political – meanings that are influenced by global/political context[a]

Spiritual – meanings related to faith and systems of belief and ethics[b]

Cultural – meanings that are shared within a community

Family – meanings that are shared within a family

Interpersonal relationship – meanings derived from relationships

Identity/life script – personal/professional/autobiographical experiences

Episode – event which adds meaning to experience

Speech act – act and/or utterance and meanings that are communicated

Bodily sensations – bodily feelings/experiences

Content – of talk and/or experience (what happens/what is said)

RESISTANCE*
Implicative force:
The effect of particular experiences on higher levels of context.

FIGURE 3.1 CMM levels of context.

Notes
a addition made by Nimisha Patel, November 2005 personal communication.
b addition made by Karen Partridge, May 2007 personal communication.

Commentary by Nimisha Patel

Biographical background

Throughout my life, I have only ever known what it is to be a minority ethnic person, sometimes part of a large community and diaspora of Gujarati Hindus, but always living on the periphery, in various countries from Kenya, Zambia, South Africa, the UK and partly in Switzerland. Anti-colonial struggles, apartheid and social activism against the insidious effects of Thatcher's Britain were all part of the social context in which I lived and experienced oppression, violence and discrimination in all its guises, personal, institutional, professional, verbal and physical.

In the profession of clinical psychology, the intersection of race, gender, class and other inequalities were defiantly segregated, and continue to be paid lip-service to, creating new forms of marginalisation for the already marginalised. An enduring memory from the early 1990s is of being repeatedly heckled while presenting a keynote at a feminism and psychology conference, and told to 'stop talking about race when we're here to talk about gender ... go and organise your own [Black] conference if you want to talk about racism'. Even in psychology, there are margins, within margins, exclusions for those already excluded.

Occupying positions of privilege in my work, apparently belonging to a 'community' of middle-class professionals, clinical psychologists and lawyers, I came to also experience the simultaneous marginalisation and disadvantage of being a woman, Indian and visibly 'not-white'. I learnt that while my 'expertise' as a clinical psychologist in the human rights field was recognised and sought after, my name, and my gender in some situations, gave rise to other prejudices and discrimination. I also learnt that there is a profound internalised colonialism and racism, where in parts of Asia and the Middle East local staff distinguished between 'international [white] experts' and referred to me as 'different – you are an Asian/Arab expert'.

The kaleidoscopic experience of multiple privilege and multiple disadvantage have been mirrored again and again over the last three decades, in my work in the UK and internationally. To practise as a critical clinical psychologist, for me, required not a process of 'liberation', or liberating others, nor a transformation or a mystical transcendence from these positions. Rather, it has been an ongoing process of developing skills in how to live simultaneously in these multiple positions; how to scrutinise every professional interaction with a honed hypervigilance which has become second nature; and how to navigate the terrain of professional clinical psychology, saturated with hidden traps and clouded by illusions of equality, community and solidarity. To effect change, I continue to strive to learn how to occupy and even embrace, however grudgingly and however painful, all those positions, and many more; but also how not to be fixed, constrained, silenced or paralysed in any.

Several longstanding colleagues and friends have deeply influenced my thinking, my practice and skills in surviving the double-edged sword that is clinical psychology. These include: Sue Holland, the first Marxist psychologist I met, who thrust her copy of *Das Kapital* in my hands in 1990, saying 'take this, I've read it and have another copy' and later took me to Cuba with her to study their healthcare system; Mary Boyle, who opened the world of critical psychology, Foucault and feminist psychology to me, and who gave me space to ask stupid questions and to create the first 'social inequalities and clinical psychology' core course at the University of East London, in order to name the unthinkable and give me a protected space to consider the intersection of race and gender, and who has mentored me for years without even realising it; Iyabo Fatimilehin, my spiritual and intellectual companion and sounding board, as we struggled to find a language and ways to work against racism in professional psychology; Ann Miller, who was my personal tutor in family therapy training and whose wisdom I sought for years as my organisational consultant and supervisor in my work in a human rights organisation; Dave Harper, whose encyclopaedic knowledge and acute thinking led to many debates, learning and discoveries of different ways of 'doing psychology'; and Leanne Macmillan, a lawyer in human rights and international refugee law who interrogated everything I said, and opened for me a new world of activism and legal advocacy aimed at changing international legal policy and state practices.

In this journey of professional learning, liberation was not a word I have ever used, of myself or of others I work with who suffer oppression, degradation, discrimination, deprivation, historical persecution, torture, conflict and gross injustices. Liberation is not a concept I identify with, yet my work has at its core a commitment to justice in all its forms: social, political, economic and legal. Inevitably, this has shaped my reading of the contributions in this book: all courageous, moving, hopeful and creative; but what do they mean by 'liberation psychology'?

Reflections on liberation practices

Liberation psychology has been interpreted and evolved and has influenced psychological practice in various ways, in different fields, globally and in the UK, as is evident in this book. The core ambition of liberation psychology, as defined by Martín Baró (1994), remains highly relevant today: developing new epistemologies and praxis. The tasks of psychology would seem to require the awareness and 'recovery of historical memory' (Martín Baró, 1994), assuming social awareness is a prerequisite to solidarity with others similarly oppressed; a politicising of everyday oppression, dehumanisation and degradation – or a social analysis for individuals, communities and society; and mobilising people's strengths and resources ('utilising people's virtues'). The assumption that the transformative process of liberation at the level of individuals and human relationships is sufficient, in and of itself, to transform injustice, is problematic, and one which needs to be carefully examined.

The chapters in this book provide hope that many practices deemed liberation can enable and empower people, to be heard, to make demands and to make changes. However, questions to further explore include (a) who is liberating who; and (b) what is the end point of liberation, and as defined by who?

On the first broad question of who is liberating who, it is important that we critically examine the concept of liberation, and the label liberation psychology itself, which I would argue are terms that are paradoxical and somewhat grand and illusory. I believe that both concepts ('liberation' and 'psychology') neglect the fundamental question of power and I question whether psychologists ever 'liberate' people with psychological health difficulties rooted in pervasive social, economic and political structural inequalities and injustices, using psychology as a tool. We might ask also, whose agenda is liberation; and where is agency in the liberation agenda if we, as clinical psychologists, create and initiate various practices, orchestrating and directing the nature of liberation and change? The construct of 'liberation psychology' is therefore problematic, even though the principles underlying practices aimed at social change may be laudable and ones around which all contributors to this book seem to coalesce.

The second question which arises is fundamental to the whole enterprise of 'liberation practices' and liberation psychology: what would liberation look like, and who decides this – us as 'professional psychologists', or those individuals, families and communities we work with? As clinicians and activists, we each have our own interpretations of the end-point of liberation, or 'justice' – shaped by our own histories and defined by our philosophical, ideological, theological, theoretical and other biases, though disguised most often by our professional identities as 'clinical psychologists', or even as 'liberation psychologists'. Liberation psychology for clinicians is not one approach, as this book demonstrates, nor one ideology, rather a broad set of beliefs, sometimes contradictory, and inevitably pointing to shades of grey in liberation.

Empowering individuals, communities and societies in speaking out, in making demands, in creating social change, may be sufficient, for some people, within some communities, at particular points in history, in some contexts. But is it liberation? Social action may result in changes in local conditions and resources, creating certain degrees of social change – but is this liberation when oppressive social structures remain, social policy remains intact, legal policy fails to protect oppressed and persecuted people and fails to ensure protection, reparation and justice? The sustainability of these changes is crucial to evaluating how 'liberating' are the practices facilitating those changes. For oppressive practices are as adept, and swifter, in transformation, as liberation practices. Time and time again, we have seen in clinical practices and innovative social action projects, how oppressive policies and practices mutate, assault, swamp and attempt to drown emergent challenging voices and changes. Or, they assimilate, annihilate and sanitise those changes, institutionalising them and making them 'mainstream practices' in ways that render them even more oppressive and more silenced than before. In this context, an important question for the future of practising psychologists seeking sustainable social change, and justice, is: what else? What else should we being doing? Is social change enough?

The challenges, I would argue, for the future include:

1. *Re-defining 'liberation' as an agenda and as practices*, to include a multifaceted and integrative analysis of power; and to be relevant to the prevailing social, legal, political and economic contexts, globally, in which psychologists work.
2. *Working with others* – social analysis, social awareness-raising and sustainable change require that psychologists work across disciplines, across sectors, across models and methods. Psychologists are constrained, by our very training, theories, models and practices, our history of eugenics, empiricism, racism and patriarchy – our analysis and practices can reach only so far, as long as we work in silos of our niche 'clinical or 'client' areas and bound by our professional tools in psychology. Working with sociologists, anthropologists, lawyers, economists and others, a more sophisticated social analysis can be achieved and more durable and far-reaching are our practices in effecting not just sustainable social change, but also structural change.
3. *Aiming beyond social justice – towards legal justice and reparation*. Change must be at multiple levels, not only at individuals and individual wellbeing but social

and political wellbeing; change must not be simply localised for sub-groups within communities, but benefiting all communities and societies; change must be not only in social policy, structures and practices but in legal policy and practices where states can be held accountable for their failure to protect the dignity, security and integrity of all people, essential to individual and social wellbeing.

References

Afuape, T. (2011). *Power, resistance and liberation in therapy with survivors of trauma: To have our hearts broken*. London: Routledge.

Comas-Diaz, L., Brinton Lykes, M. & Alarcon, R.D. (1998). Ethnic conflict and the psychology of liberation in Guatemala, Peru, and Puerto Rico. *American Psychologist, 53*(7), 778–92.

Cronen, V., & Pearce, W.B. (1985). Towards an explanation of how the Milan Method works: An invitation to a systemic epistemology and the evolution of family systems. In: D. Campbell & R. Draper, (Eds) *Applications of systemic family therapy: The Milan approach*. London: Grune & Stratton.

Ekdawi, I., Gibbons, S., Bennett, E. & Hughes, G. (2000). *Whose reality is it anyway? Putting social constructionist philosophy into everyday clinical practice*. London: Pavilion.

Foucault, M. (1980). *Power/knowledge: Selected interviews and other writings 1971–1977*. New York: Harvester Wheatsheaf.

Foucault, M. (1982). The subject of power. In: H. Dreyfus & P. Rabinow (Eds), *Michael Foucault: Beyond structuralism and hermeneutics*. New York: Harvester Wheatsheaf.

Freire, P. (2006). *Education for critical consciousness*. London: Continuum.

Holland, S. (1992). From social abuse to social action: A neighborhood psychotherapy and social action project for women. In: J. Ussher & P. Nicholson (Eds), *Gender issues in clinical psychology* (pp. 68–77). London: Routledge.

Kagan, C., Burton, M., Duckett, P., Lawthorn, R. & Siddiquee, A. (2011). *Critical community psychology*. Chichester: BPS Blackwell.

Martín Baró, I. (1994). *Writings for a liberation psychology*. New York: Harvard University Press.

Melluish, S. & Bulmer, D. (1999). Rebuilding solidarity: an account of a men's health action project. *Journal of Community and Applied Social Psychology, 9*, 93–100.

Memmi, A. (1967). *The colonizer and the colonized* (Howard Greenfeld Trans.). Boston, MA: Boston Press.

Moane, G. (2011). *Gender and colonialism: A psychological analysis of oppression and liberation* (2nd ed.). London: Macmillan Press.

Montero, M., & Sonn, C.C. (Eds) (2009). *Psychology of liberation: Theory and applications*. New York: Springer.

Nkrumah, K. (1965). *Neo-colonialism: The last stage of imperialism*. London: Thomas Nelson & Sons, Ltd.

Patel, N. (2003). Clinical psychology: Reinforcing inequalities or facilitating empowerment? *The International Journal of Human Rights, 7*(1), 16–39.

Pearce, W.B. (1994). *Interpersonal communication: Making social worlds*. New York: Harper Collins.

Pearce, W.B. (2007). *Making social worlds: A communication perspective*. Oxford: Blackwell.

PART II
Working with young people

4

'HOLDIN' ON'

Using music technology as a tool of cultural liberation with respect to performing masculinities at a young offenders' institution

Ornette Clennon

Introduction

Music technology project

I am an Afro-Caribbean academic composer and musician (male) who has worked across virtually all sectors of the community for over twenty years. My main vehicle for exploring community issues is music. I have been drawn to working with young people because of their extraordinary capacity for invention and creativity. As a community researcher based at Manchester Metropolitan University, my research asks questions about identity and culture and what it means to be both a producer and consumer of culture. For me, these questions are of prime importance because I notice that sometimes the very culture our young people produce and consume is complicit in trapping them in a system of low aspiration and underachievement. In this chapter I will present my findings from a piece of ethnographic research[1] that I conducted at Her Majesty's Prison Youth Offending Institution (HMPYOI) Werrington between 2006 and 2007 with young male offenders. I will focus on the second project, called *Sonic [db] Music Technology Project*, a unique music technology and music industry programme that took place in youth offending institutions across Staffordshire and Stoke-on-Trent. Staffordshire Arts and Museum Service and Make Some Noise set up *Sonic [db]* with additional help from Arts Council England, West Midlands.

In this project, we worked as a multidisciplinary staff team that included artists, researchers and an HMPYOI Werrington education officer, who integrated our work with the institution's education programme. Our sessions were also attended by prison officers who were assigned to assist us during moments of physical conflict. The young men ('trainees') took part in creative writing and music technology activities. The way in which the music technology elements and creative writing activities were delivered was always trainee-led, with trainees encouraged to help and support each other, even though this very act was often a new experience for them.

The music technology teaching involved the trainees playing out 'roles' within the music industry and specifically the studio set up. We realised that each role of *artist, engineer, producer* and *songwriter* had a well-defined (although sometimes overlapping) set of skills that could be easily taught, in order to fulfil that particular function. The studio roles were always executed in teams, so team work and social interaction were necessary in order to complete a track and therefore developed the trainees' social skills. The programme was designed to be modular and to give each trainee the opportunity to own his individual learning path via the creation of an individual learning programme (ILP).

We found that over time the trainees owned the roles and the relationships the roles implied to such an extent that they no longer needed to be reminded of their responsibilities in order to complete their tasks. We invited certain trainees to assume the role of informal peer-to-peer mentor to work with, encourage and assist other trainees – a kind of 'buddy' system. We felt this needed to be implicit in the way we worked so that it would grow organically within the dynamic of the group. This form of mentoring took many different dimensions during the programme, as certain roles such as *producer* already had an element of mentoring within them in order to get the best out of the *artist*.

We encouraged the group to negotiate its own boundaries and reach a consensus about enforcing them. It was through the structured use of creative writing sessions that an attempt was made at encouraging the trainees to examine the beliefs and attitudes towards issues, such as gun crime, they brought to the group. Using their written material as a starting point, we were able to have discussions with the trainees about their lyrics and track developments in both their ideological and lyrical thinking.

As part of the programme we helped the trainees to action-plan their futures upon leaving HMPYOI Werrington, by constructing resettlement packages. The packages consisted of contacts for follow-up projects or educational opportunities that the trainees had identified as part in their ILPs. Unfortunately, it was very difficult to follow up on the progress of our older trainees on the outside due to them being transferred to the Adult Probation Service, to which we did not have easy access.

My approach to liberation psychology

In this project, I borrowed heavily from liberation psychology in the way that I encouraged the young men to use their lyric-writing as an opportunity to reflect on their pasts, in order to plot their future (Martín Baró, 1994). It was also important for them to critically evaluate their pasts against the cultural signifiers and norms they were expected to follow on the 'streets'. Encouraging the young men to see themselves as independent human actors and not just by-products of cultural norms based on violence (or its commercial representations) seemed to be extremely important. Rivera, Maldonado and Alarcon (2013) call this process of reflection a 'new praxis that emerges out of the liberation psychology perspective' (p. 35) and coin the term 'defetishisation' to describe it (whereas fetishism is the tendency for commodities to be represented in a way that obscures the means of their production and the impact of that production on the social welfare of those producing and consuming those goods, defetishisation refers to humanising people by making visible or 'surfacing' these impacts). In order to 'defetishise' the young men, I used a Map of Me (Clennon, 2013) questionnaire to facilitate dialogue (see description of research below). The questionnaires facilitated the process of 'problematisation' with respect to challenging views that were generally accepted and held as universal in order to encourage the young men to see underlying structures of oppression more clearly, such that answering reflective questions 'sensitizes, denaturalizes, and establishes the concrete and affective bases necessary to motivate changes, thus inducing concrete transforming actions' (Montero, 2009; p. 80). In this way, the young men were able to think about their 'histories' in transformative ways. I did this by inviting them to critically reflect on their self-speak and their 'world/street view'. These reflections led to realisations about themselves, their present situations and their future aspirations. I will illustrate these points later when I briefly present this process of 'conscientization' (Freire, 1973) or 'consciousness raising' through my session notes and the young men's lyrics, both sketches and finished products.

Research as intervention: music technology sessions

As the researcher, I conducted a version of performance ethnography (Carless & Douglas, 2010) where I used the processes of writing, performing and recording MC (rap) tracks as participatory tools to gather qualitative data around the participants' views about their identities and popular culture. Although we conducted music technology sessions, it was the creative writing activities in particular that helped me to engage the young men in dialogue 'on the fly' because they were often in the 'flow' of writing their lyrics (Csikszentmihalyi & Csikszentmihalyi, 1988) and as a result were less inhibited talking about their feelings, beliefs and views. In fact, the creative process enabled the young men to reflect on their thoughts and attitudes, which meant further enquiry about the material that they were writing often felt natural. We worked with eight young men, aged between sixteen and eighteen years old, in a group at any one time. We had a core of seven regular participants but over the course of the twenty-week programme we worked with fifteen individuals in total. In order to assist with the creative writing element, I developed a conversational tool called the Map of Me, which took the form of a structured mind map of the four most important things to them in that moment (see Appendix). They mapped out their issues (and sub-issues) across four quadrants on a blank piece of paper and were then encouraged to draw lines of connection between the issues and explain why they were connected. These mind maps were often the first steps in expressing some of the emotions the young men had kept bottled up. Once the Maps of Me were drawn, the trainees started constructing their lyrics based on the content of the Map of Me. I analysed the lyric sketches and my session notes using thematic analysis that highlighted crosscutting themes (Attride-Stirling, 2001) of resistance and liberation.

Keeping in mind my privileged and relatively powerful position as a researcher in this environment (Wallerstein & Duran, 2006), I sought informed consent on a continuous basis, where trainees were advised that they could participate in, or opt out of, any of the programme activities that they wanted to and not face any penalties if they withdrew from the research at any time (Daymon & Holloway, 2011).

Emerging themes from the research

The finished songs can be heard on the Werrington Album (2007). I will briefly present what seemed to be the young men's 'conscientization', using excerpts of their lyrics and my session notes, detailing their journeys from resistance to liberation.[2]

From resistance

What does being a man mean?

Many of the young men grappled with this central question during their creative writing sessions. Their identities seemed heavily influenced by their experiences on 'the streets'. Below is an excerpt of dialogue with one of the young people about his Map of Me and shows how the Map of Me was used to generate lyrics.

Dialogue

OB: Got a phone call when I was in youth club. Got to the office and went on the phone and couldn't understand much 'cause there was too much tears, until my brother told me what happened to my cousin and how he got found.... I had no feelings going through my body at the time just anger. I just wanted to catch the person who done it and put their family through the same as what mine went through

OC: Who shot your cousin?

OB: Haters – people see you with more money than usual and they owe you money and you put them in their place, ruff them up and when you get caught slipping [you get killed]

OC: What's the best way to avoid all this?

OB: Don't get involved with the streets and the streets won't get involved with you. Anger won't stop 'til someone pays for it. The best way is them to go through what happened to me.

(OB drew the word 'streets' and a circular arrow to depict his thoughts).

OC: There is a vicious circle of violence on the street.
> *(Session 3, OB's discussion of his Map of Me with the researcher)*

Lyrics

> I rep for my endz everyday until I'm older
> Times have changed the hood's getting colder
> My cousin died my mum cried, I just wanted to hold her
> Rest her olive skin, her black hair upon my shoulder
> Tell my auntie Sue her kid was a soldier
> My cousin went in style that's all I could of told ya
> Reminiscing looking at his pictures in (a) folder
> Looking at the sky as the world's getting colder.
> *(Session 10, OB's initial lyrics derived from his Map of Me)*

The lyrics above represent the ways in which, for many of the young men, their masculinities were predominantly shaped by the violence of 'the streets'. The trainee above lyrically recounted the memory of the shooting of his cousin. In an earlier session, he wrote lyrics recalling the emotions that ran through his mind:

> The beats ain't like the streets, the streets fight back
> They fight back over coke and crack
> 'Cause everyday we got enemies all around us
> They pick fights and they try to surround us
>
> This shit's deep, my cousin's dead
> Point blank straight to his head
> No hospital nurses
> No hospital bed.
> *(Session 3, OB's initial lyrics derived from his Map of Me)*

It is unclear how much of the style and lyrical content of the songs were influenced by a commercial representation of 'street life' or from the trainees' direct experiences.

Much of the creative writing activities seemed to enable the young men to consolidate and reflect on their past. They appeared to describe a type of 'normality' that was inherently chaotic while simultaneously yearning for a new 'normality' without crime:

> We live our life in the slums around drugs and guns
> Our parents got to live off benefit of government funds
> We got to sell green and crack to look after our sons
> It's the way that we're living it's the way that it runs
> I was raised on the block and I was known as a real kid

> The government judge me by the way that I still live
> Shotting drugs on the block is known as the realness
> If you've lived the life I've lived I know that you feel this'
> *(Session 16 OB's final lyrics; Werrington Album, 2007)*

Being tough

Newton (1994) suggests that in prison the 'siege mentality' (Bar-Tal, 2012; p. 996) derived from prisoners' perceptions and experiences of 'street culture' is often translated into a 'hierarchy' of 'dominant masculinities' where 'the prisoner's masculinity is in fact besieged from every side: through loss of autonomy and independence, enforced submission to authority, lack of access to material goods, all of which are central to his status as a man' (p. 197). Sykes (1958) also describes a prisoner's experience of being reduced 'to the weak, helpless, dependent status of childhood' (p. 76). The stress that this experience causes was briefly alluded to by one trainee, A1, who wrote a piece called 'Jailhouse':

Jailhouse

> Every new day in jail you see new faces
> If they're suicidal they take their shoelaces
> Couple guys are safe then you meet a few racists
> Catch them slippin' out on social then do basic
>
> I remember the day getting 2 do 2 year
> I told my mum that my time will come near
> I gotta keep my head up in dis jail a fun fair
> I know my real boys cos its starts to come clear.

A1's lyrical intervention revealed the debilitating stress of incarceration that Sykes (1958) describes. Although A1 said that it made him feel upset for his peers who self-harmed, it was unlikely that he would have openly revealed his own feelings ('I gotta keep my head up in dis jail a fun fair'). Newton (1994) suggests that a show of vulnerability of this kind could leave the inmates prone to subordination by others, as they would be perceived as being 'weak'.

Maintaining your distance

Connell and Messerschmidt (2005) describe the avoidance of any perceived vulnerability as an aspect of 'hegemonic masculinity', which they describe as a constructed ideal of masculinity. They continue to explain that this concept of masculinity, originally postulated by Connell (1987), embodied the most honoured way of being a man, required all other men to position themselves in relation to it and legitimated the global subordination of women to men (Connell & Messerschmidt,

2005). When we touched on homophobia during one of our lyric-writing sessions, this performative[3] form of masculinity was played out 'through a series of hierarchical relations: rejection and suppression of femininity and homosexual desire, command and control' (Segal, 1990; p. 205), as described in my session notes:

> During the ILP (Individual Learning Plan) assessment, L expressed his personal views about homosexuality and religion. L said homosexuals should be stoned for being who they are. When challenged by OB, who asked him what his family would do if someone in the family were found to be gay, L said that his family would disown them. After an intervention from me, reminding him that people such as Hitler also held such views, L adjusted his thinking slightly and said that they would be punished by God but he himself did not condone harming (killing) gay people (or anyone else). L explained that he was conditioned to think in a homophobic way from his Jamaican upbringing and did not really know any other way of viewing the subject until the dialogue that ensued.
>
> *(Session 6 notes)*

What is interesting to note from the above is how the process of problematisation encouraged the young men to think critically about where their homophobic opinions originated. This led one of the trainees to defetishise the culturally normed homophobic views being expressed by humanising the discussion with the introduction of the topic of family. The almost redemptive or liberating effect of re-locating their masculinities into the context of family will be discussed shortly.

Musically, the most prominent aspect of hegemonic masculinity was expressed in their attitudes towards those who were deemed to have broken their 'solidarity and the unwritten code' (Newton, 1994; p. 195), usually constructed in opposition to the authority figures in the institution. The young men appeared to form a fratriarchy (patriarchy and fraternity combined) that Remy (1990) describes as a system 'based simply on the self-interest of the association of men itself' (p. 45). However, people perceived as breaking the solidarity of the fratriarchy were called 'snitches' (Werrington Album, 2007), as in the case of these lyrics:

> I've got these bitches that irritate me
> Like itches that turn into snitches every time they got beefs.
> *(Session 2 OB's initial lyrics for 'Snitches'; Werrington Album, 2007)*

OB implies in his sketches that the fratriarchy expects issues to be dealt with 'in house' without going to the authority figures who are sometimes seen as the 'oppressors'. OB's use of the word 'bitches' is a clear example of Connell's 'hegomonic masculinity', where its purpose is to exclude and subjugate women while placing other men into an ordered hierarchy. Reflecting on the ways in which women were being placed at the bottom of the order, by highlighting that any man caught being a 'snitch' is automatically relegated to this lowest order within the fratriarchy, enabled OB to reflect on the use of his language differently.

Towards liberation

Here is an excerpt from my notes which traces what seems to be a process of 'conscientization'.

'Nigger' and slavery

> F revealed that his upbringing has been challenging as he, his mum and brother moved from flat to flat on a regular basis. This transient upbringing led him to sell drugs in order to raise money for the family, in his earlier days. However, F soon found legal ways of making money through music (in partnership with a producer) by selling instrumental tracks to Producers, Managers and the like.
>
> F's family loves his music, which is not normally gun related. F said that he never uses the word 'nigger' in his lyrics because it 'creates more wars'. When asked about the idea of reclaiming the word towards desensitising it, F said that he believed his peers are only 'copying or using it to be offensive' and no real thought was put into its usage on their part. F said he would only use the word to refer to and contextualise Slavery.
>
> For F the word 'nigger' opens up a line of thought towards his emerging Black consciousness (awareness of History). *'It's good to know your roots'* F said as he described that he was brought up by his white 'nan'. Because of his cultural awareness, the word 'nigger' does not 'phase' him. F's appreciation of Black History also manifests itself in his taste in music and how he feels that without Motown and the music of Sam Cooke there would be no Hip-Hop, as he feels that especially the music of Sam Cooke deals with the experience of slavery.
>
> *(Session 15 notes)*

The excerpt above charts the significance for F of 'recovery of historical memory'[4] (Martín Baró, 1994; p. 30) and the implied importance of his family.

The recovery of historical memory

Rivera, Maldonado and Alarcon (2013) write about both the contextual and symbolic use of language in defining the terms of personal liberation. They assert that 'language serves as a social mediator between the person and his/her community, and between the individual experience and the social order' (p. 33). In other words, for Rivera *et al.*, language shapes an individual's perception of reality, so working within a liberation framework, it is really important to understand how an individual uses language. For F, 'nigger' represents a historical narrative that encapsulates the experience of Black people during slavery. For F, the concept of the African diaspora is one of hybridity, as he counts his 'White nan' as part of his diasporic existence. Hall (1996) talks about the 'diaspora experience', which is about the 'process of unsettling, recombination, hybridization and "cut-and-mix", in short a process of cultural diaspora-ization' (p. 448) which is constantly trying to make sense of its reconstructed recollection of Africa. It is this 'cut-and-mix' view of his historical memory that F values and communicates through his use of the word 'nigger'.

F's view of hip-hop and its political debt to Sam Cooke illustrates the value that he attaches to this process of 'cut-and-mix'. As F says, *'it's good to know your roots'* because in this way F can re-claim the value and esteem of his cultural heritage and carry that with pride as part of his resistance against the desire of the dominant power structure to use his historical memory to oppress him. It is F's process of 'conscientization' that enables him to challenge his peers about their more commercial usage of the word 'nigger', which *'creates more wars'* and involves *'copying or using it to be offensive'*.

The importance of family and defetishisation

F talks about his family loving his music, which is not normally about gun crime. F reflects a common theme among the group of young men, where it was thinking about their families that defetishised them from thinking of themselves as reluctant contributory factors in the cycles of 'street violence' to human agents with families able to make choices about their situation. K illustrates this in the excerpt below.

> When I went inside for stupid crimes that if I thought about how much I would have missed my friends and family [I would have done something different] ... I'm not coming back.
>
> *(From K's Map of Me)*

K translated this into lyrics:

> When I went inside for stupid crimes
> Got pushed in my cell
> And I lay down
> Started to cry
> Missing my mummy
> Missing the road side
> Don't mess up
> Stay on the outside.
> *(Session 2 notes)*

Conclusion

This chapter has attempted to give a brief insight into the creative process of song writing and its application in liberation psychology, illustrated by songs from the

Werrington Album. It would appear that liberation for the young men came from thinking about the impact of their actions on their families. The need to be part of a family unit and the desire to show people how they felt seemed to be important turning points in the reconstruction of their masculinities and a force for resistance against the hegemonic masculinities they were encouraged to perform while on the inside and out on 'the streets'.

Being deprived of their family's everyday love and support seemed to galvanise the intentions of some of the young men towards personal reform. Here is a brief case example of one young person's journey that illustrates this view of liberation and personal reform.

Discussion with OB

> OB reflected on his previous behaviour prior to arriving at Werrington and said that it would be the main cause of problems for him upon his release, as he still maintains that people will have grudges against him so his working in 'Avenues' [a youth project] will not be a smooth ride for him. OB said that he also would not have the same quality of time to write as he does in Werrington. However, OB feels that he has grown up in Werrington, as he has spent two and half years on the inside. He also recognises that some of the people on the outside who hold grudges against him will have also grown up and have jobs. OB agreed with the Researcher's assertion that he must show how he has changed by living his life differently by giving people respect and curbing his outbursts and frustrations at not being listened to. OB agreed that he had to find positive ways of expressing himself, as he wants to achieve and not find himself back in jail. In order to facilitate a smooth transition to the outside, OB intends not to tell anyone from his wider community about his release for three to four months, whilst he sorts himself out. OB was eager to record his new lyrics that he had written in the morning because he said that he was using words and writing about subjects that he had not done before. His remix of Holdin' On was about love and had a softer vibe to it, as it was inspired by Mariah Carey's *We belong together*.
>
> *(Session 20 notes)*

The excerpt above highlights two aspects of personal reform: improving wellbeing and conscientization.

Improving wellbeing

OB felt that he had grown up over the two and half years he had spent at HMPYOI Werrington. *Sonic [db]* had helped him to reflect on the progress of his personal development, as he acknowledged that he had to find more constructive ways of expressing himself, especially when he was frustrated. OB's realisation about his ability to be creative rather than destructive in resisting adversity illustrated an important outcome of his discovery of a more diverse, inclusive and expressive form of masculinity.

'Conscientization'

In OB's defetishisation process, he realised that as a human agent he was able to make choices for himself about his future. In addition to looking at employment opportunities and joining youth projects, like Avenues (Avenues Youth Project, 2014), OB wanted to carry on the 'conscientization' process with other young people, as a means of helping them to make alternative lifestyle choices that did not lead to crime. This desire to 'consciousness raise' with others seemed to be motivated by his personal 'recovery of historical memory' where he appeared to take responsibility for having been a 'tearaway determined to follow his own path, when he was younger' and his reflections on the social and political context with respect to, for example, challenging homophobia in the group. Finally, OB's journey towards liberation is musically reflected in the song, 'Holdin' on' (Werrington Album, 2007), the title of this chapter, where his more expressive and inclusive masculinity finally allowed him to write about love and relationships.

The case example above is significant because it was clear that the young people had been enculturated both on the inside and on the outside to consider themselves to be insignificant cogs (dehumanised elements) in a system of oppression that they were forced to maintain. Working in a creative way with the young men enabled us all to explore some of the complex and deep-seated issues around received masculinities that kept them from realising their potential as self-determining human agents.

Appendix

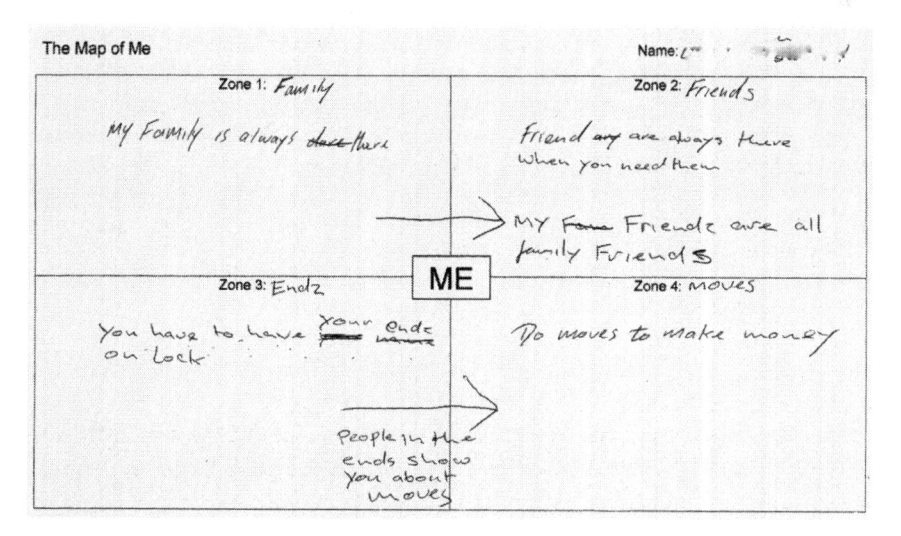

FIGURE 4.1 The Map of Me.

Notes

1 While the young men were involved in the music technology project, their musical and lyrical material formed integral parts of the overall research data. In this way the research and intervention combined to form one piece of social action.
2 Actual dialogue is in italics and lyrics written are in single quotation marks.
3 Butler (1997) describes a process of 'performativity' where we act out what society expects of us but then we own this 'acting out' as though it is our very own identity that comes from us and not societal expectation. Butler uses the word 'power' to describe societal norms and 'power' to describe our owning of it as our authentic expression of self. Butler asserts that we are brought into social existence through 'power' while at the same time wielding power of our own which has the capacity to change the very 'power' that brought us into existence in the first place.
4 Martín Baró (1994) argued that in order to achieve liberation, we have to re-evaluate our histories because our memories of our histories (both personal and cultural) have often been shaped and crafted by our oppressors. In other words, because our histories have been framed to highlight the negatives, it is this context that forms the basis of our oppression. Martín Baró (1994) suggested that we need to reframe our histories to highlight the positives so that we can use our re-framed pasts to move towards liberation from oppression.

References

Astride-Stirling, J. (2001). Thematic networks: An analytic tool for qualitative research. *Qualitative Research, 1*(3), 385–405.
Avenues Youth Project. (2014). *Welcome to Avenues Youth Project*. Retrieved 24 April 2014, from www.avenues.org.uk.
Bar-Tal, D. (2012). Siege mentality. In: D.J. Christie (Ed.), *The encyclopedia of peace psychology*, Vol. 1 (pp. 996–1000). Chichester: Wiley-Blackwell.
Butler, J. (1997). *The psychic life of power*. Stanford, CA: Stanford University Press.
Carless, D., & Douglas, K. (2010). Performance ethnography as an approach to health related education. *Educational Action Research, 18*(3), 373–88.
Clennon, O. (2013). How effective are music interventions in the criminal youth justice sector? Community music making and its potential for community and social transformation: A pilot study. *Journal of Music, Technology & Education, 6*(1), 103–30.
Connell, R.W. (1987). *Gender & power*. Stanford, CA: Stanford University Press.
Connell, R.W. & Messerschmidt, J.W. (2005). Hegemonic masculinity: Rethinking the concept. *Gender and Society, 19*(6), 829–59.
Csikszentmihalyi, M., & Csikszentmihalyi, I. (1988). *Optimal experience: Psychological studies of flow in consciousness*. Cambridge: Cambridge University Press.
Daymon, C., & Holloway, I. (Eds). (2011). *Qualitative research methods in public relations and marketing* (2nd ed.). New York: Routledge.
Freire, P. (1973). *Pedagogy of the oppressed*. New York: Seabury Press.
Hall, S. (1996). New ethnicities. In: D. Morley & K.H. Chen (Eds), *Stuart Hall: Critical dialogues in cultural studies* (pp. 44–9). London: Routledge.
Martín Baró, I. (1994). *Writings for a liberation psychology*. New York: Harvard University Press.
Montero, M. (2009). Methods for liberation: Critical consciousness in action. In: M. Montero & C. Sonn (Eds), *Psychology of liberation: Theory and applications* (pp. 73–93). New York: Springer.
Newton, C. (1994). Gender theory and prison sociology: Using theories of masculinities to interpret the sociology of prisons for men. *The Howard Journal, 33*(3), 193–202.

Remy, J. (1990). Patriarchy and fratriarchy as forms of androcracy. In: J. Hearn & D. Morgan (Eds), *Men, masculinities and social theory* (pp. 43–53). London: Unwin Hyman.

Rivera, E.T., Maldonado, J. & Alarcon, L. (2013). From Vygotsky to Martín Baró: Dealing with language and liberation during the supervision process. *Universal Journal of Psychology*, *1*(2), 32–40.

Segal, L. (1990). *Slow motion: Changing masculinities, changing men*, London: Virago.

Sykes, G.M. (1958). *The society of captives* (1971 ed.). Princeton, NJ: Princeton University Press.

Wallerstein, N.B., & Duran, B. (2006). Using community-based participatory research to address health disparities. *Health Promotion Practice*, *7*(3), 312–23.

Werrington Album (2007). *Werrington Album*. Stoke-on-Trent, Staffordshire, UK. Retrieved from http://youtu.be/EmZ57b8EI9Q and http://youtu.be/PI4fPL_69HE.

5

'WHAT'S OUR STORY?'

Centralising young people's experiences of 'gangs', crews and collectives to promote wellbeing

Gillian Hughes and Taiwo Afuape

Introduction

Taiwo and Gillian came together through a shared concern about the way young people in our urban areas were being portrayed, the effect this was having on the choices available to them and how this was related to the media focus on 'gang'[1] violence and teenage murders across the UK.

Taiwo

Young people were among many who in August 2011 took to the streets of England to engage in anti-social behaviour and protest their circumstances and those of many in their neighbourhoods, after an unarmed African-Caribbean man, Mark Duggan, was shot dead by a police officer in London. I remember saying to my sister Sola at the time that I felt as though I was one of many adults who had 'failed our young people'. As the media focused on the harmful nature of 'gangs' in London, it seemed important to understand what function crews had for young people in an increasingly difficult and oppressive social context and find ways of addressing the anger young people were communicating, without demonising them. If ever young people are a source of scrutiny and debate, it is now. At the end of 2012 the government published an update on the *Ending Gang and Youth Violence* report (Violent and Youth Crime Prevention Unit, 2012) which revealed their emphasis on management of young people, with stricter responses towards those viewed as 'perpetrators' and support for young people viewed as 'victims'. When I was asked to put together a conference about 'young people and gangs' I felt that it should be done *alongside* young people rather than *about* them, in ways that would not fix them within oppressive discourses of 'violent perpetrator'/'vulnerable victim' in need of management/treatment, respectively. I believed that young people were ethical beings rather than criminals, creative rather than just reactive and subjects in their world with something to say about their experience, rather than passive objects of history and circumstance. I was aware of the variety of views, moral dilemmas and divided opinion about the appropriateness of the term 'gang'. Personally I felt that the term was overused given the implications of defining groups of young people in that way. It therefore felt important to open up the term 'gang' to include 'groups', 'collectives' and 'crews' and reflect on the variety of experiences young people have, not all of which are negative.

Gillian

In my role as a psychologist in the Child and Family Refugee Service at the Tavistock Centre in north London, I have had many conversations with parents about one of their greatest fears – their teenage children getting involved in criminal activity and violence through gang association. These concerns have been heightened by several high-profile murders in recent years of young people from local refugee communities, caught up in gang violence. Many North London gangs are organised specifically around ethnic groups, such as the 'North London Somalis' and 'African Nations Crew'. A study carried out by the Institute for Race Relations (Wood, 2010a) showed that one-third of young people killed in London were either refugees or newly arrived migrants. This begs the question: what is making these young people so vulnerable?

Many of the teenagers we see at the Tavistock Refugee Service feel they are on the margins of society and they talk about their struggles with issues of identity, how to 'fit in' and how to find a valued place in society. There are enormous pressures on these young people, who are dealing with racism, poverty, poor housing, insecurity in the asylum status of their parents or other family members. Often this culminates in them failing at school, which compounds their sense of not being able to fit in or realise their hopes for their future. These social pressures can make young people vulnerable to being drawn into social groupings such as 'gangs' with the promise of a sense of belonging and a means of economic advancement.

Although there is much debate within the public arena about the rise of gang-related violence, our understanding about the experience of those young people affected is still limited. Why do they make the choices they do? Without having a thorough understanding of the lives of young people, it is hard for parents or service providers to know how to respond in effective ways to keep these young people safe.

'What's our story?'

The knife crime debate has reinforced perceptions of young people, and particularly those from Black and minority ethnic groups, as being dangerous, untrustworthy and out of control. This public discourse 'leads to a punitive and misguided political climate which may ultimately fail the very teenagers it aims to reach' (Wood, 2010b; p. 97). The reality is that a very small minority are involved in criminal activity associated with gangs. Although the violence associated with this attracts great concern, as it should do, there is a big part of the story about the lives of young people that is not being heard. Wood (2010b) also pointed out that if you compare the locations of teenage murders, this correlates closely with indices of deprivation. If you are from a Black or minority ethnic community, the risk of getting involved in gang violence is greater. Research carried out by the Centre for Crime and Justice Studies (Eades, Grimshaw, Silvestri & Solomon, 2007) highlighted the relationship between social inequality and poverty, and youth violence. Minority ethnic communities are more likely to live in poverty, but this does not fully explain the statistics. Our own work with young people has shown how the experience of racism and discrimination, embedded in institutional life in the UK, can lead to alienation and disaffection of our Black youth, who might then find validation in a variety of other places.

We began to collaborate with young people on a project that the young people named 'What's Our Story?' (WOS). WOS aimed to provide a platform for young people to describe their experiences of growing up in London, and an opportunity to share their views about gangs, crews and collectives. The project aimed to generate dialogue between young people, adults and those providing services in order to promote understanding of the complex issues at work. We took a liberation psychology approach, which centralises the voices of disempowered young people so that they can begin to lead the debates about the issues impacting on their lives. This chapter will describe how the project evolved using social media and the creative arts to stimulate dialogue, and how young people were at the heart of it.

A liberation psychology approach to working with young people

A liberation psychology approach is about standing alongside the oppressed, excluded and exploited members of society, and using this standpoint to interrogate social structures in relation to emotional wellbeing, including psychological theory and practice. This project was therefore guided by the following principles:

- Understanding wellbeing in its social context, leading to collective action and change (Holland, 1992; Moane, 2011)
- Critically examining our methods and approaches so that they can be a force for transformation rather than conformity (Martín Baró, 1994)
- Critiquing dominant discourses and rejecting the idea of a universal, individual, impartial and technical approach to social problems (Freire, 1973)
- Drawing on and utilising the creativity, resistance and resourcefulness of everyday people (Afuape, 2011; Hughes, 2014)
- Working alongside marginalised people to shape, influence and transform their circumstances as well as our practice (Martín Baró, 1994).

From the start it was important to interrogate the term, and ideas about, 'gangs' circulating in the public media and being perpetuated by powerful voices and institutions. We decided to utilise the term 'gang-affected young people' who are:

those who have been affected by the use of the term 'gang', touched by 'gang' activity itself, at risk of being involved in 'gangs' or have something to say about the range of experiences (both positive and negative) of being part of groupings and crews. We felt this position would help us engage young people in dialogue, and enable us to revise our views as we learnt from what the young people said.

Using creative means to generate dialogue with young people

We wanted to draw on forms of dialogue that fitted with youth culture and enabled creative modes of expression. As well as aiming to create a platform for young people to share their views, it was also important to ensure the project offered the chance for participants to increase their social capital (Bourdieu, 1986). We achieved this dual aim in various ways, including:

- bringing together a group of young people to act as consultants to this project at every stage, to ensure that the voices of young people remained central;
- seeking out young people through local youth clubs, to film and record their views;
- using a form of communication that was congruent with youth culture – namely the internet and social media, which led us to working with Google;
- engaging young people in creative projects, such as our collaboration with the hip-hop artist Akala;
- supporting young people in their own initiatives, which led us to make a film based on a script the young consultants had written.

Creating the youth consultant group

Gillian met Naomi Kyezu, a fifteen year old girl of African origin, through her work in the Tavistock Refugee Service. Naomi had written a powerful script during a week of work experience, called 'My Life', about a group of young people who get drawn into a gang, and what happens to them. Although fictional, the story was based on her personal experiences and those of her friends. Gillian and Taiwo began meeting with Naomi and her friends Reme, Osama, Hamid, Abdul and Jessica, to engage in dialogue about their lives and how we might work together. The young people were excited about being recognised as having important knowledge to contribute, and were keen to collaborate with us on what became their project. Their enthusiasm was infectious, and spurred us on to seek out ways of working that were innovative and that challenged common assumptions, to enable the disempowered young voices to be heard. In a brainstorming exercise the young people decided to call the project 'What's Our Story?' and reserved a site on You Tube under this name. The aim was to use the site to post videos made by young people to generate dialogue around the theme of *'what gangs mean to me'*, and then show the results of these dialogues at an event with service providers, commissioners, schools, carers and other young people.

Dialogue through youth congruent media

During a consultation with Sola Afuape it was suggested that, as the internet is now so integral to youth culture and a universal medium through which young people express themselves, it would be helpful to approach Google to see how they could support us. Rick Jones arranged a workshop and a tour of the Google offices for the young people from WOS, as well as arranged for a YouTube star, Louis Cole (of 'Fun for Louis' fame), to join us to discuss how to use YouTube to facilitate dialogue. Louis helped the young people make a short film about their motivations for getting involved in WOS and their hopes for the project. The young people were very excited to be at a prestigious location, as a comment from Reme shows: 'on the way here, there was a person on the train that just looked at me like "Why are you dressed like that? Where are you going? What suspicious things are you up to?" [I thought] "If only you knew that I was going to be in the Google headquarters!"'

Feeling inspired by the young people, Louis Cole offered to promote the project through his daily vlog (video log); his vlog which included this workshop had been viewed, at the time of writing, by over 66,000 people (www.youtube.com/watch?v=_nM6zei2Hrk). This was a platform wider than anything we could have imagined for WOS. However, as practitioners working within a state institution (the NHS) with responsibility for ensuring the safety of young people, we found ourselves in a dilemma. We were not sure what the consequences might be for the young people of putting up a posting of them, on the internet, and felt that we had a duty to them and their carers to explore this carefully so that their consent could be truly informed. Following a liberation approach, we took time to include the young people at every stage of reflecting on these dilemmas with us. They were very thoughtful and much more knowledgeable about the social media world in many ways than us. For example, when we had originally set up our WOS YouTube site, the young people had wanted it to be clear the Tavistock Centre was hosting the project because they felt this would make intimidating postings in response to their work less likely. As the young people were fifteen years old, we acquired informed parental consent before posting anything.

While Taiwo was on maternity leave, Gillian returned with Reme, Naomi and Osama to the YouTube studios at Google for a second time, in order to film a discussion about 'what it means to be a young person in London'. Free access to the studios and their equipment had been negotiated, and the workshop was filmed as material to post on the YouTube channel when it was launched. There was a box of props and clothes in the studio which the young people gravitated towards and started to play around with. Using these props they decided to act out a short scene of an interaction between an elderly White couple and a young Black man. They decided to do this three times, based around the themes:

1. How people see us (Black youth in casual clothing).
2. What it is really like on the streets.
3. How we want it to be.

After each performance the young people discussed what they were trying to show in the different vignettes. They talked about how poverty and the environment young people grow up in shapes them:

> When you live in a deprived area, you get used to seeing crime, you get accustomed to it. You can't go around being happy, you have to constantly be alert. That makes teenagers like 'I need protection'. The habitat where you are brought up defines you as a person.
>
> (Osama)

They described how they had to deal with the prejudices of others, and how this affected them:

> We are judged, by what we look like.
>
> (Naomi)

> If we try going to a prestige shop, people will look like 'What are you doing?' … They don't see the good things that are happening. It's just 'youth are bad'.
>
> (Osama)

> I don't feel comfortable asking people [for help] because the way that people look at me is not very welcoming.
>
> (Reme)

> If we are with just two other Black people, we would get stopped and searched [by the police]. … If you treat me like trash, I'm going to act like trash.
>
> (Osama)

Because of the news coverage of gang violence, the positive aspects of gangs, crews or collectives gets missed, and with this omission we miss out on fully understanding why people are drawn to be part of these groups:

> A gang becomes a negative connotation. Like us three and plus two other Black boys, that can be considered like a gang and then its positive connotations are suddenly removed from that and we are symbolised as a problem.
>
> (Reme)

> I am still in contact with those people, because it is like family. Once you get involved, it is more family … if your brother gets hurt, you want to help. … They are a group of friends rather than a gang. It starts as a group of friends, being bored.
>
> (Osama)

Gangs were also talked about as a way of gaining power in a world where members are at the bottom of the pile:

> They believe that life is like survival of the fittest and if you are not strong enough, you are going to be cut. If you are not part of the post code family. Everyone wants to be the big man. Everyone has the type of mentality where it is money over everything. What they don't think about is that means money over Mum, family, God, respect for women, respect towards other people, your morals, all of that is gone because of the material thing. It is not worth it.
>
> (Reme)

The gang debate has focused almost exclusively on young men, but in the YouTube studios we talked about what role young women play, and how their position of disempowerment within a gang can lead them into violence. This prompted another role play showing a young woman being used as a pawn to trap a young man in order to carry out a revenge stabbing:

> Girls play a bigger role than what is portrayed. But a lot of the time it isn't their fault. But once they are in it and have the power, they feel like 'I can be like one of the guys now', and some are thinking 'I can be even more, I can be even worse than the guys, I can stab someone in the back without even noticing.'
>
> (Reme)

> She would have suffered the consequences as well as him [if she had refused], and they would have got to him anyway. She was just looking out for herself.
>
> (Reme)

Drawing on young people's creativity

It was evident from the visit to the YouTube studios that our use of creative means (performance) enabled the young people to express themselves very eloquently. We decided to follow this by hosting a workshop at the Tavistock Centre run by Music of Black Origin (MOBO) award-winning hip-hop musician Akala and the charity he founded, the Hip-Hop Shakespeare Company. With the help of Aisling Kelly, trainee clinical psychologist on placement with Gillian, and Brice Tahati, assistant to CAMHS service manager, we brought together young people using youth services across north London for this event.

Akala began the workshop by exploring with the young people the parallels between Shakespearean verse and modern hip-hop, and then shared some fascinating history about the origins of hip-hop music, taking everyone back to its African roots. He invited the group to explore the importance of creativity in challenging inequality and oppression, reflecting on the role of love, relationships and struggle. The afternoon culminated in participants writing and performing their own lyrics, drawing on their personal experiences of being a young person in London. Two young people, Zubair Bazwan and Plamedi Dikanda, agreed to share their work in this chapter:

Zubair's rap:

> I think our country sinks beneath the yoke
> Power and money, it divides up our folk
> There are powerful winners and poor losers
> In a better world, we would all be choosers
> Who is to say people can't change?
> People can rise.

Plamedi's rap:

> I have defeated them all,
> but have not won the war.
> Still struggle to survive,
> families struggle for their lives.
> Tryna get out of jail,
> my life's been put on bail.
> Tryna get my message across,
> but I'm locked in a box.
> No job, no money,
> so I can't help Mummy.
> Soon come I'll be making big p's
> so I can help my real g's.
> Once they notice me the government will see
> poverty is pain and pain is not a game.

The young people said that although they felt quite nervous about the workshop initially, they found the experience highly valuable and inspiring. One young person described Akala as a 'genius' and said that the workshop would have a lasting influence upon him, with respect to using creativity to continue to reflect on his experience. Akala's advice to the young people was to keep working on developing their writing skills. He talked about how important it was for them to communicate their experiences and views, whether this be in the creative arts, at school or in the work place, and how this would support them to transform their lives for the better. We, as project coordinators, could see how the young people were connecting with these inspiring messages, coming from someone who they could both admire and relate to. Ricky Murphy, who came to the workshop with some young people from a drugs and alcohol service in Barnet, made a video of the event which can be found at: www.youtube.com/watch?v=su8x6YaJRTA&feature=youtu.be.

'My Life'

From the start of our collaboration with the group of youth consultants, we began working to get their 'My Life' script made into a film, which the young people hoped could be used to benefit others. Although Naomi had written the original draft, the others helped her finish the script and add to the authenticity of the story. They wanted their message to be: (a) young people often get drawn into anti-social behaviour because they are experiencing emotional and social difficulties; (b) young people often feel alienated from adults around them, which makes them more vulnerable to unhelpful influences; and (c) '*you cannot change your past but you can shape your future*' (their words). We were able to recruit two film school graduates to join this project and eventually secured enough funding[2] to go ahead.

Naomi, Reme and Osama all starred in the film, led the auditions for other parts and contributed at various other stages in the production and editing of the film. The soundtrack was written by Reme with support from a successful drama and film music composer, Martin Phipps, which offered further opportunities for valuable experience in the entertainment industry. The young people all learned a great deal about the processes of making a film, which added hugely to their social capital. It was extraordinary to witness how much they grew in confidence and stature throughout the project, and it was clearly a very special experience for them:

> Shooting the film was amazing. We were all so close, it felt like we were one family.
>
> *(Naomi)*

We were able to premiere the film at a small cinema, where key people from health, education and social care were invited, as well as family and friends. The young people introduced the film and hosted a discussion with audience members about it afterwards. They spoke confidently and articulately about their ideas, in spite of being extremely nervous about performing. The discussion generated some interesting questions: *Why had the young people chosen to cast their gang members as exclusively Black youth? Had they fallen into stereotyping Black youth as criminal? Is selling drugs a creative, albeit criminal, way out of poverty using useful entrepreneurial skills? Would this film be anxiety provoking for parents to watch as it offers a bleak picture of young people in gangs? Would there be a sequel which could offer some messages of hope?* One audience member reflected that although the film showed how lack of support from parents struggling with social disadvantage, and teachers struggling with school pressures as well as other social pressures, contributed to young people getting involved in criminal gang activity, it did not give clear suggestions about what prevents gang involvement. Osama's response to this was:

> Our film promotes what happens in crime, but we want to promote that we want to feel accepted. That's another thing we want to show with our project;

if you accept us, maybe we will speak out more and stop [getting involved in criminal activity]. Most people do that stuff to rebel, to show that they aren't being heard. People have to take it into their own hands to get what they need. 'If you are going to shut down all my youth centres then this is what I am going to do.'

Following this premiere, we decided to run a bigger event, which Rick Jones from Google invited us to host in their London offices. This event included young people, parents and staff from youth projects, schools and mental health and counselling services from across London (including those working specifically with gang-affected young people), as well as key service providers. In order to ensure that the young people had a voice, and were positioned as 'experts' on their lives, we jointly facilitated the event with our young people consultants and used methods that would enable quieter voices to be heard. We were clear that for 'true dialogue' (in Friere's sense) to take place, we needed to move away from the more traditional conference format based on professional 'experts' sharing their knowledge with a passive audience. As people arrived, we invited them to share their responses to questions posted on the walls, using post-it notes. We introduced the project with a discussion between those who had been central in its development, in front of the audience. Having seen the film, we invited the event participants to get into groups, with each group taking the perspective of one of the characters in the film, and discuss:

1. What do you think was motivating this character?
2. What life circumstances might have been contributing to the choices they were making?
3. Who (or what services) might have made a difference to the choices this character had available to them?
4. What social, community or political changes might need to happen to support the life of this character?
5. What do you think should happen next in this story? Why?

Each group was asked to write down themes onto post-it notes that they put onto flipchart paper relating to each character, after their discussion.

Following this, we used a fishbowl[3] format to generate dialogue; people from the audience volunteered to represent one of the characters in the film and sit in the front to discuss with each other themes that came up for their character. After this discussion, the rest of the audience was invited to make reflections based on the discussion between representatives of the film characters, and based on their own group discussions.

The evening generated very lively and passionate dialogue, in which many people shared their personal experiences and how this has shaped their thinking. Reflections varied from those who suggested that young people were responsible for their own behaviour and those that suggested that young people get caught up in criminal gang activity as a result of their life circumstances. Young people in particular talked movingly about grouping together in order to feel safe, wanting to be included, the impact of educational and social exclusion and feeling underestimated and misunderstood by adults. When asked (in a questionnaire at the end of the event) what people would take away from the evening, many adults said they would try to listen more to what young people have to say:

> and appreciate them without judging them ... listen to them.

> To be brave to approach young people and talk to them, even though we may feel they may not be interested.

> I will be more open to young people in future.

The evening helped people reflect on the role of the wider social context in shaping the lives of young people, which moved away from the individualising and pathologising discourses that so often surround young people:

> As a society, we need to create a better narrative of young people and their experiences ... too often young people are seen as the problem rather than responding to wider problems.

> More needs to be done surrounding the inclusion of young people in society at all levels.

In response, people talked about the need for a more collective response to the difficulties young people face. This chimes with the ethos of liberation practice, which is about bringing people together and creating opportunities for dialogue that move people to collective action:

> Young people need communities to raise them.

> [Following this evening,] ... I will take my responsibility as a 'village elder' to be part of the village that raises the child.

Young people were positioned as part of this process, rather than passive recipients of change, as one person's call to action showed:

> We can all blame society for the decisions kids make but we need to realise we *are* society and if we don't look in the mirror and make changes, nothing will change.

The evening had demonstrated how important it is to find a language that enables subjugated voices to be heard when we are working with people who are habitually marginalised by social discourses. Our use of creative means not only gave the young people a form of expression that fitted for them, but also enabled them to shine, which gave them the confidence to speak out and share their views. An audience member said:

> This project shows what can happen if we encourage voices, and believe in the talent of young people ... show their ability to express themselves through the medium of film and music.

There was discussion about where the project could go next and how the film could be used. People wanted to take it into schools and youth clubs, and use it as a resource for adults providing mental health services to dialogue with young people about their experiences. There was excitement about getting the film out and continuing the dialogue, as one person suggested: '*Set up pop-up meetings EVERYWHERE to show the film and open dialogue in every community between people of all ages, like we did tonight.*'

There were also calls for social action to result from the film and the event, with one person commenting that Google should set up apprenticeships for young people and a number of teachers reflecting on changes that need to happen in their schools. In fact, since the event, we have been approached by a number of schools and youth clubs inviting us, including our youth consultants, to run workshops with their young people. The consensus was that the power of the film to change perceptions lay in hearing the responses of the young people to it, and the dialogue that it had the potential to generate.

Reflections

Given the presence of service managers and commissioners at the film event, this project continues to move towards social action in supporting the wellbeing of young people who are 'gang-affected'. It was also an intervention in and of itself, supporting the wellbeing of all the young people and adults who took part in it. At the film showing many of the crew commented on how meeting and working with the young people impacted positively on their lives. Rather than turning in on themselves as vulnerable individuals who needed support, the project respected the young people as creative, reflective agents. It also actively sought to provide the young people with the means to challenge some of their circumstances (social capital and skills development).

To truly align ourselves with those we work with and critically examine our methods and approaches so that they are transformative rather than ameliorative, we also have to be creative in order to open up dialogue about issues that are pertinent to the lives of those we are working with. Interestingly, when exploring what it was like for young people on London streets, the young consultants talked just as much about experiences of racism, sexism and oppression from adults in authority, such as the police, as they did about violence from peers in 'gangs'.

As facilitators, actively aligning ourselves with our ethics seemed to generate forms of energy and opportunities previously not present; although this was not an uncomplicated experience. For example, Google, we are aware, is a multinational company whose central aim is to generate profits. Was this collaboration compromising of our ethics, or was it an opportunity to use the structures of power to get usually marginalised voices heard? Working as part of an institution meant that the power of our intervention was limited by the need to balance the safety of those we were trying to support with creating opportunities for them. It raised the questions: If we set up a successful YouTube channel that attracted many viewers, would we have the resources to manage it? Could we trust that young people will know what is safe when the culture of instant fame is so alluring, and where does this leave us as professionals? Where do we stand with a liberation approach if we are stepping in because of our concerns about risk and giving the message that we don't trust young people to know? Despite useful suggestions from the young consultants who were explicitly asking for a contract with the institution we work in, this institution seemed paralysed by anxiety about risk and service guidelines that did not initially accommodate this type of work. This created delays and cost precious relationships with some of the young people who dropped out of the project.

There is also some tension between the importance of collaborative working with young people that involves asking them their ideas and views about important issues impacting on their lives, and not expecting young people to have 'answers' to complex issues that extend way beyond them – to the influence of the family, community, social and political context.

Trying to set up a project that is truly youth-centred can be challenging: getting the right balance between following the lead of young people and sharing our knowledge of how their ideas can be realised effectively, without taking over; knowing how much to draw on the young people as a resource so that they remain central but not using them as unpaid labour; creating the time and space to meet in ways that suit young people, in the context of demanding work schedules; and keeping the pace up so that the young people remain engaged. We lost a couple of young consultants in the early stages of the project while we spent time searching for funding.

However, what we want to convey more than anything is how important it is to align ourselves with our ethics despite these challenges. In fact, we found that when we did align ourselves with the values of working alongside others, centralising the voices of young people and believing in and utilising their virtues, extraordinary things happened that enabled us to create extraordinary work together.

Notes

1 We use the term 'gang' throughout this chapter (as well as critique it) to refer to any group, crew or collective of young people, who are not necessarily involved in criminal activity.

2 Which included Gillian doing a half-marathon fundraising run and funding from the Tavistock Clinic Foundation charity.
3 The 'fishbowl' method involves a group of people (in this case, representatives from each of the small group discussions) sitting in a circle and having a discussion, which others (the rest of the audience) observe as if looking into a fishbowl. The observers then talk together, sharing their responses to what they have heard. This structure helps less dominant voices to be heard, and multiple opinions to be expressed.

References

Afuape, T. (2011). *Power, resistance and liberation in therapy with survivors of trauma: To have our hearts broken.* London: Routledge.
Bourdieu, P. (1986). The forms of capital. In: J. Richardson (Ed.), *Handbook of theory and research for the sociology of education* (pp. 241–58). New York: Greenwood Publishers.
Eades, C., Grimshaw, R., Silvestri, A., & Solomon, E. (2007). *'Knife crime': A review of evidence and policy* (2nd ed.) London: Centre for Crime and Justice Studies.
Freire, P. (1973). *Pedagogy of the oppressed.* New York: Seabury Press.
Holland, S. (1992). From social abuse to social action: A neighborhood psychotherapy and social action project for women. In: J. Ussher & P. Nicholson (Eds), *Gender issues in clinical psychology* (pp. 68–77). London: Routledge.
Hughes, G. (2014). Finding a voice through 'The Tree of Life': A strength-based approach to mental health for refugee children and families in schools. *Clinical Child Psychology and Psychiatry, 19*(1), 139–53.
Martín Baró, I. (1994). *Writings for a liberation psychology.* Cambridge, MA: Harvard University Press.
Moane, G. (2011). *Gender and colonialism: A psychological analysis of oppression and liberation* (2nd ed.) London: Macmillan Press.
Violent and Youth Crime Prevention Unit (2012). *Ending gang and youth violence report: One year on.* London: The Stationery Office.
Wood, R. (2010a). Youth deaths: The reality behind the knife crime debate. *Institute of Race Relations Briefing Paper No. 5.* Retrieved 9 January 2015 from www.irr.org.uk/publications/issues/briefing-paper-5.
Wood, R. (2010b). UK: the reality behind the knife crime debate. *Race and Class, 52*(2), 97–103.

6

A CLINICAL SERVICE FOR GENDER NON-CONFORMING YOUNG PEOPLE

What can a liberation psychology perspective contribute?

Bernadette Wren

Introduction

The aim of this chapter is to explore how the values and practices of liberation psychology might be applicable in a state-funded clinical service in the UK for gender non-conforming children and adolescents. The service already espouses affirmative aims and practices, attempting to nurture the confident development of the young people's unconventional gender identification, while acknowledging the impact of living in a social world where poorly informed and negative attitudes towards gender variance are widespread. Still, as a clinical psychologist and family therapist with many years' experience in the mental health field, I often feel troubled about the responsibility to guide these young people in coping with a predicament which has no established psychological causation and which does not yield to change through psychotherapy (Drescher & Byne, 2012). I am interested in how a critical perspective directed towards principled social change, such as liberation psychology, can generate fresh insights into how stigmatising and shaming practices work, how psychological difficulties for these young people may be 'privatised', how conventional discourses of sex and gender may narrow options – and how these forces may be contested. In developing this analysis, I consider how different aspects of the social and cultural context might be seen to constitute 'oppression' for this group of marginalised young people, with different consequences for treatment and activism.

Dialogues with a range of colleagues, clinicians and activists, who vary in their gendered self-definition, have challenged me to justify, clarify or modify a number of my assertions and arguments, and I have been similarly held to account by service-users present at a conference where I gave a version of this paper, and by the editors of this volume. In this chapter I prefer the term *gender non-conforming* when referring to people whose gendered sense of self is at odds with the body and with the expectations associated with the sex assigned to them at birth. It is a relatively neutral term with respect to causation. I also use the new term *trans★* (with an asterisk), which has come to signify the range of variation in gender non-conformity.

The context in which the service operates

Despite the playfulness in popular cultural references to trans★ lives, people with a non-conforming gender identity are still often positioned in public narratives as abnormal and incomplete. Trans★ people in all their variety are mainly notable, in Goffman's phrase, for '*a deeply discreditable, undesired different-ness*' (Goffman, 1963). Parents of gender variant children may see themselves constructed as reprehensible for having produced a child with a transgender identity.

Evidence has accumulated over the last few decades that gender non-conforming young people live with the threat of abuse as well as actual violence (e.g. Goldblum *et al.*, 2012). Stigmatising public attitudes to gender variant people sanction such attacks. Only recently in the UK have gender variant people become protected by law, with substantial rights enshrined in the Equality Act of 2010. The empirical data on the mental health of gender variant young people demonstrate plenty of evidence of social suffering: fear, anger, self-doubt (Wallien, Swaab & Cohen-Kettenis, 2008). It seems that the normative criteria for judging one's worth do not remain as judgements from outside, but rather they may be internalised (Russell & Bohan, 2007).

Despite this, many gender non-conforming people function extremely well, forming friendships, finding love, getting jobs and generally thriving. In addition, most of those who undergo physical re-assignment are reported to have no regrets about their transition (Singh, Hays & Watson, 2011). Those young people who achieve good outcomes, despite the oppressive social context, are more likely to be those who have experienced lifelong gender non-conformity and who start off with significant social advantages – chiefly, the absence of any serious psychological difficulties and the presence of strong family support (de Vries, Steensma, Doreleijers & Cohen-Kettenis, 2011).

The clinical service

Our service sees young people, aged up to eighteen years, whose experience of the body is at odds with their assigned gender. These are young people without observable bodily anomalies, who have come to feel that their sense of self does not fit with the assignation of male or female. Most are preoccupied with unwanted and incongruent aspects of the body (for example, the chest and the genitals) and others are uncomfortable with the imposed social expectations of their assigned gender.

The service was established twenty-five years ago in response to an unmet need in publicly funded child mental health services. Knowledge and experience of how to support these unconventional children and adolescents built up slowly in partnership with families. The service is now led by mental health clinicians (psychologists, psychotherapists, social workers and psychiatrists) working alongside endocrine colleagues. Clinicians in the service accept that gender non-conformity cannot be explained adequately within any monolithic theoretical model, and that explanations are probably multi-factorial. As a systemically trained practitioner, my clinical stance is underpinned by a particular set of theoretical and ethical commitments which involve understanding individuals and their difficulties by taking into account the complex web of family and social relations and the social order in which they live. Other clinicians bring therapeutic frameworks from psychoanalytic psychotherapy, attachment models and cognitive behavioural therapy (CBT). More recently, some of us have been attempting to integrate perspectives from critical psychology, feminist scholarship and post-modern gender studies into our practice (Wren, 2014a; Zitz, Burns & Tacconelli, 2014).

Most of us take the view that causal stories are a distraction, where the evidence is so flimsy. Our approach is broadly affirmative, in not seeking to directly undermine people's gender self-narratives, but to support them and their families to explore meaning around the experience of having a gender non-conforming identity and to focus on active coping and problem-solving. Many of the young people coming to the service suffer considerable distress with a high degree of mood problems, anxiety and self-harm (di Ceglie, Freedman & McPherson, 2002). In alleviating these problems there is often a clear role for mental health clinicians, as there is in working with concerned and bewildered carers and relatives, and other important members of the child's network, to appreciate the profound and unwilled nature of gender identification.

Family and individual sessions are provided, plus regular groups for young people and their parents/carers. Network meetings with key agencies in the young person's life are arranged; training and consultation to such agencies is also offered. We host family days, to include siblings, with a view to connecting families to each other for solidarity and support, and to encourage a view of their struggles as socially shared.

In recent years, the emergence of effective endocrinological interventions to delay puberty and to alter the development trajectory of adolescence can provide young trans* people with the opportunity to live with a body that makes a better fit with their gender identity. A strong case can be made that the only way to circumvent negative social judgement for these young people in later life is for them to transition to the preferred gender as soon as possible and be helped to do everything possible to achieve the body to fit (Wren, 2000). Parents are often the strongest advocates for this early physical intervention, to enable their child to live in their preferred identity and body 'by stealth', and survive in an intolerant and discriminatory social world. Whether a 'stealth' identity is consistently desired by the young people themselves, as they move through adolescence, is often a focus of discussion in clinical conversations.

Following a series of consultations with the young person and family/carers, and depending on the young person's stage of pubertal development, there are likely to be discussions about whether to embark on our staged programme of physical intervention. The service protocol is kept under review and evolves in relation to ongoing discussions between professionals, parents and young people. The service has no record of refusing anyone who continues to ask for physical intervention after the assessment period. Some young people back off from physical treatment at an early stage, but the majority stay on the programme and continue through to adult gender services, where surgery becomes an option.

The significance of dialogue

As a service we are in regular (if sometimes tense) dialogue with advocacy and support groups to receive feedback on our clinical approach, and to discuss the meaning and implications of research findings and of initiatives for new approaches to treatment. Previous and current users of our service usually present their perspectives at conferences we organise, and clinicians speak at events run by support organisations. Such an exchange of perspectives has, over the years, shaped professional perceptions, understandings and language, as well as our intervention protocols. For example, changes have been made in the provision of outreach clinics in the UK, in the availability of early intervention at the start of puberty, and in the regular offer of family days.

But dialogue can also lead to sharp divisions. Presentations I have made recently at conferences, opening up the debate on such issues as non-binary patterns of gender identity development (Wren, 2014b) and on adolescent impulsivity (Wren, 2013), are not well-received by some delegates, although welcomed by others. Some families and advocacy groups see mental health clinicians as over-cautious, sceptical gatekeepers. They take the view that young people are inarguably the authoritative resource for their own gender (their sense of being male, female, both or neither), rather than this knowledge being the outcome of an 'expert', purportedly neutral, psychological evaluation. On this view, medical treatments (reversible and irreversible) should be offered to young people more or less on demand. Other parents and professionals argue for a more tentative approach, reflecting the dearth of solid knowledge about outcomes for young people treated early. Arguments are made that the service may be too ready to speak for, rather than with, children and families.

So, it is clear that the issues raised in this work are psychological, as well as ethical – to do with the capacity and entitlement of young people to determine their own physical development, the pressing need to challenge negative public perceptions of trans* youth, the responsibility of clinicians to support reflective decision-making, and the assumption that physical intervention provided early to enable 'passing' as the 'other' sex is the best way for these young people to achieve good psychological adjustment. I now consider whether a liberation psychology perspective has the potential to illuminate these debates.

A liberation psychology perspective

Liberation psychology offers a political analysis of the predicaments of people helped by psychologists, taking it as given that societies are unequal in terms of power, and therefore in the degree of discrimination, exclusion, stress and even violence that people suffer. Much social and psychological suffering is due, it is argued, to the political, economic and cultural structures and ideologies that underlie oppression. The central idea of liberation psychology is the need to acquire a critical consciousness of how oppression works (Burton & Kagan, 2005). Social justice is a core value, and the task is to work for change that transforms relations of power, rather than just ameliorates distress (Orford, 2008).

Crucially, liberation psychology resists the tendency to reduce complex social phenomena to individual psychological ills (Lykes, 2012). Liberation psychologist Martín Baró criticised the 'fictional commonsense that nurtures the structures of exploitation and conformist attitudes' (Martín Baró, 1994). Furthermore, important links can be made between the conditions of oppression and associated psychological difficulties, such as a sense of inferiority and helplessness. These difficulties can be a barrier to action and thereby serve to maintain oppression (Moane, 2003).

The 'tools' of liberation psychology, as is well documented elsewhere in this volume, include 'conscientization' – Freire's word for the work of helping people become more aware of the oppressive processes by which they and their social contexts are constructed (Freire, 1971), with a view to helping them shift those forces of oppression and the psychological habits that help perpetuate them (Martín Baró, 1994).

> Change the lens and see mental health or illness not from the inside out but from the outside in; not as the result of an individual's internal functioning but as the manifestation, in a person or a group, of the humanising or alienating character of the framework of historical relationships.
> *(Martín Baró, 1994; p. 111)*

A liberation psychology approach in a gender identity service: a good fit?

I am attracted by this ringing endorsement of values of social justice which appear, at first reading, to simplify the therapeutic task,[1] although this is deceptive, as we shall see. Existing practices in our service are already informed by ideas about the need to open up frank dialogue with young trans* people about their lives, to challenge prejudice in oneself and others, to increase people's knowledge of their rights under law, and to help build adequate counter-narratives to the demeaning cultural story about transgender experience.

To protect confidentiality, all the vignettes that follow, although drawn from clinical practice, are composites of several scenarios, implicating no particular clients. All names are fictional.

- Liberation psychology enjoins us to articulate a moral line in our work. Clients should expect and receive an affirmative stance towards their experience and world view from clinicians. Young people often have their backs against the wall when it comes to defending their trans* self-definition; only by showing that what they say and feel is taken with real seriousness does one earn the right to probe further, for good psychological help will always challenge as well as support. *With dissenting parents, like those of thirteen-year-old Savannah, who feared that their child's assertion of a male identity was misguided and wrong, it is important to enquire about their position, too, from a stance of empathy and genuine curiosity.*
- Our preferential position should be to help clients develop an understanding of the ways that discrimination works. The psychological difficulties they face must be conceptualised as only partly a unique, private and idiosyncratic pattern of emotional distress, even less a deficiency, and strongly as a predictable response to an unsympathetic and disempowering context. *Nadia felt anxious to attend secondary school as her preferred self, always fearing exposure and bullying. She had disabling panic attacks and could not get out of the car to enter the building. The task was not to 'treat' her anxiety as a mental health problem but to engage with the teachers to help build her confidence that the school would both protect her and work to create a better-informed and more tolerant school culture.*
- A genuine 'praxis of commitment' (Martín Baró, 1994 p. 23) also means demonstrating more strongly the emancipatory element of our work – for example, making it clearer where we feel that discriminatory language and practices are operating to disempower our clients at their school or workplace, or in their contact with other health or social care, and raising our voices with those agencies to improve their practice in what may be for them an unfamiliar domain of work. *I learned that fourteen-year-old Aaron's school felt helpless to influence the transphobic attitudes and behaviour of some of their pupils: we took this to be an unacceptably passive position and offered to discuss and illustrate examples of good practice as a way forward.*
- The service should find ways to support young people to develop a better awareness of the history of the struggle for human rights for gender and sexual minority people. This would honour Martín Baró's notion of 'the recovery of historical memory' (Martín Baró, 1994). *Sixteen-year-old Tom was angry about our service protocol that he must spend a year on the hormone blocker before moving to cross-sex hormones: in his view we were rigid and unresponsive to his needs. As a way to establish a better alliance and to demonstrate the possibility for progress on such issues, I recounted a little of the history of our pioneering service and the way we have continued to make treatment available earlier and more widely. Tom relaxed a little and began thinking about how he might get through the year.*
- We should find additional opportunities to join with others to take collective action towards achieving fair and equal treatment for sexual and gender minorities in all health service settings (for example, we currently engage in policy development work with the UK Parliamentary Forum, and contribute to guidelines for national and international professional bodies seeking to increase recognition of

the needs of gender non-conforming people). We should support our young clients to get involved in activism and stress the importance not just of change coming through people acting together, but of the way resilience in a community can be built through engagement in social action.[2] *Sixteen-year-old Billy began to attend an LGBT alliance group at his school, and invited gender variant speakers to debate. Fifteen-year-old Lucy began writing to media outlets when trans* people were traduced in the press. And Alex's family talked to me about the discovery that making a compassionate response to others who are marginalised for their 'difference' has evoked in them a new quality of sensitivity to oppression which they have come to value.*

- Liberation psychology stresses the crucial practice of dialogue with those to whom 'help' is offered (Martín Baró, 1994). It challenges all the ways we talk *for* and *about*, rather than *with*, the people who are at the heart of our service. To establish plausible and effective alliances, the community of young people and families need to be more involved in informing our treatment protocol and research priorities. This needs to be a process over time, where trust is built up and topics debated, with the acknowledgement of genuine differences, and without fear of censure. Problems only occur in such partnerships when a small group seizes the agenda forcefully and proves unable to grasp the drivers for, and constraints on, action for other groups. *It was hard for fifteen-year-old Lola's parents to engage in reasoned dialogue with me as their clinician because they believed I was harming Lola by acting with caution in sticking to the staged programme of treatment; but similarly it was hard for me to build a trusting therapeutic relationship with this young person under the threat of legal action from her father.*

Broadly liberatory ideas informing future directions for the service might be resisted by some therapist groups who would see this work as beyond our remit – too partial, too concrete, too much a matter of taking sides rather than locating ourselves in a 'neutral' therapeutic space. It would also involve clinicians taking a stance that reveals a considerable degree of confidence and assertiveness, both ethically and theoretically, at a time when only practices that are fully 'evidence-based' are seen as deserving of unequivocal allegiance. But a service more finely tuned to the voices of those who seek its help will take seriously young gender variant people's parlous social status and face outward more boldly. However, it is important to acknowledge that some young people and families wish to live ordinary private lives without taking on the political issues of trans liberation; this view must also be respected (Richards, Barker, Lenihan & Iantaffi, 2014).

What liberation psychology can touch on but not resolve

Writing this chapter has helped me to see the potential value of liberation psychology ideas for our practice, but I still see some profound and complex questions left unaddressed by the call for open dialogue, affirmative practice, service-user involvement and activism. These are questions to do with how we understand the very nature of gender non-conformity, and in particular questions about what, in the predicament of gender non-conformity, counts as 'oppressive'. Read simply, a liberation psychology stance implies that the problems are in the social context bearing down on non-conforming individuals whose ability to flourish is constrained by their absence of voice and control, and by their public portrayal as deviant or incomplete. But what if the leading counter-narrative addressed to the oppressing social context is itself oppressive to some gender non-conforming groups?

We can agree that one way to resist discriminatory public narratives is to have available counter-narratives to help resist the shaming. Proponents of narrowly biomedical accounts of the causes of gender variance – whether genetic, neurochemical or anatomical – argue that such a causal account enhances the human rights argument for combating discrimination and promoting genuine acceptance of gender non-conforming people. By contrast, stories that incorporate complex and uncertain *meaning* (social and psychological accounts) are not seen to offer adequate protection against such shaming. If gender non-conformity is a bona fide 'medical' condition, then no blame or shame attaches to the child or family. And such an account creates a clear justification for intervening early – 'correctively' – to prevent the child developing the unwanted secondary sexual characteristics that may need rectifying later in life if they want to successfully 'pass' as the 'other' sex. A liberation psychology stance might see this causal story and its consequences as unproblematic if the task is to build solidarity and confidence in the face of stigmatising and discriminatory social narratives.

However, we need to consider the risks to the gender variant community of a biomedical causal model, based thus far on limited data,[3] that risks limiting and oversimplifying ideas and concepts of sex and gender. Four decades of highly contested research on what makes boys different from girls (Fine, 2010) should make us uncomfortable with uncomplicated and fixed conceptions of masculinity and femininity. Gender is more justifiably seen as the unfolding of a complex set of exchanges between self and others in which gender constructs can take on a rich variety of meanings, and gender performances are put to a wide range of uses (Harris, 2005; Goldner, 2011), with biology and physiology only setting the boundary at the most extreme limits (Fausto-Sterling, 2012). When our sense of embodiment is so crucially mediated by cultural meanings, it is hard to see the experience of gender non-conforming people as purely a biological 'given'. To do so, it might be argued, is precisely to draw attention 'away from structural issues and towards subjective factors' (Martín Baró, 1994), focusing too much on people's individual profiles and not enough on the wider context of their lives.

As those who have endorsed a biomedical explanation of homosexuality can attest, theories that at one time prove liberating and fruitful may at another time prove a liability. If placing all hope in an essentialist biological explanation leads one to promote a biological 'solution' to gender incongruence, then the problems of oppression and intolerance might be sidestepped. Individual young people may feel under pressure to choose early physical intervention, with consequences for those who choose not to 'pass', or who try but 'fail' (Roen, 2011). Once young people are positioned by a demand that identity *must* be underpinned by biological change, then we risk gender variant people winning social recognition *only if* they conform physically to normative conceptions of how a male and female must look. Is this not in itself oppressive?

My concern is that representing physical intervention as the most desirable goal for gender non-conforming young people represents a potentially oppressive acceptance of a version of gender that many – not just gender non-conforming people – experience as limiting, precisely because it demands conformity of body and mind to a narrow binary discourse. A non-essentialist view of gender offers conceptions of gender as to a large degree multi-layered and evolving over time, as well as involving pre-natal, parental and wider social forces. From such a perspective we are surely bound to interpret the urgent requests of young people for hormonal and surgical sex reassignment as *sometimes* demanding too much coherence and clarity (Wren, 2014a). At the least, we should be promoting a grasp of the possibilities of varied trans★ identities, in order to encourage thinking critically about conventional notions of masculinity and femininity, and to challenge a passive relationship to diagnosis and classification. Add in a concern, within a society that widely promotes body dissatisfaction, that young people may be led to idealise the transformation of the body, with the limitations of physical intervention poorly understood.

In conclusion

I have argued for the importance of our service repeatedly opening up opportunities for dialogue about the possible trajectories of gender development within a highly charged sociopolitical landscape where the voices of trans★ people are marginalised and their opportunities for self-determination narrowly constrained. This is especially critical given the power imbalance in services where young people may not always give us, or their parents, the full account of their motivations and desires when they ask for treatment. But a delicate balance is crucial: the need for thoughtful consideration of a range of alternative ways of struggling with and resolving gender non-conformity should never be presented in a way that could itself be experienced as oppressive to those young people who have evolved a settled binary sense of their gender; there is a danger of ignoring their unique experience and point of view too.

Incontestably, as liberation psychology approaches assert, there is urgent work for psychologists to do to support young gender non-conforming people in the negotiation of their social identity and to explore how that positioning constrains or enables them to achieve what Butler (2004) calls 'a liveable life'. Only if the lives of gender non-conformist people, in all their variety, are celebrated and made more visible, will young people be in a position to make better decisions about how to live their gender. But it is a distortion of the liberation psychology approach to think we can empower our service users purely by challenging oppression on their behalf and offering them simple medical solutions to complex predicaments.

Precisely because the process of gender identity development is likely to be so rich and layered, the pathways to gender non-conformity are surely legion. Trans★ people do not form a monolithic group in terms of how they experience their gender and their bodies, in their relationship to distress and disempowerment, or in their demands for support and treatment. For many, the incongruence between gender identity and body creates a form of psychological distress in the deep relationship between the self and the body (Prosser, 1998), with a profound sense of bodily discomfort seeming to lie at the heart of transgendered lives. We are not in a position to say how far this distress might be experienced even in a more accepting social context. Reluctant as we may be, as 'liberatory' clinicians, to draw attention towards individual and subjective factors, we cannot be too knowing about how far a negative and demeaning public profile is what distresses them, or, alongside that, how far the solution must be sought in a more private and intimate reckoning with what is possible in reconciling body and identity.

Acknowledgements

I would like to thank the people who heard or read versions of this chapter and made helpful observations, especially Jay Stewart of *Gendered Intelligence*.

Notes

1 To be sure, the oppressed people in Martín Baró's world were typically in extreme need of food, shelter, health and work. But Martín Baró insists that even in such circumstances they do have other – less pressing, but equally serious – needs for humanising relationships, for love and hope in life and for identity and social standing (Martín Baró 1994). The young clients in my service are less likely to be short of a home and food, although the absence of needs at this level cannot be assumed.
2 Testa, Jimenez and Rankin (2014) demonstrated this effect empirically.
3 For a good overview of research on the sexual differentiation of the human brain, see Bao and Swaab (2011).

References

Bao, A.-M., & Swaab, D.F. (2011). Sexual differentiation of the human brain: relation to gender identity, sexual identity sexual orientation and neuropsychiatric disorders. *Frontiers in Neuropsychiatry, 32*, 214–26.
Burton, M., & Kagan, C. (2005). Liberation social psychology: Learning from Latin America. *Journal of Community and Applied Social Psychology, 15*, 63–78.
Butler, J. (2004). *Undoing gender*. Abingdon: Routledge.
de Vries, A.L., Steensma, T.D., Doreleijers, T.A., & Cohen-Kettenis, P.T. (2011). Puberty suppression in adolescents with gender identity disorder: A prospective follow-up study. *Journal of Sexual Medicine, 8*(8), 2276–2283.
Di Ceglie, D., Freedman D. & McPherson, S. (2002). Children and adolescents referred to a specialist gender identity development service: Clinical features and demographic characteristics. *International Journal of Transgenderism, 6*(1). Retrieved 17 September 2014 from www.symposion.com/ijt/ijtvo06no01_01.htm.
Drescher, J., & Byne, W. (2012). Gender dysphoric/gender variant (GD/GV) children and adolescents: Summarizing what we know and what we have yet to learn. *Journal of Homosexuality, 59*(3), 501–10.
Fausto-Sterling, A. (2012). The dynamic development of gender variability. *Journal of Homosexuality, 59*(3), 398–421.

Fine, C. (2010). *Delusions of Gender: How our minds, society and neurosexisim create difference.* New York: W.W. Norton & Company.

Freire, P. (1971). *Pedagogy of the oppressed.* New York: Continuum.

Goffman, E. (1963). *Stigma: Notes on the management of spoiled identity.* London: Penguin.

Goldblum, P., Testa, R.J., Pflum, S., Hendricks, M.L., Bradford, J. & Bongar, B. (2012). In-school gender-based victimization and suicide attempts among transgender people. *Professional Psychology: Research and Practice, 43*(5), 468–75.

Goldner, V. (2011). Trans: Gender in free fall. *Psychoanalytic Dialogues, 21*, 159–71.

Harris, A. (2005). *Gender as soft assembly.* Hillsdale, NJ: Analytic Press.

Lykes, M.B. (2012). One legacy among many: The Ignacio Martin-Baro Fund for Mental Health and Human Rights at 21. *Peace and Conflict: Journey of Peace Psychology, 18*(1), 88–95.

Martín Baró, I. (1994). *Writings for a liberation psychology.* Cambridge, MA: Harvard University Press.

Moane, G. (2003). Bridging the personal and the political: Practices for a liberation psychology. *American Journal of Community Psychology, 31*(1/2), 91–101.

Orford, J. (2008). *Community psychology: Challenges, controversies and emerging consensus.* Chichester: Wiley.

Prosser, J. (1998). *Second skins: The body narratives of transsexuality.* New York: Columbia University Press.

Richards, C., Barker, M., Lenihan, P. & Iantaffi, A. (2014). Who watches the watchmen? A critical perspective on the theorisation of trans people and clinicians. *Feminism and Psychology, 24*(2), 248–58.

Roen, K. (2011). The discursive and clinical production of trans youth: Gender variant youth who seek puberty suppression. *Psychology & Sexuality, 2*(1), 58–68.

Russell, G.M. & Bohan, J.S. (2007). Liberating psychotherapy: Liberation psychology and psychotherapy with LGBT clients. *Journal of Gay & Lesbian Psychotherapy, 11*(3), 59–75.

Singh, A.A., Hays, D.G. & Watson, L.S. (2011). Strength in the face of adversity: resilience strategies of transgender individuals. *Journal of Counselling and Development, 98*, 20–7.

Testa, R.J., Jimenez, C.L. & Rankin, S. (2014). Risk and resilience during transgender identity development: The effects of awareness of and engagement with other transgender people on affect. *Journal of Gay and Lesbian Mental Health, 18*(1), 34–56.

Wallien, M.S.C., Swaab, H. & Cohen-Kettenis, P.T. (2008). Psychiatric comorbidity among children with gender identity disorder. *Journal of the American Academy of Child & Adolescent Psychiatry, 46*(10), 1307–14.

Wren, B. (2000). Early physical intervention for young people with atypical gender identity development. *Clinical Child Psychology and Psychiatry, 5*(2), 220–31.

Wren, B. (2013). Treatment for adolescents with gender dysphoria: future perspectives. Talk given at the *Amsterdam Gender Identity Meeting, Symposium and Workshops on the Occasion of the Retirement of Prof. Peggy T. Cohen-Kettenis*, VU University Medical Center Amsterdam, the Netherlands, 7 June 2013.

Wren, B. (2014a). 'Thinking post-modern and practising in the Enlightenment': Managing uncertainty in the treatment of transgendered adolescents. *Feminism and Psychology, 24*(2), 271–91.

Wren, B. (2014b). Working with gender non-conforming young people: What can a liberation psychology perspective contribute? Talk given at conference *A Stranger in My Own Body: A Festschrift for Domenico di Ceglie*, Tavistock Centre, London, 13 June 2014.

Zitz, C., Burns, J. & Tacconelli, E. (2014). Trans men and friendships: A Foucauldian discourse analysis. *Feminism and Psychology, 24*(2), 216–37.

7
THE USE OF FILM AND CREATIVE MEDIA TO LIBERATE YOUNG REFUGEE AND ASYLUM-SEEKING PEOPLE FROM DISEMPOWERING IDENTITIES

A dialogical approach

Sue Clayton and Gillian Hughes

Introduction

Coming from different practices, Gillian Hughes (clinical psychologist, systemic family therapist and lead of the Tavistock Child and Family Refugee Team), and Sue Clayton (screenwriter, film-maker and academic) came into dialogue over a concern for young people who arrive in the UK alone from war zones such as Afghanistan and face complex legal issues. As minors they are protected by the Children Act (1989), but because of this initial protection their asylum case is not fully considered until they turn eighteen. Then, having thoroughly established their life and identity in the UK, they are faced with the real threat of violent and abrupt return to their home countries.

This racist and discriminatory system as evidenced in the mass media, government policies, and UK institutions, is played out in social relationships in which young asylum-seeking/refugee people experience multiple disqualifications of their identities. With the backdrop of loss of family, community and homeland, and often a history of trauma, these young people are faced with the Herculean task of re-constructing their identities and sense of home. These issues can have a devastating impact on wellbeing, although many survive and grow in remarkable ways through their experiences (Tedeschi & Calhoun, 1995). Accessing discourses of survival and resistance can be crucial in supporting recovery and the development of positive futures for these young people.

Gillian and Sue are both involved in work with this aim, using film and creative media. In this chapter, they explain what they each brought to the task; how they worked together and synthesised practices and insights; and what this has meant not only for the young people with whom they work, but for their own understanding of issues around power, identity, belonging and liberation.

Sue

The first issue that struck me when I began to work with separated young male Afghan asylum-seekers was that on arrival they seemed to have great difficulty in articulating their 'own' stories – their selves, effectively – which caused them considerable distress, making it hard for them to function in daily life. Only later did I come to appreciate that the trauma of arrival in the UK, the subsequent culture of disbelief and subtle or blatant racism to which most are subjected, can potentially have a more crippling effect on their sense of self than the trauma they experienced in their home country.

It is estimated that each young person is interviewed, often in a confrontational and disbelieving way, over twenty times in the first months of arrival, by Home Office, police, and other asylum agencies, which can make them reluctant and scared to reveal personal histories (Asylum Aid, 1999). As a researcher in narrative storytelling, I was curious as to what life stories these young people would feel able to present in a non-'official' and non-threatening environment.

I had read the work of *Children of the Storm* and *Salusbury World*, both pioneering groups for young asylum-seekers set up in London schools, where poetry was used as a way to encourage storytelling that would, it was hoped, reconnect them to their former histories and strength. From this work I noted many 'voices' – from the longing in the poem of a young Bosnian girl who described the broken Mostar Bridge in Bosnia, as a 'father', tactile, familiar and dear, to the shockingly adult and possibly angry voice of a Bosnian boy in Newham in his poem *Sorry*:

> Sorry...
> Sorry that we are here
> That we take your time
> Sorry that we breathe your air
> That we walk on your ground
> That we stand in your view
> Sorry Yes sorry
> Sorry that we look like we do
> Sorry that we disturb your rest...
> ...Sorry that we sit in your trains and buses
> And on your benches in the sun
> And sorry that we brought nothing
> And the only thing we have is a story
> Not even a happy story...
> *(Salusbury World, 2008)*

This powerful play of emotions – of guilt, longing and angry defensiveness – drew me to study the psychological aspects of these young people's lonely journey to create a self-hood, and the obstacles they face. This is why I have found Gillian's therapeutic work and insights so valuable.

Gillian

In my work with separated children seeking asylum, I notice a constant struggle between our efforts to help these young people develop identities that support their wellbeing and self-esteem, and enabling them to survive within a system that is deeply oppressive. As one young Afghani man said to me '*It is like constantly being told you are a nobody, that you have nothing to offer, that you are not wanted.*'

Our identity positions us in relation to others and opens or limits choices for how we can act. As the Russian linguist Mikhail Bakhtin (1984) explains, identities are created through social interaction in which stories are generated about us, and which locate us in the context of social narratives. Where dialogue is possible, there can be a process of constant re-interpretation, and opportunities for each speaker to define themselves. In contrast, a 'monologic' discourse implies a fixed identity behind the narrative, with no space for the dominant view to be questioned. For example, the monological descriptions of asylum-seekers in the media as 'bogus' invites the perception that all asylum-seekers are untrustworthy, which then permeates everyday social interactions. As family therapists White and Epston (1990) highlight, these dominant social narratives can become internalised, and can grow into identities which limit opportunities for future action. The accounts people then give of themselves can function to reproduce and legitimate the very social order that is oppressing them. This was encapsulated in the words of a young Afghani man I will call 'Rohullah';[1] when expressing his frustration about not being believed by the home office, he said '*Send me home and I will become a drug dealer or a terrorist.*' Wellbeing is therefore closely connected to the identities emerging from broad social discourses, but these narratives are also historically situated. They are shaped by relationships forged within colonialist systems (Moane, 2011) which place some in positions of power over others, and are also embedded in cultural and community practices. When attempting to counter these oppressive processes, it is therefore important to look to people's social histories to uncover alternative and more enabling discourses which have the potential to serve for their liberation. Martín Baró (1994) described this process as *the recovery of historical memory*, and one of the central tasks for liberation psychologists. By inviting people to recover an identity and pride of belonging rooted in their tradition and culture, this enables them to make sense of their current circumstances. It also connects them with aspects of their identity which offer opportunities for resistance against oppression.

In the Tavistock Child and Family Refugee Service, we have responded to these ideas in our work with separated young people seeking asylum through our use of narrative practices. White (2004) describes how to create 'alternative identity projects' with people, helping them uncover alternative understandings about their life and their preferred ways of living, which fit with their personal moral codes and preferred identities. Particularly for separated children seeking asylum, we have found this to be a powerful method to help them make sense of their pasts, and build enabling narratives about themselves and their communities to carry into their futures.

I was excited to meet Sue and hear how she was using film and creative media, as this seemed to offer possibilities to enhance the processes that we were working with. Many years previously, in East London, I had collaborated on the 'Making Waves' project supporting Black men who had used mental health services to make a radio programme about their experiences (described in Chapter 1). It was extraordinary to witness the powerful effect on the men of being able to have a voice and a platform which authenticated and valued their words, within a system which they had experienced as so disqualifying of them. Meeting Sue reminded me of the possibilities this work opened up.

Sue

In 2003 I became involved with Project Phakama, a participatory theatre group that supports artists, musicians and performers in sharing their skills with young asylum-seekers in the UK. I became the technical trainer in video and sound, but was keen also to observe the ways in which these young people might use creative opportunities to stretch the boundaries of expression and throw off the conventional ways in which they are perceived and perceive themselves. For the 2004 Phakama show *Strange Familiars* both the trainers and young people were resident for a week in an ex-children's home in North London – and for the young people, their rooms became places transformed into performance spaces. Audiences arrived to first find themselves herded into a chaotic and intimidating reception space and ordered about by the young people in a Babel of nonsensical languages that they could not understand or follow: the young people acting out their subjective experience of a detention centre. After their initial disorientation and discomfort, the audience acknowledged the serious point being made, but also the playfulness behind the idea. Further anarchic reversals – the marching of the audience in and out of the scenes of the play, the flying of a giant fat lady kite as a symbol of the caring asylum they all seek, the commandeering of a harmless tea-trolley as prop to be a killer army vehicle – recalled for me Bakhtin's work on carnival and play. Bakhtin wrote about the carnivals and popular festivals of the Middle Ages and Renaissance, tracing the history of class distinction as expressed in what he called 'dialogic' modes of communicating (discussed above). He viewed carnival as an act of rebellion, one of satire and playfulness. He suggested that an individual in the Middle Ages lived two lives – an official life subjected to the hierarchy of the social order and everyday existence and an unofficial carnival life freed of daily social norms and restrictions.

For Bakhtin (1984) 'the unofficial carnival is people's second life, organized on the basis of laughter' (p. 8). Child psychologist Lynne Cohen interprets his view as follows:

> Carnival is a way of breaking down barriers, of overcoming power inequalities and hierarchies. Festive life is achieved through the playful mockery of hierarchical order by individuals oppressed by it. Through free and familiar

interactions, carnival offers a temporary way of experiencing the fullness of life.

(Cohen, 2011; p. 178)

This kind of inventiveness, and using the imagination to create new ways to present stories, was also evident in the way the young people presented carefully composed scenes in each of their rooms. A Somalian boy covered his room entirely in white sheets. He wore all white, and sat reading a book whose pages were all white and blank and said: '*Nothing to hurt me here!*' A young girl set her bed as a picnic table for her family – with plates, fruits and flowers special to each of them – a family who had all died in Sudan. A former Liberian child soldier sat in his room reciting his detailed biography but insisted that the audience be moved on at a random moment midway through: '*The Home Office never wanted to listen to my whole story. So I'll tell it forever and ever, but the audience won't get to hear the end.*'

What excited me here as an artist was the way that the young people created rich and diverse artistic styles that challenged the stereotype of the refugee as passive, objectified victim. '*Strange Familiars*' and the next Phakama play, *Breaking the Glass Box* (2005) also intrigued me because of the ways in which the young people developed strategies to reach back toward their own history. For instance a scene of attack and murder is mimed behind a lit coloured sheet; the figures appear to us as shadow-shapes only. The music that accompanies it comes from the girl behind the screen who sings a long-remembered lullaby from her own country. These are young people who listen to rap and hip-hop on their mobile phones, but when they perform they combine snatches of old song, rhythms, dance moves and gestures from home. As Martín Baró (1996) described, this 'recovery of historical memory' enables a reconnection with modes of expression and identities rooted in their past, which can then become integrated into their developing sense of self.

I saw that their sharing of these stories and memories, though painful, produced a sense of purpose and agency that was lacking before, and therefore positioned them in a stronger and more powerful place. For instance, one boy, Jacob, was 're-settled' by the Home Office to Manchester during the rehearsal period. He knew no-one there. The others went to Euston to see him off, as grave as if he was being deported to another country. He responded to their concern and sneaked back to London the next day, where he was received back in rehearsals like a hero. This echoed with Gillian's quoting of White (2004), above: the young people refused to accept the *diktat* that asylum-seekers shall be randomly re-settled, simply because they have been re-settled once before – and exerted their own agency to keep Jacob with them.

Gillian

In the Child and Family Refugee Service, we have been offering a number of narrative groups in schools, youth clubs and sports centres for young people from refugee communities (Hughes, 2014; Hughes & Kaur, 2014). These groups have been based on the 'Tree of Life' methodology developed by Ncube (2006), which invites young people to map out their lives in the form of a tree, identifying their cultural heritage (roots) and communities of support (shoots), and how these have nurtured the development of their strengths and skills as well as hopes and dreams for their future (fruits). This narrative map offers people a safe base from which problems can be explored, and a way to develop 'an alternative territory of identity' (White, 2005), as well as a method for the recovery of historical memory (Martín Baró, 1994).

We have used this methodology to help young people understand their struggles within the context of a history of oppression, challenging the story that so many come with – that their struggles are a consequence of personal failure. Through narrative 're-storying' (a process of identifying alternative, more enabling descriptions of what lies behind the struggles), we help people connect with their position in the context of postcolonial relationships, and talk about stories of resistance. For example, in a group with Somali boys, there was talk about what it was like being connected to a homeland where there was ongoing conflict. The conversation progressed from narratives of confusion and shame to those of pride and resilience as they began to realise how this history of struggle had made them strong. They began to identify stories of Somalis in the UK who had been able to stand up to injustice, and they were then able to connect these to their own lives. When people understand that external circumstances, not personal or internal characteristics, are responsible for their distress, there is often a radical shift towards wellbeing.

We decided to run a Tree of Life group with the unaccompanied young men from Afghanistan using our service. Although for some of them, it was painful to reconnect with their social histories because it reminded them of all they had lost, the process of talking together enabled stories to emerge about strength through struggle, and the importance of community.

The group itself developed a strong and supportive identity, and people were eager to contribute to each other's stories about skills and abilities they had noticed in each other. It was clear that the group was experienced as validating of the young people. As one person said about the group facilitators, at the end: '*They listened to us, showed us respect, they were prepared to get down on the floor with us. This never normally happens to us.*' Also that it had helped connect people with positive aspects of their identity; for instance, one young man commented '*Everyone helped me feel proud of myself and realise my qualities.*'

Everyone was keen to continue to meet after the group ended, although they did not like the fact that the group had taken place in an institution (the Tavistock Centre) and said they would have felt more comfortable meeting outside in a natural setting, as this would connect them with their home experience. They also felt that the method of using pen and paper to record their responses was limiting, as writing was a struggle for many of them. We therefore agreed to plan a follow-up day in Richmond Park, where we would continue the conversations, which would be recorded using hand-held video cameras. We took a picnic to share and a football, and when we arrived in the park I handed the cameras over to the young people so they could take ownership of what was recorded.

The day turned out to be a great success which everyone seemed to enjoy. '*We changed a lot. I feel much better ... when I came back [into London] I was saying ok, I'm fresh now, I can do whatever I want*' (Roshan).

By giving the video cameras to the young men, they became authors of their own stories – they had control over the questions asked as well as the responses, and this seemed to position them as survivors rather than victims. Izat commented: '*I got to interview my friends. We talked about how to help people who have just arrived in the UK. It was good.*'

Being in an environment (a rural setting) that connected the young men with home prompted conversations about their cultural history. It seemed we were witnessing the recovery of the young men's historical memory in a way that had not been so possible within the confines of a Tree of Life therapy group, located in an institution that they had no historical connections to.

> It was a natural place ... it reminded me of what we had, and we talked about how life was [back home].... When we came back, we went to Farid's house, and we stayed there and talked about the things that we did. And we had pictures ... on our mobile phones – a lot of pictures, a lot of memories. We all talked about it afterwards.
>
> *(Shamal)*

It seemed important for the young men to have records of the day so we agreed to edit the footage from all the films and make it into a short video to complement their personal photos.

White (2007) describes how, once people have identified the self descriptions that they want to embrace, the process of 're-telling' these preferred stories helps them become fully embedded in their lives and relationships. White (1995) developed narrative techniques he referred to as 'definitional ceremonies' – a process which offers people ways of telling or performing the preferred stories of their lives before an audience of carefully chosen 'outsider witnesses'. These witnesses honour the stories told by responding with what has resonated personally for them, and how their lives have been touched by hearing these stories. Self descriptions become more tangible through hearing they have had an effect on others. I therefore asked the young men if I could show their film during systemic teaching I was offering with Taiwo, and recorded the responses of the audience/witnesses, which I then took back to the young men.

The witness responses were remarkable. People were deeply moved by hearing the young men talk about how they had overcome adversity and oppression in their lives. They were struck by how the young men could join together and celebrate their cultural roots in spite of all that they had lost. People talked about how the film had influenced their ideas about their future practice – for example: going out for walks with clients to avoid the limiting effect of the clinic setting, talking more with clients about how they have sought to overcome oppression, and discussing strength and resilience. As one witness commented: '*The young men have inspired us all.*'

When I went back to the young men and shared the witness responses with them, they responded with amazement and awe. Mohammed was initially speechless, then said '*I had no idea we could influence people like that. It is so . . . so good hearing how we can help other people.*'

This confirmed for me that it is not enough to offer people space to have a voice unless there is the opportunity to influence others with that voice.

Sue

The Richmond Park film interested me a great deal as I had observed the young men in therapy at the Tavistock Clinic, and then the same young men in the park. The aspect of 'play' or inventiveness that I have spoken of earlier was apparent in Richmond Park. Whereas in therapy they appeared in a way as 'victims', people with problems, in the park they talked more openly about their journeys here, and freely turned the camera on each other, breaking the hegemony of its gaze and catching each other in the filming – a further example of Bakhtin's dialogic.

Alongside the theatre and video work I did with separated young people, I have filmed with them over ten years to build up a longitudinal sense of their stories and struggles, a practice which resonates with the Martín Baró (1994) 'task' of *de-ideologizing everyday experience* in order to be free of its constraints on personal identity. This footage is being assembled as an online archive (www.Bigjourneys.org). One such archive story expanded into my film *Hamedullah: The Road Home* (2011), which has been widely screened in the UK and worldwide.

I met Hamedullah in 2008 when filming with separated young people in Kent, where many of the Afghan boys are housed after arriving via the UK port of Dover. When Hamedullah was arrested and detained, he accepted my offer to take back to Afghanistan a small video camera, and on it chronicle his life as a forced returnee. For over a year he sent me emails and digital video (DV) footage of his life and his attempt to reconcile the stages of his life to date – that of a child fleeing alone to a foreign country; an asylum-seeker here, prematurely adult; and his forced return to ... what?

Considering the film project in terms of Gillian's Tree of Life concept, I observed Hamedullah on his forced return grasp instinctually at what Gillian would call the 'roots'. In the first days back he drew on his absent parents' wisdom, saying: '*When I was a child in my sleep time, my parents would tell me stories and say humans must be harder than rock and softer than a flower. I did not know what this meant – now I know what it means*' (ibid.). And instead of remaining in Kabul – the only Afghan city the Home Office deems safe for returnees – he risked going to settle in the far north, in a rural area west of Mazar-e-Sharif, where his family had lived years before. This posed risks as there were no opportunities for work, severe climate conditions and both famine and drought.

As well as physically hard times, Hamedullah struggled to resist the repressive identities imposed on him. He reported that distant relatives were suspicious that he had been deported back. Looking conspicuously Western and with acquired

Western values, he was not easily accepted back into Afghan society. He had committed no crime, yet both Afghanistan and UK cultures branded him criminal. He also struggled to deal with impending adulthood: 'I don't know how to be the man that I am supposed to be' (Clayton, private email correspondence with Hamedullah, 28 November 2008).

However, filming proved beneficial by offering Hamedullah, first, a different 'eye' – that of the outsider or the observer; and, second, an audience, someone to witness his courageous journey. He progressed from speaking only of his sense of alienation – *'everyone is strange to me, and I to them'* (Clayton, 2011) – to recording what he saw happening to people around him. Whatever their nationality, or ethnicity, they were poor, and they were crippled by the war. Hamedullah films boys selling tea and plastic bags for virtually nothing; men who squat around fading fires in wasteland; the barricaded Red Cross building which denies him admission. This recalls Martín Baró's notion of reconstructing psychology from the perspective of the 'other' – here, it is his voice, his view, his Afghanistan that we see. *'This is my bed, my room and my blanket. All the time it is dark, dark place. There is nothing here for me'* (ibid.) In this way Hamedullah progressed from using film to simply describe what he was doing and how he felt, to how he saw his country, and what the future must be. *'We need a settled government'* he says to camera. *'It is not just the Taliban, there are lawless people everywhere'* (ibid.). This raises the question – who is this new 'we', this new 'I'? – and brings us back to the branches of the Tree of Life – the aspirational drives of self that move us forward. Chase and Allsopp (2013) argue that migration policy in the EU and member states is predicated on the idea that young people who arrived after difficult journeys here 'belong' back in their countries of origin – even though much evidence, including my own with Hamedullah, strongly suggests that most cannot construct a stable life when returned, and because of danger factors are very likely to leave again to pursue further options. It is these young people's plans and aspirations to which we must work to respond, at both a policy and a therapeutic/support level, rather than seeking to contain the young person as 'victim' or 'problem' to be sent back. Hamedullah refers frequently in his film material to his own aspirations, and attempts to envisage a new and different future for himself. His ability to articulate his world view, and to express anger, frustration and hope for a better future, is inspiring to those like myself who continue to fight for changes to the policies and attitudes that so harshly impact on so many young lives.

Conclusion

What was interesting to both of us was a deeper understanding of how film, creative writing and performance can work as effective tools to de-ideologise young people's potentially restricted views of self. The creative process can provide a means of accessing the original experience of individuals and groups, and return it to them as inspiring and potentially liberating stories, shared within a social context. The audience, by witnessing the enactment of these stories, can provide validation for these new ideas of self, and through their responses, further reinforce these preferred versions.

We would argue that the process goes beyond simply retrieving past experience, and involves accessing earlier cultural memories in order to integrate them into complex and ever-changing views of self in ways that are liberating in the present context. Lone young asylum-seekers are likely to experience particularly complex models of self because of the multiple oppressive, and often conflicting, contexts they have had to negotiate. This complicates the notion that there is a cohesive 'past' that, in and of itself, provides the answer to questions of identity posed in the present, and that may take a young person forward into the future. However, examples from both the Tree of Life and the *Hamedullah* film (where Hamedullah is forced to return to his own region even though there is seemingly nothing there for him) support Martín Baró's emphasis on the importance of historical memory.

We have learnt a great deal from working with these young people about the process of the ongoing development of self within a social context and how that can be oppressive and/or liberating. We believe that we have a role and a responsibility to use our professional skills to get the unheard stories of the marginalised heard, and create opportunities for their impact to be felt by others. For example, having made the Hamedullah film, Sue made sure it was seen by all relevant organisations, submitted as evidence in Immigration Court appeals, screened to the UNHCR Policy Unit in Geneva[2] and its evidence submitted to Parliament (Parliamentary Select Committee, 2013). Gillian not only used the Richmond Park film in teaching events, where she recorded audience responses and fed this back to the young men who had created it, but also showed it to the commissioners of the Refugee Service who agreed to support more of this type of work in the service.

The process of making and showing creative work illuminates not only the therapeutic journey for those who are defining themselves, but also the effect on others who to a greater or lesser extent recognise themselves in the stories and the emotions produced. This is evidenced in the countless debates that have taken place around the *Hamedullah* film, such as that at another young asylum-seeker's site (http://lifeafterdeportation.wordpress.com). Indeed, viewing someone you can identify with can be as transformative as directly taking part in a creative process, which was the idea the 'outsider witness' process with the Richmond Park video drew on. And such processes – for both makers and audience – help provide the symbolic recognition that young asylum-seekers need. It can also provide opportunities to step outside the assumed role that even benign well-wishers can force upon them – that of helpless victim. The dynamism of the creative process can therefore be a powerful tool in the process of liberation from oppressive identities and the re-defining of relationships. Thus we will go on seeking in our future work to explore this rich vein – the benefits of creative interaction in helping young people move towards a more nuanced and liberating sense of self, and ourselves towards more profound and socially committed empathy with them.

Notes

1 Real names are not used for any of the people referred to in this chapter.
2 UNHCR Policy Unit Geneva 16 July 2013: *Falling Through the Cracks: The Fate and Future of Unsuccessful Asylum Seekers*. Screening of *Hamedullah: The Road Home* and presentation by Sue Clayton.

References

Asylum Aid. (1999). *Still no reason at all: Home Office decisions on asylum claims*. Retrieved 20 August 2014, from www.asylumaid.org.uk/wp content/uploads/2013/02/Still_No_Reason_At_All.pdf.

Bakhtin, M. (1984). *Rabelais and his world* (Hélène Iswolsky, Trans.). Bloomington, IN: Indiana University Press.

Chase, E., & Allsopp, J. (2013). 'Future citizens of the world'? The contested futures of independent young migrants in Europe. *Refugee Studies Centre Working Paper*, paper series 97, 1–38.

Clayton, S. (2011). *Hamedullah: The Road Home* (UK, 2011, 23 min). Eastwest Pictures UK (see www.hamedullahtheroadhome.com).

Cohen, L.E. (2011). Bakhtin's carnival and pretend role play: A comparison of social contexts. *American Journal of Play*, 4(2), 176–203.

Hughes, G. (2014). Finding a voice through 'The Tree of Life': A strength-based approach to mental health for refugee children and families in schools. *Clinical Child Psychology and Psychiatry*, 19(1), 139–53.

Hughes, G., & Kaur, P. (2014). Young men from refugee communities score goals for their future using the Team of Life. *Context*, 134, 25–31.

Martín Baró, I. (1994). *Writings for a liberation psychology*. Cambridge, MA: Harvard University Press.

Moane, G. (2011). *Gender and colonialism: A psychological analysis of oppression and liberation*. London: Palgrave Macmillan.

Ncube, N. (2006). The Tree of Life Project: Using narrative ideas in work with vulnerable children in Southern Africa. *The International Journal of Narrative Therapy and Community Work*, 1, 3–16.

Parliamentary Select Committee (2013). On the human rights of migrant children. Retrieved from www.parliament.uk/business/committees/committees-a-z/joint-select/human-rights-committee/news/publication-of-first-report-human-rights-of-unaccompanied-migrant-children-and-young-people/.

Salusbury World (2008). Poem by a Boy from Bosnia. Retrieved 20 August 2014, from www.salusburyworld.org.uk/childrens-poems.php.

Tedeschi, R.G., & Calhoun, L.G. (1995). *Trauma and transformation: Growing in the aftermath of suffering*. London: Sage Publications.

White, M. (1995). Reflecting teamwork as definitional ceremony. In: M. White (Ed.), *Re-authoring lives: Interviews and essays* (pp. 172–98). Adelaide: Dulwich Centre Publications.

White, M. (2004). *Narrative practice and exotic lives: Resurrecting diversity in everyday life*. Adelaide: Dulwich Centre Publications.

White, M. (2005). Children, trauma and subordinate storyline development. *International Journal of Narrative Therapy and Community Work*, 3/4, 10–22.

White, M. (2007). *Maps of narrative practice*. New York and London: W.W. Norton and Company.

White, M., & Epston, D. (1990). *Narrative means to therapeutic ends*. New York: W.W. Norton & Company.

PART III
Working with adults

8

'KEEPING IT REAL'

Oppression, liberation, creativity and resistance

Ornette Clennon, Elisha Bradley, Taiwo Afuape and Amelia Horgan

Inspired by the online phenomenon 'rapper tag', this chapter includes the voices of young people Taiwo and Ornette have worked with. A 'rapper tag' is a non-interrupted, responsive and consecutive battle rap, in which one rapper performs a rap (spits a verse), then tags another, who spits a verse in response, and so on.[1] This chapter starts with an excerpt from a 2007 BBC interview with Fender, an eighteen-year-old male Ornette worked with, about the impact music had on his rehabilitation as an inmate. Ornette picks up on some of Fender's themes before tagging twenty-year-old Elisha and Taiwo simultaneously. Taiwo and Elisha respond to Ornette, before Taiwo tags in nineteen-year-old Amelia. They all share reflections about how we liberate ourselves and contribute to the liberation of others.[2]

Extract of 'Blockz' by Fender

> It might've sounded good, people talking about killing parents and killing each other. It made the younger youth around react different. They started picking up guns, twelve year olds going jail.... It was nothing to be proud of. I've been in jail for two years now. It was really a tough road for me. Mum was there. Didn't want to see her hurt but in a way I'm glad I'm in jail 'cos I'd be out there now, guns and things like that. Instead I write lyrics nearly every day, it relates to what I've been through on the streets.
>
> I was proud to write lyrics. We're trying to get across to guys that gun crime is not the answer. In music you can chat about life, lifestyles and politics and things like that and let other people enjoy it. You haven't got to talk about killing people. I've just really been enjoying writing love songs and things like that. It's a big change.

> Music's given me a new life.... A lot of Black lads have been coming to jail for murder and things like that. I want to get that message out there. If my music can achieve that, I'll make my mother the proudest woman ever.
>
> *(Fender, 2007)*

───◆───

Title: 'Keeping it Real'
Submitted by: Ornette D. Clennon
Category: Urban culture

For me, an African-Caribbean male composer, musician, academic and arts-led community development worker, *'keeping it real'* summarises street culture, the value of authenticity within street culture and the commercialisation of that authenticity. It was a phrase that was often used by young people at HMPYOI Werrington, where I worked with Fender. Since the two-year Werrington project, which involved writing and recording music, I wanted to explore how the concept of 'keeping it real' impacted on the cultural and personal identities of the young inmates, in terms of both their concientización[3] and their social orientation.[4]

Cultural oppression and the market

Given what is reflected back at us from reality TV shows and music videos, how can we ever hope to keep it 'real'? Popular culture is market-constructed because youth culture and anything *'urban'* makes money; but not for the young people who inspire these urban art forms. Talented urban artists, busy making a name for themselves in MC battles, spitting about issues important to them in their communities, might gradually get exposure for their talent on the likes of SBTV (a broadcasting company that makes YouTube rap and pop music videos), YouTube and BBC one Extra. They might grow an underground fan base and, if really lucky, they might get noticed by an important promoter or record label. However, what starts out as a genuine expression of where someone comes from (the 'real' bit) gets subtly transformed into 'something else': a commercial representation of itself.[5] This 'something else' has a semblance of reality but also isn't real. In order to become commercially attractive, and shift products, endorsements and modern celebrity, this product has to sell fantasies.

When an MC's track and video becomes available, in order to promote them the artist will need to have been packaged by a promoter and local recording studio; this involves taking the essence of who the artist is and turning them into a market projection that becomes less specific to the artist and more general. Their image, which will be the main vehicle for carrying their music, will need to attract as large an audience as possible, especially in this age of the single track download. In the case of hip-hop, perhaps the largest selling urban genre around the world, the consumer tends to be White middle-class males.[6] This is important because the consumer may not be interested in the 'reality' of where the music came from, but in what the music represents; a representation which no longer reflects its origins but an oppressive fantasy. This fantasy can only exist if the raw cultural experiences of the artist are merchandised. Artists may be promised success by being shown role models in the industry who have made it. But what they haven't been shown is how these artists have been manipulated to fit an industry stereotype that keeps power firmly with the market and industry. Bourdieu calls this 'mis-recognition'.[7] It's this promise of success that keeps artists producing the raw materials for the cultural merchandise that are sold to consumers at 'street value'. Street value gains its monetary value from its disposability and accessibility.[8] So a download, which typically is low cost, gains its value from not only its amount but its 'likes', which directly reflects its ability to generate higher revenues by attracting advertising. In other cultural sectors, such as galleries, the artist's merchandise is sold to consumers at 'rarity value', the one-off, customised, one of its kind piece that can be sold individually at an extremely high cost (see Velthuis, 2003).

Cultural liberation and the people

In order for artists' tracks to 'succeed' in the market they need to be packaged in such a way as to be commercially appealing, which means promoting oppressive fantasies. For example, urban youth culture is based on stereotypes about what being Black is – 'Blackness' – a commercial concept and marketing/branding tool.[9] In this context, 'Blackness' does not refer to ethnicity, but, like a fashion accessory, something that someone can wear at any time to make themselves more commercially desirable. This refers to youth style: fashion, music, the way people speak or sing and how they carry themselves. Ironically, style should communicate authenticity, originality, rebelliousness and innovation, but in order to appeal to a mass audience, its form and content is manufactured and mass produced. The surface qualities of 'real-ness' become market tools and not the real thing at all.

This is worrying because youth culture, and its principal driver, music, is dominated by stereotypes of 'Blackness' based on a dangerous form of exaggerated hyper-masculinity (female artists can wear it too although it will mean slightly different things for them). This commercial 'Blackness' is a fantasy based on violence, aggression and sexual exploitation. If our young people see these images but no commercial alternatives, they may think that they are the only way to perform masculinity. This 'fantasy' may also condition young women to accept the misogyny that is part of it, such as the depictions of young women in music promos 'performing' in ways often described as 'sexy'; but sexy for whom? We see the dangers of this commercial fantasy of 'Blackness', and the homophobia prevalent within it, in its resolute refusal to accept any other forms of masculinity or 'Blackness'.[10] This commercial fantasy does not accept that Black men can be educated, or soft,[11] but cleverly obscures the actual experiences of Black men and women:

Britain's colonial history, racial tensions and institutional discriminatory practices, and the history of the Black experience[12] that informs its cultural merchandise, such as the Windrush generation's Toasters.[13] We need to educate our young people to look more closely at the culture they are consuming. The continual consumption of this toxic diet of cultural products and merchandise maintains the status quo. But what is even more disturbing is how this toxic diet co-opts young people or those who are oppressed, to do the oppression on its behalf. This cycle must be broken. A shout out to Elisha and Taiwo...

Title: Young women and the commercialisation of perfection
Submitted by: Elisha
Category: Women and youth culture

As a twenty-year-old female student, the effect of the commercialisation of youth culture and the domination that comes with it is obvious to me, particularly its effects on young women. Throughout history it has been young people who have challenged authority and believe that they can create change. It has been young people who have been instrumental in bringing new ideas to politics and culture; while their views may at times have been extreme, they have helped to balance out the apathy of older generations. As far as I can tell this is no longer the case.

In the past youth cultures and subcultures have been directly influenced by young people themselves. However, due to commercialisation, ideas that would once have inspired a generation, are filtered through managers and those funding musicians and filmmakers. The result of this process is a watered-down version of the original idea, designed as a one-size-fits-all, conventional and marketable profit-making tool. Women are hit by this process the hardest, as women are only able to make a profit if they fit into a certain mould. Even if we are strong, independent and talented, to be commercially viable we also apparently need to be skinny, but not too skinny, pretty, but not unobtainable, sexy, but never intimidating. As author Chimamanda Ngozi Adichie said in her 2012 TED talk: 'We should all be feminists:'[14] 'You should aim to be successful, but not too successful, otherwise you will threaten the man.'

This obsession, in the entertainment industry, with perfection (but not too perfect, mind) has an unhealthy impact on the young women of my generation. Popular culture tells us that we must be perfect, but the image we are presented with is one no one will ever obtain. Young women are turning their backs on feminist ideas that should surely be so important to them. I recently had a discussion with two friends of mine about maternity leave; both of these intelligent young women, no doubt with promising careers ahead of them, believed that maternity leave should be a privilege, not a right. Young women are so busy trying to reach an unobtainable height of commercialised attractiveness they have no time to consider if their own basic rights as women are being respected. Often it seems to me that for some young women at university, it is more of a status symbol to have a boyfriend than a First.

In the end this process of striving for commercially fabricated perfection becomes a full circle. Social media allows us to create our own illusion of perfect lives akin to those we think our celebrity idols lead. Instagram filters allow 'selfies' that erase all our perceived imperfections, and those of our friends. Social media has become less a way of staying in touch with friends, and more a vicious, unspoken competition: *Look, look at me, I'm one step closer to perfection than you.*

Attractiveness becomes a sense of worth. Apps like 'tinder' allow us to make snap judgements about people's appearances, accepting or rejecting them on nothing but that basis. On 'Pinterest' you can create a 'dream wedding' board before any hint of an engagement, or even a serious relationship, because of course marriage is a competition now too. If your wedding didn't cost more than your entire degree, it basically doesn't count and your marriage will never last, right?

More young women need to wake up to the way they are being manipulated by the media, the entertainment industry and each other. Women should act and dress in the way they want, and if this happens to be in the commercially attractive way the media dictates, that's fine, but make sure it's because YOU want to, not because you think you should.

◆

Title: Creativity can uphold power and resist it
Submitted by: Taiwo Afuape
Category: Creativity and resistance

Liberation requires dialogue, so it is important to listen to people as they are, in the ways they want to speak and not only create space for people to say what we want to hear or to speak with voices we find 'acceptable'. A rapper-tag invites us to listen to different voices, as well as produce texts that are not finished or monovocal. Ornette described the impact of powerful institutions, such as the music industry, on individual creativity and Fender described the potential of creativity as a form of liberation, even within an oppressive context. As a Black working-class African feminist/womanist socialist/anarchist woman and psychologist, I am drawn to the links between creativity and resistance.

I was surrounded by music growing up, and the ways in which it can represent a sign and tool of resistance and liberation. I was inspired by the resistance histories of diverse communities around the world and in my quiet spaces I grew more resilient and connected to life's possibilities. I was particularly drawn to street-based creativity (such as punk and hip-hop culture), filling up areas of deprivation and turning emptiness (lack) into space (possibility) with body art, graffiti, dance and music. Hip-hop currently outsells every other type of music globally, and yet it owes its beginnings to 1970s South Bronx – a notorious borough of New York marked by racism, unemployment, poverty, dereliction, violent crime, gang activity and drugs. At that time mainstream Black music was mainly disco pop, which felt out of step with the lives of the urban American underclass. From breakdance and rap battles, hip-hop developed a rich tradition of improvisation and experimentation based on expressing and reflecting on the reality of Bronx life. Restrictions on personal and cultural identity can be harmful but can also, ironically, lead to creative forms of expression. Hip-hop MCs must be flexible and responsive to the various challenges of their craft, constantly trying out new ideas in an attempt to push themselves in their performance, reading and responding to the audience. Creativity reminds us that we draw on resources when surviving oppression that might otherwise go unnoticed and unutilised.

Music, lyrics, artists and audiences exist within market situations, oppressive social structures and discourses of misogyny, homophobia, hyper-masculinity and individualistic materialism. It can be difficult to develop a progressive and 'local' market in a context in which global influences are so dominant. Instead, artists may conform to Eurocentric, sexualised and sexist stereotypes in order to 'succeed'. Ways of thinking and acting that promote the dominant culture and existing power structures are rewarded with fame and fortune and those that don't are often rejected. And yet, by creating music the artist insists on the right to have a voice, to interpret experiences and to bring to public view ideas that are obscured by official ones. Creativity provides opportunities for those who would normally be on the margins to take centre stage; creates pauses within the relentlessness of despair; involves coming back to the same topic from different angles, developing our reflections; opens up the limits of what can be expressed, and often emerges when we run out of options. Creativity does not just reach deep into the core of us but also connects us to others, producing a kind of pleasure that is hard to rival. Potentially, it is genuine openness to otherness; a commitment to understanding experience beyond the limits of our personal understanding. Creativity does not just reflect our experience, but actively *shapes* it; hence it comes with great responsibility to self and others. As Fender argues, creativity is most fulfilling when it liberates us from oppressive ideas, rather than upholding them.

Working in the mental health system, it is clear to me that people are inherently creative and *always* resist experiences of subjugation, prejudice and harm, even if these forms of resistance are invisible to others and confined to the privacy of our internal experience. We could even view 'mental health problems' as forms of protest and resistance. Refusing to be content, coherent and comprehendible may be an invitation to look outwards – to the nature of oppressive circumstances – rather than towards the inner-life of the protester. Whereas oppression orientates us to the contours of emptiness, creativity reconnects us to the potential of space. As Maya Angelou suggests in her poem *Ailey, Baldwin, Floyd, Killens, and Mayfield*, spaces, far from being void, can be filled with an 'electric vibration'.[15] I don't think it is any coincidence that in Pali, the language of the Dharma (Buddhist scriptures), 'Dukkha' – often erroneously translated as 'suffering' – can be understood as 'restricted space'.[16] Creativity can open up areas that initially feel fixed, tight and constricted. It does this by helping us notice and appreciate the moments of beauty and possibility that surround us, and exist within and between us, that oppression would have us blind to.

Resistance can be *creative* (creating opportunities), or *restrictive* (harming others) or a combination of both. Creative forms of protest often take on a contradictory manner because they are also implicated in the status quo. But as Fender explains, creativity is never finished; it can be reworked to move us closer to a place that liberates ourselves and each other. If the corporate world has stolen hip-hop, there are many stealing it back (for example, Akala and The Hip-Hop Shakespeare Company[17]). All of us are involved in a complex process of complicity with dominant cultural interests as well as resistance to it. However, we are never fixed in any particular identity or state of being, but continue to create who we are in a world of others.

Young people regularly tell me about their forms of creativity (parkour,[18] skateboarding, music, writing, reading, photography, acting, knitting, designing, fashion, boxing, cooking, martial arts, dancing, drawing, sculpting, writing, sports and so on) that enable them to resist adversity and oppression and open up new avenues for action. When everyday acts of resistance are noticed and valued by a community of others, as forms of creativity, they can provide foundation for further liberatory action. To see potential, art, something special in another person, is a form of love and it liberates us and liberates that quality in them; like Michelangelo's angel in the stone: '*I saw the angel in the marble and carved until I set [her] free.*'

I remember talking with Amelia about the power she had when taking photographs, to look for beauty in the most unlikely places. We talked about what her creativity had her thinking about herself that she wanted to take into her future life, and what her camera saw that her 'dread' did not. Amelia talked about the ways photography requires concentration and mindfulness in order to see new things and how it both captures time and time is forgotten. We talked about the values and commitments inherent in her creativity in terms of the type of world she wished for. I described her as an ongoing moment in history, and asked what legacy she wanted to create. Amelia talked about wanting to be part of a movement that empowers, rather than 'treats', women:

> With our self-promoting fervour
> which sees weakness at her seams
> with the unease of wings caked in phlegm,
> all we can be is mental saviour.
>
> With our desire to cure and calm
> her battered dreams,
> our soothing balm, fails to condemn
> *their* abuse, *their* harm.

All we can see is blinded fate,
sculptress' fingers numb to shape.
She might become our silence,
part cataract, part bruise,

If not for the protest
arising from her core,
inviting us to join her insistence
'no!' to harm; 'no more!'

From our stagnant forlorn
to her Oya, laoch, Amazon,
playing leaves like flutes,
while wisdom sings her roots.

Only now might we be free
like dolphin arias, delight not ashamed.
In nick of time we might be saved
– think lonely rats surfing a maze –
we might just learn[19]

Over to you Amelia…

Title: Lost and found
Submitted by: Amelia
Category: Women, community and resistance

When I was younger I thought my salvation lay in controlled isolation. I'd take myself and my camera off, frame the image, and feel those split seconds of silence, of me directing my life. My creativity lay in solitude, in my unstoppable desire to feel in charge of my life, even if only for a second. I located my agency in myself alone, as I'd never felt I had any chance of controlling my life; never felt I could be calm, or get better, or even just get outside of my head.

Since then I've learnt. Going to university I first learnt the kind of Knowledge you're supposed to have to Make It Big. All the big dates, the big men in their big ships, history as a (tempered now they've added caveats to their claims) march of progress, European capitals, women in silks, men with swords or pens. I thought I'd found my way in. Done with capturing the present, I thought I could creatively rediscover the past. With time, I realised the only creative rediscovery was their refashioning of history – writing out the struggles, the torment inflicted on the many by the few.

But I was still confused. One night I felt so alone that I thought if I read all these books, all these old white men on dead white men, I might find the answer – I might find the part of myself, that part that's always been missing. I might find it in some dusty old book in some dusty old library. I thought I'd found my way out of sadness by entering into esteemed dialogue with the dead. I thought I'd found my community, some rarefied, heavenly salon where we'd discuss the Great men and the Great matters, resolve the questions of all ages. Really, my creative faculties were just as desiccated as their rotting corpses. The thing about being taught (rather than learning) is that it's not what they teach you that's really interesting, it's what they miss out.

The books didn't work; I couldn't fit myself into their stately waltz of progress, the gentle stream of history. When things started to go wrong around me – friends revealing their own stories of violence, abuse, survival; all the while nothing seeming to happen to change, to help, to help me, to help *us* – I realised the enormity of my error. My community was not in a constructed past. My community had been around me all the time.

A friend of mine once told me that once you get two women together, of any age, and they start talking, really talking, something happens; there's a completeness to women, from years of living in their own heads, kept quiet, trying to keep pretty, but underneath it all quietly thinking. And across these decades of silence, a connection is forged. It's an idea I haven't been able to get out of my head.

Although I'm worried about its claim to universality – the idea of a universal womanhood, beyond our different experiences, stratified by class, race, sexuality, geography – when conversations happen, when real communities are made (communities that value difference, that see sisterhood not as a thing to be assumed but as a process of understanding, of realising our individual experiences are marked by sharp differentiations of privilege) something special happens. The first time you hear that someone else has felt that thing you've felt, when you know you're not alone, and when (if?) you can use that moment to learn, or to destabilise, or even take on, harmful power structures, is a moment so powerful, so creative in its potential for change, self-development and self-love. Having been socialised to see other women as competition (who can get the man, who's got the best hair, the best clothes, who can sit pretty, perfect, beautiful with her suitors lined up in a row), I was in awe of how powerful we were when we got talking, when we got planning. I learnt to love women and to stop competing.

We, this growing group of women, would talk about our experiences, some of us as women living with mental health problems, but all our lives scarred by sexual violence, domestic abuse, harassment, frustration and loneliness. What got us really talking was how our sadness, our anxieties, were not welcome, not up for discussion in the world outside. These were supposed to be our private sufferings, not evidence of structural violence, and talking about them was somehow unseemly. From our talking, we realised that often women's depression is seen as a personal failure, whereas men's, at least in literature, is seen as the result of an unfair world, a too powerful intellect, a romantic tragedy. We had the mad women in the attic against the dreamy Byronic hero. We stopped seeing ourselves as screw-ups and failures, and saw ourselves as a community struggling for safety, survival and recognition. In talking, listening and respecting, we've given each other strength, found new strategies for facing misogyny and violence, and we've found ourselves in *our* pasts.

When you learn to love yourself, your sorrow included, learn to love and support those around you, you find yourself in your past and your history; a creative and powerfully subversive force in a society that seems set on the erasure and forgetting of the lives of women and other marginalised people. The act of (re?) discovering self, the selfhood stripped away by years of silencing and powerlessness, is perhaps the ultimate act of creativity, of resistance. I'm glad I could find some directionality at last in myself, but that agency, that political, emotional and psychological force, we hold, when we as women get talking, get thinking, get acting for and with each other, is even stronger. Now I take photos of the women who inspire me, not just controllable landscapes.

Notes

1. The rapper tag phenomenon was started on YouTube in 2010 by Melbourne rapper '360', based on the 'Rap Tag Game' developed by US Emcee Ramzo (rappertag.com).
2. Each contributor has given as much information about themselves as they would like to give.
3. Roughly translated as 'consciousness-raising' (Freire, 1973).
4. Meaning the acknowledgement that sociopolitical history plays an important part in being able to understand oppression happening in the present (Burton & Kagan, 2005).
5. Baudrillard (1981) describes the media's four different forms of reality where (1) it gives an honest account; (2) it distorts reality and this is obvious; (3) it distorts reality but pretends it's real; (4) it distorts reality but doesn't need to pretend it's real because it can use other fantasies to legitimise its version of 'reality'.
6. As described by Yousman (2003).
7. Sometimes known as 'false consciousness', coined by the German social scientist, author, political theorist and philosopher Friederich Engels (see Bourdieu, 1984).
8. Baudrillard (1972) describes four types of consumer values attached to objects/culture: (1) functional value (doing what it is supposed to do); (2) trade value (how much you get for it); (3) symbolic value (what it means to its owner); (4) sign value (what it represents to others).
9. See Kvifte (2001), who talks about this.
10. Frank Ocean is an exception to the rule but remains the only out gay man in hip-hop.
11. See Frosh, Phoenix and Pattman (2002) for details.
12. Martín Baró (1994) describes how the re-writing or erasure of a people's history can be used as a tool of oppression against them.
13. Toasting, chatting or deejaying is the act of talking over a rhythm or beat by a deejay, which originates from the griots of Africa. Toasting has influenced the development of rapping in African-American hip-hop, dancehall in Jamaica, as well as grime and various types of dance music, such as UK jungle and garage.
14. www.youtube.com/watch?v=hg3umXU_qWc.
15. Extract from Maya Angelou's poem 'Ailey, Baldwin, Floyd, Killens, and Mayfield' (1995).
16. Contemporary translators have emphasised that 'suffering' is too limited a translation for 'dukkha', and have preferred either to use terms such as anxiety, stress, frustration,

unease, unsatisfactoriness and 'dissatisfaction' or to leave the term untranslated, given that no single English word effectively conveys the same range of meanings and connotations as 'dukkha'. Winthrop Sargeant (10 December 1903–15 August 1986) was an American music critic, violinist and writer who had an interest in the sacred Hindu text *The Bhagavad Gita* and published his own English translation in 1979. With respect to the etymology of the word 'dukkha' Sargeant argued that *dus* is a prefix indicating 'bad' and *kha* means 'sky', 'ether' or 'space'. Thus 'dukkha' could be understood as restricted space.
17 www.hiphopshakespeare.com/site.
18 A physical and mental discipline (philosophy and way of life) which uses jumps, vaults, climbing and swinging to enable a person to overcome obstacles and go from place to place in the quickest and most efficient way possible.
19 Poem written by Taiwo Afuape inspired by Amelia and Taiwo's commitment to empowering rather than 'treating' women.

References

Angelou, M. (1995). *The complete collected poems*. London: Virago Press.
Baudrillard, J. (1972). *For a critique of the political economy of the sign*. St. Louis, Missouri: Telos Press Ltd.
Baudrillard, J. (1981). *Simulacra and simulation*. Michigan: University Michigan Press.
Bourdieu, P. (1984). *Distinction: A social critique of the judgement of taste*. (R. Nice, Trans.) Cambridge, MA: Harvard University Press.
Burton, M. & Kagan, C. (2005). Liberation social psychology: learning from Latin America. *Journal of Community and Applied Psychology*, 15, 63–78.
Fender. (24 July 2007). *Sonic [db] Music Technology in Prisons*. (M. Lee, Interviewer) BBC. Radio Stoke, Stoke-on-Trent Retrieved from http://youtu.be/65Hu7vi7Ykc.
Freire, P. (1973). *Pedagogy of the oppressed*. New York: Seabury Press.
Frosh, S., Phoenix, A. & Pattman, R. (2002). *Young masculinities: Understanding boys in contemporary society*. Basingstoke: Palgrave.
Kvifte, T. (2001). *Hunting for the gold at the end of the rainbow: Identity and global romanticism on the roots of ethnic music*. Retrieved 26 July 2013, from www.popular-musicology-online.com/issues/04/kvifte.html.
Martín Baró, I. (1994). *Writings for a liberation psychology*. Cambridge, MA Harvard University Press.
Velthuis, O. (2003). Symbolic meanings of prices: Constructing the value of contemporary art in Amsterdam and New York galleries. *Theory and Society*, 32, 181–215.
Yousman, B. (2003). Blackophilia and Blackophobia: White youth, the consumption of rap music and white supremacy. *Communication Theory*, 13(4), 366–91.

9

'WOMEN CAN BUILD A NATION. OUR DISEASE, HIV, CANNOT STOP US TO BE MOTHERS BECAUSE WE ARE THE MOTHERS OF THE NATIONS'

A liberation approach

Angela Byrne, Jane Tungana,[1] *Upenyu, Monika, Devota, Janet, Fay, Rose, Rukia, Wonderful, Patience, Becky, Mary, Hope, Lizzy, Linda, Barbie and Uwamaria of Re:Assure Women's Project at Positive East*

Introduction

Re:Assure Women's Project[2] is a community project for refugee, asylum-seeking and migrant women who are living with HIV. It is a project of Positive East[3] and was developed by one of its African communities' workers, Jane Tungana, and its clinical psychologist, Angela Byrne, supported by the African communities' staff within the charity and the work of the wider organisation.

Jane is originally from Burundi, where she was a teacher and journalist; Angela is originally from Ireland. We have both worked in HIV services in London since the 1990s and came together because of our shared passion for working with women and our interest in issues affecting women, human rights and community approaches. Jane uses her position as a refugee woman living with HIV to provide peer support, which is frequently described as a source of great hope and inspiration by women who participate in the project. Angela also discloses her HIV negative status and women often comment on how inspiring it is to witness us working together in harmony despite our differences.

Our service model is influenced by Sue Holland's social action psychotherapy approach (Holland, 1992), as described in Chapter 2, and provides peer support, outreach activities, psychological therapy, group courses and community events. Women who participate in the project contribute to service development and delivery in numerous ways, including promoting the project, co-facilitating workshops, speaking at conferences and activism for the rights of migrants and people living with HIV. Women have gone on to create their own projects and networks both in the UK and Africa. In this chapter we discuss how liberation psychology principles link to our work.

The dialogue

This chapter is based on dialogue between women who participate in the project. We developed questions in dialogue with Taiwo and Gillian and came together to eat and discuss oppression, liberation, wellbeing and the role of Re:Assure Women's Project. We tried to include voices of women who were not present by incorporating their ideas into our questions. It is impossible to capture the energy and exchange of ideas on these pages, but we have tried to highlight moments of laughter and celebration in the quotes.

Oppression in context

A key concept within liberation psychology, critical consciousness, entails moving from an individual to a social focus in theory and practice, such that distress and wellbeing are understood in their social contexts. Therefore, we began by asking about the contexts in which women came to our service and whether (and how) they see their experiences as being connected to processes of oppression.

> As a woman, and a migrant for that matter, and I live alone, I am a marginalised person to start with. So there are a lot of issues already before even bringing ... HIV into it.
>
> *(Upenyu)*

The concept of intersectionality (Crenshaw, 1989) is useful in understanding the inter-connectedness of different forms of oppression and how they shape each other. Women discussed the impact of poverty, racism, stigma and discrimination with multiple dimensions – as women living with HIV, as migrants, refugees and asylum-seekers. In the UK, migrants are often wrongly blamed for spreading disease and exploiting the NHS and welfare system (Dodds *et al.*, 2004), and women discussed the hostility and lack of understanding that they face.

> Most people here, British people, don't understand why we come to seek asylum or why we want to live in another society.... I'm talking about people who come from countries in war, for example, no one understands how it could be really depressing to be in a country you were born in and you feel that you need to escape. It's the heaviest feeling you can have.... And deep down, when you know your reason for coming, you know it's not reasons you want to discuss with anyone passing.
>
> *(Monika)*

Stigmatisation and discrimination impact on the material conditions of women's lives and can undermine their strategies for resistance. In the extract below, Devota describes the response she received when, having been sent out of London due to the policy of 'dispersing' asylum-seekers, where she experienced racism and discrimination, she and her daughter returned to London to reconnect with their only social network.

> The housing people said I made myself homeless. This woman said to me 'now look at you! You leave affordable housing and come to make yourself homeless, you better go back on the street, there is no houses for such a person like you'.
>
> *(Devota)*

Living with HIV brings further experiences of oppression. HIV-related stigma is heavily reliant on other forms of discrimination, such as racism, homophobia and misogyny, as well as anti-immigrant discrimination (Dodds *et al.*, 2004). Women highlighted the gendered aspects of HIV stigma in which they may be judged as prostitutes, promiscuous women and unfit mothers.

> They think you have been promiscuous and sleeping around and they can even say it is a punishment from God.
>
> *(Janet)*

> Even those who are educated, they only have one thing in their mind. They think you are a prostitute.
>
> *(Fay)*

HIV-related stigma and discrimination serve to maintain social inequalities through processes of exclusion and the creation of stigmatised identities (Parker & Aggleton, 2003). Women's rights to have relationships and children were contested, both within their families and communities and in mainstream services.

> a relative of my partner ... started disclosing to social functions, so my partner was terrorised, like 'You should leave this woman, she's HIV positive'. I could not attend any social function without being pointed at, even now.
>
> *(Rose)*

> Most of us have been judged, like we're not supposed to live because you're HIV positive; you're not supposed to have a relationship because you're HIV positive. When we go to mainstream services, the moment you mention you are HIV positive, it's like 'So now, why are you having those children? Why are you doing this?'
>
> *(Rose)*

Refugee, asylum-seeking and migrant women living with HIV in the UK are thus faced with the problem of resisting multiple stigmatised identities, in the context of isolation from family and community, making this resistance much more challenging. These experiences can have a profound impact on women's emotional wellbeing.

> When you're walking down the road, you feel that people are pointing at you. You don't trust nobody.... You feel guilty ... like you've done wrong and that you are a sinner ... you cannot even walk or go into a shop or a church or a mosque ... Sometimes it's so hard for me to cope with these things. It's really hard.
>
> *(Rukia)*

A liberation psychology approach acknowledges that women resist such social and emotional abuses in many ways and their accounts of oppressive experiences almost invariably include accounts of resistance. For example, Devota, who described her experience with the housing department above, responded '*I said, "You are lying. Let me continue my life."*'

Liberation in context

Who defines liberation is an important issue of power. In our dialogue, women defined liberation as freedom '*from being judged all the time*'; '*from fear, shame, and stigma*', '*freedom from discrimination*'; '*from lack of confidence*'; '*Free to live, free to love*'; '*Freedom to talk freely ... to move around*'. These definitions can be understood in the context of oppressive experiences, which constrain women's freedom of movement and speech; question and judge their rights to love and live as they choose and involve stigmatisation and discrimination.

Liberation practices and Re:Assure Women's Project

Psychology, liberation and oppression

A key idea in liberation psychology is that of reconstructing and critiquing psychology from the perspective of those who are marginalised or oppressed (Martín Baró, 1994). An important part of our approach is to invite women's critical perspective on psychology. When asked whether psychology has contributed to liberation or oppression in their lives, women reported many oppressive experiences, including being rejected from services, offered only medication and treated as if they have no choices. More than thirty years after Sue Holland's work, women were still beginning their journeys as 'patients on pills'. Almost all women present spoke of being offered anti-depressants or other psychiatric drugs, which they found unhelpful or harmful.

> My doctor sent me to a psychiatrist. This man, the way he interrogated me, put me like I was at a police station. At the end of it, he said 'don't put your frustration or whatever on your child' and he gave me medicine. I even thought, maybe it's me that's wrong. Am I really bad to my daughter?
>
> *(Wonderful)*

> I used to see a male psychologist who used to just sit and look at me. And I would cry and cry because my mother died and I couldn't go to bury her and he would just sit there. It used to really frustrate me because there was no dialogue between us and then he would go and record what I had said ... and they gave me anti-depressants but I didn't need anti-depressants.
>
> *(Upenyu)*

These accounts highlight how psychology can reinforce isolation and pathologisation (see, for example, Patel, 2003). We aim to support women to critique and challenge these oppressive processes.

> They give you [anti-depressant] medication and say you have to take it but it has side effects. I took them and got some bad effects so I was glad when Angela said 'you don't have to take them, see how it goes, you have options'. But the way they talk to you in the hospital, it's like you have to. I don't want to say people shouldn't take medicine but you have to have the right not to be forced to take it.
>
> *(Wonderful)*

> Psychologists try to blame you. They try to put their words to you, not your own words.
>
> *(Patience)*

Patience's comment above also highlights something important about whose words and understandings are privileged. Our approach is concerned with co-creation of meaning and focus on the client as expert in their own lives. Thus women define their own outcomes. An important aspect of the work also involves engaging women in discussions about how they have protested and resisted the abusive and oppressive experiences they have faced (Wade, 1997). These stories of resistance help them reconnect with their strengths, both individual and collective.

Geraldine Moane (2011) writes about the 'cycle of liberation', which encompasses the personal level (building strengths), the interpersonal level (making connections) and the political level (taking action), and this provides a useful framework for thinking about our work.

The personal level

As with Holland's (1992) model of social action psychotherapy, Re:Assure Women's Project has a place for individual psychological therapy and peer support sessions. These are supported by practices such as outreach to HIV clinics, support groups and community events, where we seek to demystify psychology and encourage self-referral. Self-referral is important, not only in terms of ease of access, but being able to refer yourself, describing your difficulties in your own words and defining your own outcomes, positions women very differently compared to their experiences in mainstream services. Women have often found psychology services extremely difficult to access and have undergone assessments only to be rejected from services for reasons that are often unclear, related to their immigration status or lack of available childcare.

> The process took more than three years.... I was assessed at my GP's and referred to a very far place.... I went for assessment three times ... then after ... they said no they can't take me.... I thought maybe ... are they discriminating me because of my origin? Are they discriminating me because of my HIV status? Why?
>
> *(Patience)*

> My doctor referred me to a psychologist but she told me they can't see me cos I'm not ill and because I've got immigration problems, so I can't access the service there so I should go back to my GP, and get onto medication. ... But I said 'Listen here! My problem is not medication, I just need to speak to someone. I've got this problem and I feel guilty because it's like I'm turning it onto my child and I don't want my child to be taken away from me tomorrow and you're telling me I need to find childcare or I can't come and see no one here? What planet are you from?! What can I do? I can't afford childcare. The father is not available when I need him but I need to speak to someone. These are my problems, can someone help?'... So, I come here and Jane says brings all your papers and she talks me through everything and I see Angela ... and that was what I needed. I didn't need medication. It's just ridiculous, I mean do I have to go on a stretcher so I can see a psychologist?
>
> *(Becky)*

In contrast, women referring themselves (or being referred) to Re:Assure Women's Project are not assessed, screened or required to fill forms in order to access the service. To support access we provide a crèche for group sessions and fares for those with no recourse to public funds. We also offer joint sessions where language or cultural support is needed or where women feel unsure about seeing a psychologist and want Jane's support.

The interpersonal level

A crucial aspect of our work involves women coming together in groups, where they can develop collective strategies to challenge the operation of stigma in their lives. We run a course, 'Self-expression, sex and relationships', which involves seven workshops covering topics such as sexuality, having a baby, domestic violence and disclosing HIV status. It grew out of our discussions with women about common difficulties they face, such as feeling that they must stay in abusive relationships in which their partners might be using violence or threats to disclose their HIV or immigration status in order to control them. We invite women to think about their own wishes and desires before focusing on intimate relationships. We inform women about their rights, which is especially important for those without leave to remain in the UK as they are often unaware of how they can leave abusive relationships. Particularly important is enabling dialogue that shares ideas and knowledge between women.

> I'd like to take you back to the first session we had … everyone was talking, it wasn't Jane talking or Angela talking, everybody was participating, and even demonstrating things that other people didn't know. We all felt really really liberated when we got in there. And people (outside the session) were asking 'What's going on in there?' Do you remember? There was so much laughter, so much sharing and people didn't want to go home. We lingered around because we wished it could carry on. It's such a lovely lovely thing. Professionals are usually talking in terms that most people wouldn't understand and they don't care as long as they've delivered what they've planned, which is so different to here.
>
> *(Upenyu)*

Women who have attended the course play a significant role in delivering the course, co-facilitating and sharing their experiences on issues such as surviving domestic violence, dating with HIV and having a baby. This aspect of the work is highly valued by participants.

> We need to learn from people who've lived with HIV. That's an inspiration.… Jane, you really gave me the strength to talk about my status because I didn't know how to disclose to anyone but when you stood there and said you're HIV positive, I was so amazed. Honestly you should have seen my face! I couldn't believe it. There isn't anyone who's ever said that to my face. That just gave me the confidence and the strength. When you said it, I was like, 'if she can say it, then why not me?'
>
> *(Becky)*

Community level: 'Ubuntu'

We came to articulate 'Ubuntu' in a group session following a difficulty that arose between participants and a discussion about how we want to treat each other in the group. Most women knew the term Ubuntu and all were familiar with the concept, which includes a sense of collective responsibility and care:

> For us, we normally say don't cook just for who is at home, we cook for anybody, any passerby can stop.
>
> *(Mary)*

The articulation of this concept, rather than traditional 'ground rules', served to promote the sense of a collective identity and endeavour, which was articulated as follows.

> In Burundian and Rwandese culture, if somebody says 'that person has Ubuntu', you trust them. They have all it takes for you to trust them.
>
> *(Monika)*

> we respect each other, we are chatting on the same level, so it's beautiful. And it brings out the humanity in all of us.
>
> *(Rose)*

> then also, it brings a sense of belonging. You belong somewhere.
>
> *(Patience)*

Women complete the course with a graduation and celebration event and we also organise community events to celebrate International Women's Day or World AIDS Day. These events are extremely popular and challenge isolation and stigma. They include various ways of celebrating achievements, including presentations, group discussions, music and dancing. Women contribute in numerous ways, including writing and performing plays, giving testimonies and presentations, cooking and facilitating discussions.

We also encourage dialogue on a wider community level – for example, a recent International Women's Day event explored 'gender based violence'. Five women shared their experiences, a local HIV consultant presented her research on intimate partner violence in the lives of women living with HIV, and men in the audience were invited into dialogue in order to respond to what they had heard. This led to a rich, though at times difficult, discussion about issues of blame, responsibility and men as both victims and perpetrators of violence.

One of the strongest themes in women's dialogues is Re:Assure Women's Project as a family. When asked what makes it a family, women identified a number of practices:

> As a family, you have to join like this, eating.
>
> *(Hope)*

> Exchanging contacts, so that when you're low you can speak to someone who understands you from your own perspective.
>
> *(Patience)*

> Hearing about [a woman who died]. This one called me and said 'We have to organise ourselves and be there'. That's what a family means.
>
> *(Lizzy)*

Women have also organised themselves to support each other in attending immigration tribunals, given that many women cannot include their families of origin, who may be unaware of their HIV status. Women accompanying each other for support demonstrate that they have established family and community in the UK.

> We can visit each other and know each other and our children grow up knowing each other. That's the most important thing, yeah, being a family. Let's conquer our fears.... It's taught me how to talk. I never knew how to talk.
>
> *(Devota)*

As Devota explains, it is this sense of family that enables the conquering of fears and speaking for oneself and others. Upenyu elaborates the impact of these connections in terms of support and understanding:

> we are all cultures, and we share ideas that you go out there and use from other countries. It's not like, '*you* are from Nigeria, *you* are from Zimbabwe, *you* are from Zambia'. You know, it's like we are a family, our own community. We've formed friendships, right? We phone each other, 'are you ok?' finding out. Nobody else will do that for you.... Wonderful there, she will pick up the phone and say 'Hey woman, what are you doing? You haven't phoned me!' (Laughs). And Barbie there, she was bragging that she was eating this and that and that when she went home to Zimbabwe but she knew she was talking to somebody who would understand what it means to go home after such a long time being here. It's such a lovely feeling to know you can pick up the phone. Re:Assure cemented our friendships, made us a family and I value that very much.
>
> *(Upenyu)*

As Upenyu notes, this community is diverse and participants of Re:Assure Women's Project often speak of the pleasures of these bonds between women from different countries and what they gain from these relationships. This includes learning from each other and helping each other resist discrimination and racism. As a Caribbean woman, Linda discusses her membership of this family.

> I've been here since I was seven and there were African people where I used to work and, ok, my ancestors were probably African, and although there were African people there, I was never really their friend, but.... I'm really glad that I found all of you lot, as African girls, and to me you're like my family now. So, although my diagnosis is not a good thing, I found a family I never had.
>
> *(Linda)*

Women elaborated the concept of the HIV family, in which the shared experiences of living with HIV become a source of strength – for example, Lizzy discusses her relationship with Linda which enables her to resist the stigma she experienced in her family of origin.

> For me, I've even told my sister that she's my family, because she's my HIV family. If they don't want to accept me as a person with HIV, she's

my HIV family. Even when they see her, they will start walking away, and I say 'good!'

(Lizzy)

Foucault (1985) wrote about forms of resistance to stigmatised identities, including 'counter-identification' in which stigmatised identities are subverted and taken on by individuals and groups in different forms. This construction of the 'HIV family' may be an example of this and, as Linda explains, this family may be preferable to other kinds of family, even when they are supportive.

My family ... always want me to come around for tea and they know my status and they're very supportive but I say, 'no I'm seeing Lizzy', she's HIV like me and we can talk about the same sorts of thing and she understands and I understand. And I'd rather see her.

(Linda)

Taking action

Through participation in Re:Assure Women's Project, women have taken action both individually and collectively. Some of these have already been described, such as supporting each other to deal with the immigration system, bereavement and isolation and entering into public dialogue with men around gender-based violence. Some of the many other ways will be described in this section.

Challenging discrimination and stigmatisation

Part of our work involves supporting women to know their rights and to challenge discrimination in their lives, as Rose explains.

Someone from social services learned that I was [HIV] positive and it just kicked off from there. Whenever I had an appointment, people came out to look at me. My appointments were cancelled. I reported it and they said 'No, this person cannot do something like that'. So, I had no one, I did not know the system. But through Re:Assure I was pointed to the right direction, to the right people to deal with this and now no one can put me down.

(Rose)

Women related numerous experiences of challenging stigmatisation and discrimination in their personal lives and within systems, both on their own behalf and on behalf of others:

If I go to the hospital and say I'm HIV positive, if you try to bring any discrimination I will just tell you.... 'I've told you I'm HIV positive, so what of those who don't tell you? Do you know everybody's HIV status? I tell you

> to protect you ... why should you start behaving that way? If you don't want to touch me, then go and somebody else will come and touch me.'
>
> (Janet)

> Now I work at the hospital and I see how sometimes they treat people. Well I do challenge them. If this patient is HIV positive, they say to me 'Janet, your people are around'. Although they don't know my status [Laughs], they just say 'Come come come, we have somebody with immune suppression'. I say, 'What does that mean? Why are *you* not going there?'
>
> (Janet)

Rose describes how the process of challenging discrimination can in itself be empowering.

> Because I was given five years to live, that person [family member] was telling people, 'you wait and within five years she will be gone'.... So I sort of kept to myself and then through coming here, I got myself up and said 'You know what? Get up, and get out there and challenge them'. I can now sit with them and look at them. I ask them with challenging eyes, my head held up high, we are there together seated at the same table, because I've been empowered like all of you have said, I've been empowered so much that some of them have learned to appreciate me.
>
> (Rose)

Positive East is active in trying to influence policy around issues affecting the lives of people living with HIV and women involved in the Re:Assure Women's Project have taken a significant role in this, addressing politicians and commissioners about issues that concern them such as the impact of welfare cuts and the immigration system.

Living and loving as resistance

As described at the beginning of the chapter, women's rights to loving and sexual relationships and motherhood were contested, as were their rights to move freely and pursue their goals. These freedoms were important aspects of their concept of liberation. In this context, action taken by women in pursuit of these desires can be seen as a form of resistance.

> I just can't wait to come here because what I've learned, it has actually turned me into what I am today – I'm a mother and I couldn't ask for more. After I found out about my diagnosis, I thought I would never be a mother but thanks to Re:Assure, I've been more than reassured and I'm having a second child now as everyone can see.
>
> (Becky [Cheers, applause, 'Yeah!'])

> Prior to coming I didn't think I'd get a partner but after the course, I felt empowered, I found a partner and we've been together for two years now. We're a happy couple!
>
> (Barbie)

Similarly, women talked about and celebrated how they have come to pursue other goals such as working and studying.

> At first I was not working, cos I was always thinking that anywhere I go, people will think 'Oh she's HIV positive'. I even kept my child away from people, but now I have confidence.... At first I was a cleaner, now I'm a health care assistant.
>
> (Janet [Cheers, applause])

> When I came here I was like a mad woman. I thought my life was finished. But when I came here I was reassured that I can make something out of my life. And now people can see something about me, they say 'now you are glowing, your beauty is coming out now'. I'm happy. Even at college. I came out with distinctions in all my courses.
>
> (Fay [Cheers, applause])

Creating networks

Women have taken action to bring what they have gained to others in various ways. This includes volunteering, providing peer support, promoting HIV awareness and establishing their own networks and projects. One woman set up a charity with women widowed by HIV in Uganda, and Uwamaria below describes her project with Rwandese women in the UK.

> I've done a big thing because I tried to bring our Rwandese women together and we started a prayer group, slowly, slowly so these women said ... 'This mission cannot stop here.... We are going to find a name where we can bring every woman together and build something which will help the next generation.' We are having a conference to empower women to understand that they are powerful, that they can stand together and they can build the country and build the nation.
>
> (Uwamaria)

In conclusion, participating in Re:Assure Women's Project enabled women to create family and community that sustain them and enable them to take action, resisting stigma and oppression in their lives. They transformed the stigmatised identity of HIV, creating the concept of an 'HIV family' in which the shared experience of living with HIV became a source of liberation. This is perfectly encapsulated in Uwamaria's vision of how women's collective transformation of a stigmatised identity has the potential to bring about social change.

> Women can build a nation. Our disease, HIV, cannot stop us to be a mother because we are the mothers of the nations, we are the mothers of community. If we stand without fear saying that we have HIV, we are going to give birth to those things, we are going to put down all those kinds of things which are trying to put down our countries, which are trying to put down ourselves, which are trying to put down our community ... we have something here which we can bring out and help the country to move on with peace and joy.
>
> *(Uwamaria)*

Notes

1 The names of the following Re:Assure participants have been changed to ensure confidentiality.
2 Currently funded by City Bridge Trust and Comic Relief.
3 Positive East is an East London-based HIV charity (www.positiveeast.org.uk).

References

Crenshaw, K. (1989). Demarginalizing the intersection of race and sex: A black feminist critique of antidiscrimination doctrine, feminist theory, and antiracist politics. *University of Chicago Legal Forum, 140*, 139–67.

Dodds, C., Keogh, P., Chime, O., Haruperi, T., Nabulya, B., Ssanyu SSeruma, W., et al. (2004). *Outsider status: Stigma and discrimination experienced by gay men and African people with HIV*. London: Sigma Research.

Foucault, M. (1985). *The history of sexuality, Volume 2: The use of pleasure*. New York: Random House.

Holland, S. (1992). From social abuse to social action: A neighbourhood psychotherapy and social action project for women. In: J. Ussher & P. Nicholson (Eds), *Gender issues in clinical psychology* (pp.68–77). London: Routledge.

Martín Baró, I. (1994). *Writings for a liberation psychology: Essays, 1985–1989* (ed. A. Aron & S. Corne). Cambridge, MA: Harvard University Press.

Moane, G. (2011). *Gender and colonialism: A psychological analysis of oppression and liberation*. (2nd ed.), London: Macmillan.

Parker, R., & Aggleton, P. (2003). HIV- and AIDS-related stigma and discrimination: A conceptual framework and implications for action. *Social Science and Medicine, 57*, 13–24.

Patel, N. (2003). Clinical psychology: Reinforcing inequalities or facilitating empowerment? *The International Journal of Human Rights, 7*(1), 16–39.

Wade, A. (1997). Small acts of living: Everyday resistance to violence and other forms of oppression. *Contemporary Family Therapy, 19*(1), 23–39.

10
LIBERATORY PRAXIS ALONGSIDE ELDERS

Maria Castro Romero

Introduction

Liberatory praxis is often associated with high levels of activity or activism, in turn associated with younger generations; the underlying (and mistaken) assumption being that 'older people' do not have the energy or level of activity necessary to make social changes. In the UK, liberatory praxis has not focused specifically on older generations. This chapter will provide an overview and include stories of liberatory praxis alongside elders.

The chapter has been constructed from numerous dialogues I had over seven years working as a clinical psychologist in the National Health Service (NHS) alongside elders who came into contact with older people's mental health, social services and voluntary organisations. It is also the result of dialogues and joint teaching over the last five years with Joyce Mangan (now eighty), with whom I had therapeutic conversations in 2004. Joyce later became a consultant to services and educator, from primary school to doctorate level. Although Joyce's current caring role has not allowed involvement as co-writer, we discussed an earlier draft of the chapter and this final form includes her invaluable contributions.

In the act of writing, I am in dialogue with myself, holding in mind the voices of elders in my personal life too. I also hope that in reading, you, the reader, will enter into a dialogue with me, rather than take my statements as final or *truth*.

I think these dialogues, highly enriching and transporting, have been made possible by actively positioning myself *alongside* elders who accessed help (and their family, friends and carers), so that I was not a *helper* but, as Joyce says, 'a friend' in solidarity. 'I am thinking of a solidarity that is constructed by therapists who refuse to draw a sharp distinction between their lives and the lives of others, who refuse to marginalise those persons who seek help' (White 1993; p. 132). Or, as Martín Baró wrote, one more among *the people*: 'Socioeconomically, the people is those who *accept* the other and seek to *become* the other. Politically, the people is those who are *open* to the other. Historically, the people is those who *look for* and *struggle for* the other' (1994; p. 183, my emphasis).

I will return to these ideas, as they form the basis for liberatory praxis alongside elders.

Language and identity: elders

The language we use allows particular identities and positions and hinders others.[1] UK discourses about older generations generally refer to *older people* or *older adults*, which implicitly sets some kind of comparison – older to whom? We are always older to ourselves, older in relation to some groups, while younger regarding others. Who is older is socially and culturally defined, and a distinction is generally made in our cultural context between people born before 1948 (19.5 per cent of the UK population over the age of sixty-five, mostly female), and people over eighty, sometimes over eighty-five, generally referred to as the fourth age, older-older or oldest-old (Office for National Statistics, 2013). However, utilising age to *other* a particular group systematises discrimination on the basis of age – that is, legitimises ageism (Bytheway & Johnson, 1990).

By contrast, the term *elder* (more often used in cultures in the majority world) communicates an acknowledgement of having lived longer and being worthy of respect, in which accrued wisdom is made visible. Elders are positioned as valued members of, and integral to, their communities; for example, taking roles in providing guidance to younger generations. In my experience, elders have seldom self-identified as older people/adults, seeing themselves just as individuals, with their own principles and lives lived through particular historical moments. Joyce's preferred term, if one has to be given, is *senior citizen*, highlighting both the elder/senior position and the importance of 'civic, political, social and cultural rights and responsibilities' (Phelan, 2008; p. 325).

Social constructions of ageing

Considering reality as socially constructed places a question mark on *who* defines old age, who has the power to do so and with what effects? The linguistic production of elders as a homogeneous group overshadows the diversity within older generations, and groups within generations. This also renders invisible the social inequalities, marginalisation, and oppression of elders with respect to the intersectionality of age, gender, ethnicity, level of (physical and cognitive) ability, and so on. For example, an eighty-four-year-old Chinese woman living in poverty in West London may be subject to multiple discrimination and limited access to resources, but more so if she is living with a diagnosis of dementia in a care home where no one speaks her language.

Contexts of oppression

Gross and multiple inequalities affect elders' wellbeing (Higgs *et al.*, 2005). Broadly, they can be captured within three interlinked contexts of oppression: historical, political and socioeconomic.

Historical

Current UK elders have lived within particular historical times that need to be taken into account.

> The link has been broken between families, it started with the rebuilding of the UK after the war, the younger family members went to new estates and their seniors stayed in their family home, so they were left and communication broken down.
>
> *(Joyce)*

Other context factors worth mentioning are:

- During World War II family life was disrupted, young children were evacuated[2] out of London, while older children witnessed bombings and their horrid consequences (for example, an elder shared with me his childhood experience of searching for neighbours in the gravel where their house once stood). However, elders born during the post-war baby boom and the birth of the NHS in 1948, as the UK started rebuilding a future, often experienced a sense of hope and solidarity. So the 1950s brought a very different socioeconomic and security context to some of today's elders' lives.
- Immigration borders were opened in the 1950s to support the economy after the war, with people arriving from Commonwealth states (mostly former colonies of the British Empire), notably from Caribbean islands, India and Pakistan and, in the 1960s, from African countries. Now Black and minority ethnic groups account for 16 per cent of the population of England (greatly concentrated in London), and 8 per cent of those aged 60 and over. These elders endure the oppression of colonial history, racism and immigration.
- Same-sex physical affection and sexual activity was only decriminalised in the UK in 1967 and it was coded in The International Statistical Classification of Diseases and Related Health Problems until the ninth edition in 1977. Despite the gay liberation movement of the 1970s and increasing civil rights, gay, lesbian, bisexual and transgender elders have suffered the criminalisation and pathologisation of their sexuality earlier in their lives and, currently, homophobic discrimination and stigma, and ageism that conceptualises them as no longer sexual.

Socioeconomic

A great proportion of elders in the UK live below the poverty line, recently counted at 1.7 million, of which one million live in severe poverty (Department for Work and Pensions, 2012), yet this serious inequality has not been redressed. The current economic recession has had dramatic consequences for the general population, but particularly for elders' social and financial status.

> Lots of people had not prepared for that, perhaps they did not think they would live so long, and no one can live on state pension!
>
> *(Joyce)*

As Phillipson (1982; p. 3) argues, the 'logic of capitalism as a productive and social system is irreconcilable with meeting the needs of elderly people'. The introduction of a retirement age, a relatively recent historical development (1908), brought with it for many elders loss of status, income and valuable work relationships, which inevitably affects elders' wellbeing (Higgs *et al.*, 2005). Poverty leaves little opportunity for elders to '*do the mundane but also do something completely different to give yourself a little treat*' (Joyce), which is important for elders too because '*pampering oneself here and there is good for your soul. You come away feeling really good and able to cope with anything*' (Joyce).

Political

Material constraints will also have an effect on elders' capacity for political involvement. Confronted with the dilemma of eating *or* heating the home, it is difficult to think beyond the day-to-day. Where there are mobility limitations, the lack of a car coupled with poor public transport connections can make it difficult for elders to maintain their political presence. Nonetheless, elders are more likely to vote than younger generations and they are progressively involved in new forms of political participation which is non-institutionalised,[3] previously typical of younger generations (Goerres, 2009).

> There is more involvement now but is there enough being done as a result? I don't think so, but if people were prepared to listen [to elders] they would gain something themselves.
>
> *(Joyce)*

Negative political discourses about old age and the ageing population are nothing new, but they seem to have been aggravated in recent times, placing elders as 'one of the main threats to Britain's economic future' (Walker, 2012; p. 812). This powerful discourse encourages elders to be viewed (and often to see themselves) as a burden to the nation. The fact that elders have contributed to social and economic capitals throughout their working lives and continue to participate in civic provision through voluntary or informal caring roles is rarely storied.

Rethinking ageing: myths and 'counter-myths'

The mistaken assumptions oppressing elders, and constructing not only societal views of elders but also how they view themselves, must be recognised as problematic (Martín Baró, 1994). Some preconceptions held by society generally and, more specifically, by some psychologists and other professionals, are:

- The dominating fatalistic *natural decline* discourse, which highlights that elders will have increasingly greater levels of disability, including reduced mobility and memory loss, despite the fact that elders now have lower levels of disability and greater longevity than in the past (Manton & Vaupel, 1995; Martin, Schoeni & Andreski, 2010).
- The discourse of elders as a burden to society overshadows the fact that, for example, people over the age of sixty-five provide over one-third of care to elders and do much of the voluntary work and childcare in the UK (see Box 10.1), making them an invisible workforce.
- The Freudian discourse of elders as unwilling to listen to advice or unable to benefit from psychotherapy, as their minds lack the mental elasticity necessary for therapeutic change. This preconception often results in exclusion from psychological intervention and research trials on the basis of age – hence, elders are underrepresented in published studies and in shaping services and policies. However, more recent psychodynamic therapists reject these earlier assumptions (for example, Hildebrand, 1986).
- The belief that *inevitable* memory loss will mean that elders will be unable to make decisions. Care planning for elders with labels of dementia often leaves them aside, and illegally detaining them in hospital units (without formal capacity assessment and against their will) is still common practice. This is despite the introduction of the Mental Capacity Act (2005), which recognised that even with dementia diagnoses elders can make decisions.[4]

Box 10.1 The invisible contribution of elders

- Of the two million older people with care-related needs, 800,000 currently do not receive any formal support.
- About 960,000 people aged sixty-five and over provide unpaid care for a partner, family or others, but only 93,000 of these receive any carer-specific support services.
- One-fifth of all carers (20 per cent) aged seventy-five and over provide fifty or more hours of informal care each week.
- 2.8 million people aged fifty and over provide unpaid care and 5 per cent of people aged eighty-five and over provide unpaid care.
- In 2006, among families where the mother was in work, 31 per cent of

> lone parents and 32 per cent of parent couples relied on grandparents for informal childcare.
> - Recent research has estimated that older carers (aged over sixty) in the UK are providing up to £4 billion in unpaid volunteering and up to £50 billion in unpaid family care.
> - *Grandparents plus* estimate that there are 25,000 grandparents over the age of sixty-five raising 30,000 grandchildren in the UK and that, if the children they are caring for were in independent foster care it would cost £1.4 billion in care costs alone each year.
>
> Source: Age UK June Factsheet (Age UK, 2014; online)

The systematic marginalisation of elders since the rise of industrialisation and capitalism (Phillipson, 1982), and continuous subjecting of older generations to gross inequalities, leads to isolation, unhappiness, greater disability and, thus, state dependency (Equality Trust, 2012). 'Women, minorities, and persons of low socio-economic status are especially vulnerable' (Freedman, Martin & Schoeni, 2002; p. 3137). Arguably, it is not ageing but the oppression elders face that may create the conditions for elders to be a *threat* to the UK's economic future.

Liberation: a new praxis

Siding with elders in the process of *conscientização* (Freire, 1972), or conscientization, liberates and humanises health and social workers and services, and the rest of the population for the wellbeing of all. However, power can hinder or promote the fulfilment of personal, community and relational needs; the basis of wellbeing. 'The overwhelming evidence is that [these] three domains of wellness must co-occur for life satisfaction to ensue' (Prilleltensky, 2008; p. 123). The imbalance of elder power is apparent in conflicts of interest between elders, families, and professionals/institutions, when the latter will have the final say, even in violation of elders' rights and the consequent detrimental effects.[5] Power must be used alongside elders, advocating and attaining their rights in praxis and not just conceptually (*true word* instead of *blah, blah*; Freire, 1972).

The United Nations (1991) grouped the human rights of senior citizens around five overarching ideas: independence, participation, care, self-fulfilment and dignity (see Box 10.2). However, this is just a departure point, because it is together with elders that their entitlements and responsibilities must be constructed. For example, while physical, social, psychological and spiritual wellbeing are referred to, there is no direct mention of quality of life. Joyce pointed to the need for '*changes in legislation, because each person should be able to decide what happens at the end of their lives*'. This raises ethical considerations, in particular concerning terminal illness/end of life, which can only be addressed by reflecting alongside elders on their preferences.

Box 10.2 Summary of elders' rights

- *Independence*, regarding access to basic needs (food, water, housing and clothing); health care; work, means to earn income and determine their own retirement; education and training; and safe environments (according to preferences and ability).
- *Participation*, social integration, policy development and implementation and knowledge and skills sharing; continued service to the community (e.g. as volunteers); and involvement in social and political groups.
- *Care* and protection by family, community; health systems, for optimal functioning and wellbeing; legal and social services, for enhancement of autonomy; institutions providing humane and stimulating environments for rehabilitation; and care settings respecting their fundamental human rights and freedoms (e.g. privacy, beliefs, needs and decision-making).
- *Self-fulfilment*, continued self-development; and access to social, educational, cultural, spiritual and recreational resources.
- *Dignity*, safety (free from oppression and abuse); equality (no matter their age, gender, ethnicity, sexuality, level of ability and so on); and being valued.

Source: United Nations Principles for Older Persons (1991)

Personal and collective wellbeing

Wellbeing is linked to greater health, longevity (Diener & Chan, 2011; Lima-Costa, De Oliveira, Macinko & Marmot, 2012) and more social engagement (MacKean & Abbott-Chapman, 2012). In turn, activity (social, leisure, productive or helping), lifelong learning (formal and informal) and social integration and engagement positively affect physical and emotional wellbeing (Lu, Kao & Hsieh, 2010). These lead to less use of health and social services and to higher quality of life and personal wellbeing (Louh & Herzog, 2002; Merriam & Kee, 2013). Isolation, accessibility and mobility issues can be tackled by functioning from local community centres (such as the local ideas store, library or drop in), arranging transport to get elders out of the home environment for social activities and connections (with mobility mini-buses, 'dial-a-ride' or 'shopmobility'). Whenever this is not possible because of great disability or frailty, going to elders' homes, which necessitates a willingness on the part of psychologists (and other professionals), to step outside controlled clinical spaces and into peoples' own *territories*.

Elders' involvement in community life has been highlighted as making an important contribution to the wellbeing of the community (Merriam & Kee, 2013). That active and socially integrated elders contribute positively to community wellbeing is unsurprising, given that the wellbeing of individuals is interlinked with the wellbeing of the collective (Prilleltensky, 2008; Brookfield, 2012). In particular, elders' vast knowledges and skills, acquired through their rich life experience, are a precious resource for our communities, as is their desire to *give back*, for example, through volunteering.

> Churches are playing a big part, there are many people wanting to volunteer, they want to do good work but then they get put on to do more and more, demeaning the volunteer. It is important to *really value* volunteers.
>
> *(Joyce)*

Elders in their communities

Liberation can only be achieved through action *alongside* elders. Regrettably, most times things are done *for* elders. About ten years ago, I was approached by the Alzheimer's Society (AS) to run a memory group, as they were doing in other parts of the UK. I thanked them for contacting me but suggested that there are alternative views about what can help people with memory problems[6] and, instead, we could find out from local people with memory problems themselves what they would consider most useful. A group of about fifteen elders (some with formal diagnoses, some not) and I got together. With incredible ability to listen to each other and integrate their different wishes with respect and egalitarian agreement, they put forward a proposal for a fortnightly open-membership group that would alternate between: non-formal learning (such as hosting a talk from a housing officer about benefits); outings to special places, like museums; and mutual social support (unstructured time together). The idea was accepted[7] by the AS with the proviso that it could only happen monthly because of resources. The elders agreed and this became the first AS group in the UK set up by people with memory problems according to their identified needs and wishes.

Peer-run groups and organisations have a particular significance because they are 'collegial and informal rather than hierarchical and formal'. 'Peer recognition of fellow members' knowledge and skills, learned over a lifetime, and the opportunity to share these, was highly valued and encouraged a strong sense of reciprocity' (MacKean & Abbott-Chapman, 2012; p. 55). While these groups are important to regain *voice*, the process of liberation must include other members of the community, because it is through joining together that myths can be dispelled and reciprocal valuing can occur. One way in which entire communities can be joined is through rebuilding elders' historical memory in inter-generational gatherings, so the whole community connects, creating and maintaining wellbeing (Martín Baró, 1994). This is part of a more recent project, still in developmental, consultation stages, alongside my local community and colleagues, which is about creating a therapeutic space to promote and enhance individual and community wellbeing, and joining together the people in our local community to achieve social change.

Liberation: a new future

> Liberation is not the task of professionals; it happens between us in everyday life (Montero, 2007) through ethical commitment and engagement, conscientization, and what Martín Baró (1994) referred to as building on the peoples' *virtues*. Qualities such as solidarity, resilience and wisdom are common among elders, who are often ready for their *'values to be transmitted'*.
>
> *(Joyce)*

Stop, look and listen: teaching, consultation and leadership

In this heading is the title Joyce gave to our joint lecture for trainee clinical psychologists in their first year of professional training. It is a powerful, urgent call to attend to what elders have to say, beyond the words uttered; to truly *listen*, not only utilising our sense of hearing but our solidarity, joining in, feeling alongside elders. Joyce's teaching has multiple ripples. She has also been teaching primary school children in the village where she was evacuated during the war, ensuring the continuity of historical memory. After our teaching, trainees and I reflect back to her some of the important connections we make, as a result of her sharing her expertise, through outsider witness practices[8] (White, 2004) and letter writing. This is an excerpt from my last letter to Joyce:

> there were many things you shared that have really stayed with me. One is your statement about having more experience than any of us and your invitation to ask questions of all of the older people in our lives, because one day we won't be able to ask these anymore and so much will be lost. This brought to me the image of a very, very tall and leafy tree, which shares its shadow with all the other trees, plants, welcoming birds and other creatures; which is sure of where it stands, well rooted in its history and current context; which has resisted untoward conditions through the years and has become strong and wise.
>
> *(Maria)*

Elders are also keen to be involved in consultation. However, Joyce cautions that

> the problem is getting people to be consultants and then not wanting them to take a leading role ... some people have more of a voice [than others], but they [elders with more voice] need to listen to the others whose voice is not so strong too; taking all the ideas forward and take it to higher authorities so changes can be made ... but often things stop at the top.
>
> *(Joyce)*

This awareness did not stop Joyce from becoming a consultant and presenting at conferences,

> giving and giving in hope that somewhere along the way someone will do something about it. Not just about my ideas, there are many people out there trying to improve things, not just for themselves but for everyone.
>
> *(Joyce)*

However, for elders to have a real position of leadership, not only a willingness to lose one's own professional power but a desire to do so is required, and in doing so we (re)gain the greatest power of all, of humanising ourselves alongside others.

Action research and social transformation

In our dialogue, Joyce and I wondered how things would be if communities were integral to proposals and implementation of changes. For example, where would we be now if the community had really been involved in the policy shift introduced by the Community Care Act in 1990?

> Trying to keep people in their homes longer is a good idea, rather than care facilities; even if they seem very good. But Care in the Community failed along the way, it did not have the level of staffing or quality of care.... Some people are family orientated, as it used to be, but now that's exceptional because [younger generations] don't want the responsibility, they have their own life to live – you have to see the other side too – but if communities continue to disintegrate, then who will be expected to care for those who need it in future?
>
> *(Joyce)*

The above highlights the need to go beyond policies towards social transformation and for elders to be actors in the process of changing their realities (Montero, 2007). One way to do this is through participative action research (PAR), which involves elders investigating their own living conditions and conditionings, which is another form of conscientization and, therefore, path to liberation. I was once given the task of consulting families and carers of elders who accessed a service that social and health managers wanted to change. I involved the people accessing the service too. We dialogued in focus groups to allow the co-construction of experiences of the service as it was, with a mix of people with different kinds (and at different stages) of problems, and what they would like to be different. No one wanted the service to become segregated into types or levels of problems. What really stood out was how much elders who accessed the service valued each having different strengths and being able to support one another. Unfortunately, decisions had been taken in parallel to the consultation and, therefore, we were not able to truly engage in dialogue with managers. Being alongside elders is not the difficult part as they often, in my experience, have the energy and desire to transform the world. Resistance to change generally comes from professionals and services, possibly because they operate within structures of oppression (even third-sector organisations who are often dependent on government funding), which are more difficult to change. Therefore, long-term commitment to PAR and other kinds of collective participation is needed to bring about social change, for 'liberation is a never-ending task' (Montero, 2007; p. 529).

Reflections

Writing about the liberatory praxis alongside *elders* can be seen to bear a contradiction. Age differences do not tell us much about the other person, except how long they have lived. Elders have told me that they do not wish to be treated differentially nor as less than full members of society; they are who they always were.

In writing this chapter, I am not asserting that we should value elders more than anyone else, but certainly not less because of their age. I am affirming that elders must be valued uniquely and equally with reverence,[9] as all human beings.

> Ageism should not exist. People are being put in a box. Seniors should be one more part of society.
>
> *(Joyce)*

In Joyce's words, the idea of citizenship is key. Montero (2007) sees conscientization, and praxis to sustain it in our lives and the world, as central to the exercise of citizenship as it is to the process of liberation. Elders have the values, expertise and readiness to join in conscientization and liberatory praxis for their, and their community's, wellbeing – understanding that one cannot be without the other. They have a critical consciousness of their situation and the power imbalance that denies their full citizenship and impacts their ability to create necessary social change. It is only by embodying solidarity alongside elders, by engaging, often struggling, collectively in liberatory praxis that we can humanise (otherwise oppressive) structures and systems. Social transformation and wellbeing can only be realised through liberatory praxis, for liberation is the foundation of humanity.

Notes

1 Since human life, including identity, is mediated by relationships and language (Gergen, 2009).
2 Evacuation has been regarded as traumatic in many ways: children were told they were going on holiday but were stuck in remote and unfamiliar areas of the countryside without knowing when they would return home; they often did not see family again for years or at all (some were 'unclaimed' when the war ended); some were neglected or abused.
3 Forms of political activity and expression beyond voting for/belonging to political institutions and parties, such as through petitions or demonstrations.
4 By stating that: 'A person is not to be treated as unable to make a decision unless all practicable steps to help him to do so have been taken without success' (Mental Capacity Act, 2005:1).

5 More obviously, this manifests in abuse in families, care homes and health settings (leading to death in extreme cases; e.g. Francis Report, 2013).
6 Levy and Langer's (1994) cross-cultural (China–USA) study pointed out that memory performance in later life is related to positive views of ageing in the culture.
7 The shift from making services *accessible* to making them *acceptable*, when they are planned from the bottom up takes the focus to services' acceptance, rather than any group/population.
8 Outsider witness practices involve an audience or outsider witness group to someone telling a story of their life. The audience/outsider witnesses do a retelling 'shaped by a specific tradition of acknowledgement … it is those aspects of the telling that outsider witnesses were most strongly drawn to that provide the foundation for this re-telling' (White, 2004; pp. 16–17).
9 By reverence I mean a high respect and regard, true awe for the preciousness of humanity in each of us.

References

Age UK (2014). Later life in the United Kingdom. *June Factsheet*. Retrieved 30 June 2014 from www.ageuk.org.uk/Documents/EN-GB/Factsheets/Later_Life_UK_factsheet.pdf?dtrk=true.

Brookfield, S. (2012). The impact of life-long learning on communities. In: D.N. Aspin, J.D. Chapman, K. Evans & R. Bagnall (Eds), *Second international handbook of lifelong learning* (pp. 875–86). New York: Springer.

Bytheway, B. & Johnson, J. (1990). On defining ageism. *Critical Social Policy, 10*, 27–39.

Department for Work and Pensions. (2012). *Households below average income: An analysis of the income distribution 1994/95–2010/11*. London: DWP. Retrieved 15 March 2014 from www.gov.uk/government/uploads/system/uploads/attachment_data/file/200720/full_hbai12.pdf.

Diener, E., & Chan, M.Y. (2011). Happy people live longer: Subjective well-being contributes to health and longevity. *Applied Psychology: Health & Wellbeing, 3*(1), 1–43.

Equality Trust (2012). *Income inequality and participation*. Retrieved 20 April 2014 from www.equalitytrust.org.uk/sites/default/files/research-update-income-inequality-and-participation.pdf.

Francis Report. (2013). *Report of the Mid Staffordshire NHS Foundation Trust Public Inquiry*. London: HMSO.

Freedman, V.A., Martin, L.G. & Schoeni, R.F. (2002) Recent trends in disability and functioning among older adults in the United States: A systematic review. *The Journal of the American Medical Association, 288*(24), 3137–3146.

Freire, P. (1972). *Pedagogy of the oppressed*. Harmondsworth: Penguin.

Gergen, K.J. (2009). *Relational being: Beyond self and community*. New York: Oxford University Press.

Goerres, A. (2009). *The political participation of older people in Europe: The greying of our democracies*. London: Palgrave Macmillan.

Higgs, P., Hyde, M., Arber, S., Blane, D., Breeze, E., Nazroo, J., et al. (2005). Dimensions of the inequalities of life in older age. In: A. Walker (Ed.), *Understanding quality of life in old age*. Maidenhead: Open University Press.

Hildebrand, P. (1986). Dynamic psychotherapy with the elderly. In: C. Colarusso & R. Nemiroff (Eds), *The race against time* (pp. 22–40). New York: New York University Press.

Levy, B., & Langer, E. (1994). Aging free from negative stereotypes: Successful memory in China and among the American deaf. *Journal of Personality and Social Psychology, 66*, 989–97.

Lima-Costa, M.F., De Oliveira, C., Macinko, J. & Marmot, M. (2012). Socioeconomic inequalities in health in older adults in Brazil and England. *American Journal of Public Health, 102*(8), 1535–41.

Louh, M.-C., & Herzog, A.R. (2002). Individual consequences of volunteer and paid work in old age: Health and mortality. *Journal of Health and Social Behaviour, 43*, 490–509.

Lu, L., Kao, S. & Hsieh, Y. (2010). Positive attitudes toward older people and well-being among Chinese community older adults. *Journal of Applied Gerontology, 29*(5), 622–39.

MacKean, R., & Abbott-Chapman, J. (2012). Older people's perceived health and well-being: The contribution of peer-run community-based organisations. *Health Sociology Review, 21*(1), 47–57.

Manton, K., & Vaupel, J.W. (1995). Survival after the age of 80 in the United States, Sweden, France, England, and Japan. *The New England Journal of Medicine, 333*(2), 1232–5.

Martin, L.G., Schoeni, R.F. & Andreski, P.M. (2010). Trends in health of older adults in the United States: past, present, future. *Demography, 47*(Suppl), 17–40.

Martín Baró, I. (1994). *Writings for a liberation psychology: Essays, 1985–1989*, ed. A. Aron & S. Corne. Cambridge, MA: Harvard University Press.

Mental Capacity Act (2005) Retrieved 14 March 2014 from www.legislation.gov.uk/ukpga/2005/9/pdfs/ukpga_20050009_en.pdf.

Merriam, S.B., & Kee, Y. (2013). Promoting community wellbeing: The case for lifelong learning for older adults. *Adult Education Quarterly, 20*(10), 1–17.

Montero, M. (2007). The political psychology of liberation: From politics to ethics and back. *Political Psychology, 28*(5), 517–33.

Office for National Statistics (2013) *What does the 2011 Census tell us about the 'oldest old' living in England & Wales?* Retrieved from www.ons.gov.uk/ons/dcp171776_342117.pdf.

Phelan, A. (2008). Elder abuse, ageism, human rights and citizenship: implications for nursing discourse. *Nursing Inquiry, 15*(4), 320–9.

Phillipson, C. (1982). *Capitalism and the construction of old age*. London: Macmillan Press Ltd.

Prilleltensky, I. (2008). The role of power in wellness, oppression and liberation: The promise of psychopolitical validity. *Journal of Community Psychology, 36*(2), 116–36.

United Nations (1991) *United Nations principles for older persons*. Retrieved 28 March 2014 from www.ohchr.org/EN/ProfessionalInterest/Pages/OlderPersons.aspx.

Walker, A. (2012). The new ageism. *Political Quarterly, 83*(4), 812–19.

White, M. (1993). Commentary: The histories of the present. In: S. Gillian & R. Price (Eds), *Therapeutic conversations* (pp. 121–35). New York: W.W. Norton.

White, M. (2004). *Narrative practice and exotic lives: Resurrecting diversity in everyday life.* Adelaide: Dulwich Centre Publications.

11

BREAKING OUT OF THE GENDER BINARY

Liberating transgender prisoners

David Nylund and Heather Waddle

Introduction

As social justice-oriented clinicians working in the USA,[1] we are committed to working with marginalised and oppressive social structures. One such unjust institution in the USA is its prison system. The USA has the highest incarceration rate in the world, with one out of every thirty-two Americans incarcerated, comprising 25 per cent of the total prisoners worldwide (Alexander, 2010). Within correctional institutions, a particularly marginalised population is transgender inmates (prisoners). Liberation psychology, an approach that directly addresses subjugated and impoverished persons by conceptually and practically addressing the oppressive sociopolitical structure in which they exist, is essential in our work with transgender prisoners.

The term 'transgender' is an umbrella term for a person whose sex assigned at birth is inconsistent with their gender identity. Transgender persons who are incarcerated face considerable problems, including obstacles to/difficulties accessing health care, violence by other inmates and potential stereotyping by legal decision-makers and correctional staff; however, there is little research regarding these issues. This chapter will discuss the difficulties that transgender inmates face and how liberation psychology can address such problems. A case vignette will illustrate the approach.[2]

Incarcerated transgender persons

An estimated 30 per cent of the US transgender population has been incarcerated in their life (Peek, 2004). Courts have typically categorised and placed transgender inmates according to their biological genitalia. This categorisation is based on an essentialist notion of gender that conflates biology (genitalia, chromosomes, for example) with a fixed gender identity. The US Bureau of Prisons has developed guidelines for handling arrests and incarceration of transgender inmates that is consistent with these decisions. Therefore, male-born transgender persons who identify as female are incarcerated in a male facility. Inmates who realise their transgender identity after they are incarcerated have the same concerns.

Physical and mental health care become serious concerns for transgender persons who are incarcerated. For transgender persons who were undergoing hormonal therapy or sex reassignment surgery[3] at the time of arrest, the continuation of hormone treatment or other medical treatments is important to their welfare. Yet access to hormonal therapy or surgery can be temporarily or permanently suspended while incarcerated. The administration of hormones requires ongoing care by a physician, and adequate support services are required to assist in the gender transition, as noted in the World Professional Association of Transgender Health (WPATH), the organisation that outlines the standards of care for individuals who wish to undergo hormonal or surgical transition to a sex other than the one they were assigned at birth. Sudden termination of hormonal therapy can be physically dangerous and can also cause negative psychological and medical effects.

Transgender inmates may be at risk for abuse by correctional officers and other inmates. Correctional staff and prisoners alike are situated within a heteronormative and cisnormative[4] context that views transgender persons as 'abhorrent' and deviant. Pathologising transgender prisoners can justify various forms of ostracism in the institution, including violence. This potentially increased vulnerability to violence could result in constant fear for transgender inmates, or other adverse psychological effects. The policy and practice of housing transgender inmates based solely on their genitalia creates a considerable risk for rape, sexual abuse and assaults from aggressive inmates drawing on homophobic and transphobic discourse (Peek, 2004). Due to the increased risk of violence, there is also a high rate of HIV/AIDS infections among transgender inmates. Prisons have a policy that prohibits inmates from having access to condoms due to 'sex' being a rules violation; therefore, the chances of contracting HIV as a result of rape is extremely high. This fact can lead to extreme anger, shame, isolation and depression.

There are policies in place such as The Prison Rape Elimination Act (PREA) which was passed in 2003 with unanimous support from both parties in the USA Congress. The purpose of the act was to 'provide for the analysis of the incidence and effects of prison rape in Federal, State, and local institutions and to provide information, resources, recommendations, and funding to protect individuals from prison rape' (Prison Rape Elimination Act, 2014). In 2011–2012, an estimated 4.0 per cent of state and federal prison inmates and 3.2 per cent of jail inmates reported experiencing one or more incidents of sexual victimisation by another inmate or facility staff in the past twelve months or since admission to the facility if less than twelve months (Beck, 2013). By comparison, one study found that 59 per cent of transgender women that were housed in male prisons had been sexually abused while incarcerated (Beck, 2013). Unfortunately, prison rape is grossly underreported for fear of retaliation. Prisons often have certain politics or unwritten rules that label those inmates who speak out against violence as a 'snitch', which can lead to increased expectations from other inmates, such as cleaning and cooking for your cell mate, to being murdered by other inmates. This unwritten rule of being punished for snitching coupled with a MTF (male to female)[5] identity in a male prison leads to an increase in marginalisation and underreporting of rape and other abuses.

Genitalia-based placement also leads to feelings of loneliness due to being isolated from other females as well as other transgender persons. The idea of placing a female among all males for the duration of incarceration that may be years can lead to severe depression. There is an increased probability that transgender inmates with no prior mental health intervention will require mental health services at some point during their incarceration. In addition to depression, there are higher numbers of suicide attempts among transgender inmates due to these violent attacks, acute sense of isolation, discrimination and stigmatisation by staff.

It is not uncommon to hear stories of MTF inmates castrating themselves in order to end the ongoing rapes, beatings and abuse, as well as with the hopes of regaining the hormones that have been denied them. Once they have removed their genitalia, if medical officials are unable to repair the damage they may have the opportunity to be moved to a female institution. At times, medical doctors will prescribe testosterone in order to re-masculinise the inmate against their will. Finally, if this also does not work, in the medical official's eyes, then the inmate will be placed on oestrogen and moved to a female prison. This may be the only way that they see out of the situation and to gain the appropriate housing with the hope of ending the constant trauma.

In addition to safety and mental health concerns, there is a lack of medical policies on how or whether to even treat transgender inmates (Rosenblum, 2000). Several institutions have begun to make policies around hormone therapy. Some institutions may continue hormone therapy if a transgender person entered prison having previously been receiving hormone therapy in the community. Other institutions in the USA do not have policies in place and will deny the continuation of hormones based on assigned gender at birth and genitalia at the time of incarceration. When transgender females discontinue hormones, physical and mental health side-effects arise, leaving the individual feeling as though their body is unrecognisable to or betraying them.

As well as the lack of medical policies on providing hormones, there is also the issue of the lack of gender-specific treatment that MTF inmates may receive due to lack of training, knowledge and discrimination by the health care provider (Rosenblum, 2000). For instance, MTF persons who have developed breasts while taking oestrogen should be taught breast self-exams and be provided with regular mammograms after a certain age or if there is an indication, per community standards of care. There are also specific health complications that can result from hormone therapy. The lack of transgender-specific care provided in prisons can leave the client feeling even more isolated and depressed due to frustration or fear for one's physical and emotional/medical wellbeing.

Liberation psychology

As allies and activists in the transgender community, we believe that traditional psychotherapy and psychological models are ill-equipped to address gender non-conforming inmates. Dominant psychotherapeutic approaches, informed by an ahistorical and apolitical individualism, can pathologise transgender persons with such diagnostic labels as *gender identity disorder* and *gender dysphoria*. Such pathologising practices reinforce transgender as 'other' and reinforce cisgender[6] folks as 'normal'. When transgender inmates are viewed from a lens of individualism, they are more susceptible to marginalisation and discrimination within correctional systems and the culture at large.

We are committed social justice oriented therapists who are shaped by liberation psychology (Montero & Sonn, 2009; Afuape, 2011) and narrative therapy (White & Epston, 1990), and see our role as re-orienting the focus from an individualistic lens to one of a social-relational one. Hence, this approach relocates psychological issues as resulting from an understandable incorporation of the transphobic attitudes characteristic of the social structures within which transgender people live. Although traditional psychotherapy may recognise the effect of transphobia on transgender persons, it often fails to clear the person of the blame for being influenced by such views. However, a liberationist psychological approach aims to facilitate freeing the client (in this case, working with transgender inmates) of the blame for adopting the transphobic views of the society. Instead, the responsibility is on the social environment, understanding that persons are themselves constituted as persons in their social context. Such an approach understands psychological issues as intimately linked to the societal context.

From a liberation psychology frame, transgender persons are able to examine how they are a participant in the social environment and the ways in which they can take control with respect to future actions. Additionally, using the concept of concientización (which refers to the process of developing a critical awareness of one's social reality through reflection and action), transgender persons are able to critique the idea that they are responsible for changing themselves and make visible the systems of oppression so transgender inmates, joined with other transgender prisoners and allies, can challenge wider repressive systems, namely US correctional institutions. Liberation psychology positions us, as mental health practitioners, as part of an emancipatory process to both empower transgender inmates at an individual level while committing to change larger social structures and correctional policies that oppress gender minorities.

Liberation psychology and narrative therapy share a great deal in common; both work with oppressed people from a socio-political contextual perspective. One of narrative therapy's key tasks is to contextualise and deconstruct taken-for-granted assumptions of gender and sexuality that are based on the gender binary (Nylund, 2007). The gender binary is an essentialist idea that classifies sex and gender into two distinct, natural, and opposite categories – male and female. Narrative therapists and other post-structuralist theorists such as Judith Butler (1999) critique the gender binary due to its regulatory effects. Transgender persons and other non-normative sex and gender identities are stigmatised because they do not fit within the gender binary system. Genitalia-based classification of inmates in correctional settings is based on the gender binary, which marginalises transgender inmates. Narrative therapy seeks to complicate these hegemonic assumptions by offering alternative ideas based on a social constructionist view of sex and gender, to see if they are helpful or fit for transgender clients. From these perspectives, narrative therapists create dialogical spaces to challenge and resist these dominant ideas of sex and gender and encourage a celebration of difference and non-normativity. Having these deconstructive conversations with transgender inmates can be de-stigmatising and liberatory.[7] A transgender prisoner can then more fully advocate for themselves in the correctional institution with the support of their therapist. A case vignette will now illustrate a liberation psychology and narrative approach.

Natalie

Natalie (name changed to ensure confidentiality) is a thirty-seven-year-old MTF transgender inmate incarcerated in a maximum security male prison with whom I (HW) have had the privilege of working. (I work in a maximum security prison as a clinical social worker.) She was placed in an all-male institution based on the current policy of genitalia-based placement. When arriving at the reception centre, Natalie, who has been on hormone treatment since age eleven, has a feminine voice, breasts and feminine facial features, as well as mannerisms. She desires sex reassignment surgery (increasingly being referred to as gender confirmation surgery) in her near future as it is a key step in her transition process. A masculine pronoun is used at all times when referring to her except when in therapy with me (HW). She shares her attempts at requesting to be referred to by the gender neutral term 'inmate', attempting to work within the constraints of the prison culture that is based on the gender binary.

Despite these attempts to educate the employees that include her teacher, custody officers, and medical staff, Natalie is continually and intentionally called 'Mister', 'him' and 'male'. She has also been waiting four months for a bra that was ordered from medical services. If she were placed in a women's prison, she would have access to her choice of bras in the prison store called the canteen. She also showers in a T-shirt and boxer shorts for fear of being assaulted if she shows her body. Additionally, Natalie has been subjected to several years of not only discrimination and stigma, but brutal rapes and beatings at the hands of other inmates. Generally, a cell would be considered a safe space for most inmates; however, for transgender inmates there are few, if any, safe spaces in prison. She chose to fight back in order to protect herself, which conversely left her with emotional trauma and questioning her identity as well as the guilt that comes along with injuring another human. She also received a rules violation because she chose to fight back.

In addition to Natalie facing extreme violence and discrimination living in a men's supermaximum prison, she has also not had access to adequate transgender health care. As mentioned above, she began taking hormones at the age of eleven, which has produced lasting feminine characteristics consistent with her gender identity. Recently, after transferring to a new institution, her new doctors have discontinued her hormone treatments due to her decision to not take HIV medications and high testosterone levels. Natalie feels as though this is discrimination rather than based on medical reasons. The termination of her hormone treatment has caused physical effects such as increased facial hair growth and her penis having the ability to become erect again, to name a few. This has left her unable to recognise herself and feeling as though her body is betraying her. The experience of Natalie being unable to recognise herself, coupled with changing brain chemistry as an effect of the deletion of oestrogen therapy, means she has become depressed with mood swings. Natalie discusses having power over the mood swings by utilising 'positive self-talk'. This male body has been imposed on her by the criminal justice system that is required to provide her constitutionally adequate medical and mental health care.

Natalie expresses gratitude to having the opportunity to work with a clinician (HW) that is well versed in the transgender experience. As seen below and with many marginalised populations, she has been unaware of how to influence change on her and others' behalf. She has also been unaware of the types of resources and programmes available to her in order to parole successfully to the community. When I first met her, she was discouraged and depressed. Now when she comes into the session, it is generally with a smiling face, stating:

N: Hey, Ms. Waddle. How are you girl? This place is plain crazy!

HW: How are you able to stay positive in such a negative environment?

N: Girl, I have to stay positive in this environment where there is so much negativity because this is how I can show them [staff] that I am a good person so maybe they will learn to respect us [transgender inmates]. It is the only way that I can show them that they cannot break me. If I become negative then I let the environment take over and I cannot not go to that place. That is a dark, scary place.

HW: What does that say about you as a person?

N: [Pause] That I am a tough girl!

HW: Wow! That is a really powerful statement. You are definitely a person who has influenced change in your environment despite the challenges it has presented to you.

N: Yeah, I guess I have. I want to do more and help other girls in this situation when I get out.

HW: Is transitioning to protective custody an option?

N: Hell no! Why would I do that? That will never be an option. That is the easy way out. How can I hold my head up if I did that? I need to stay on this yard and do my time the right way. I want to try and change how prisons treat us girls.

HW: What might be some steps you can take in order to advocate further for transgender inmates and to influence policies?

N: I would like to help others in my situation, but I am not sure how.

At this point, ideas were discussed and Natalie took the address for the Transgender Law Center, an advocate organisation for transgender persons. Natalie has a release date from prison and is hoping to get involved in this social justice movement in order to advocate for change by telling her story and assisting in creating new policies and educating others so that other incarcerated transgender persons will not have to endure the amount of suffering she has experienced.

Conclusion

As clinical social workers we stand in solidarity with those who are in jail or prison. All people, including those in prison, deserve lives free from violence, with the opportunity to live as their preferred selves. The principles of liberation psychology assist in this social justice stance as it challenges us to understand transgender inmates' struggles within their sociopolitical, cultural, and historical context. Clinicians need to consider larger contextual and structural inequities in their work with transgender inmates. Considering the larger social context can empower transgender persons as they can become more conscious of their lives as structured by the reality of oppression. When transgender inmates make these connections between their experience and the larger socio-political structure, they become social actors and self-advocates.

In addition to empowering transgender persons in a psychotherapeutic context, it is crucial that we advocate for our clients by working to change prison policies regarding transgender inmates. For example, I (HW) gave training at the institution that I work for on how to treat transgender inmates in a forensic setting. In that training I was able to express the need for the institution to follow the Standards of Care as well as identify the need for a team that has a background in working with transgender inmates. I have also sent numerous emails on behalf of my inmates advocating that they receive hormone evaluations and bras, and advocated with various staff for the use of the term 'inmate' rather than 'Mister'.

Hence, we recommend that prisons adopt the following policies and procedures:

- End the practice of genitalia-based classification. Prison officials should classify transgender inmates in accordance with their gender identity, or wherever they feel safest. Placement based on a transgender inmate's gender identity would reduce the risk of sexual assault from male prisoners.
- Transgender inmates have the right to hormone replacement therapy (HRT) and other much needed medical care. HRT and other medical services for transgender persons are not cosmetic but a 'medical necessity'. The medical care should be provided by physicians and other staff who are culturally competent in transgender health treatment.
- Transgender inmates should have the ability to dress according to their preferences. Based on hegemonic discourses of sex and gender, too many jails and prisons limit the ability of prisoners to dress or groom in a way that is comfortable

for them. Most transgender women housed in men's facilities are denied access to bras and are forced to keep their hair at a stereotypically male length.
- Transgender inmates should have access to programmes, jobs and recreational opportunities. Countless transgender people are denied basic conditions of confinement afforded to other prisoners. Most institutions will disallow transgender inmates' opportunities to attend drug treatment, educational or other programmes because these opportunities are offered only in a gender segregated setting.

Working with the diverse transgender population in the prison setting invites the practitioner to adopt the values associated with liberation psychology. An ethical posture informed by liberation psychology assists the clinician to deconstruct taken-for-granted discourses of gender and more fully understand the unique needs of the transgender population. It is our hope that through writing this chapter we will start a dialogue that leads to the just and humane treatment and placement of transgender inmates.

Notes

1 Heather works in an adult correctional institution and David is the clinical director of an agency serving the LGBTQ population.
2 Although our chapter discusses the issues facing transgender prisoners in a US context, we think that our approach has practical applications in other Western industrial countries.
3 Sex reassignment surgery (SRS), also known as gender reassignment surgery or gender confirmation surgery, is a term for the surgical procedures by which a person's physical appearance and function of their existing sexual characteristics are altered to resemble that of the gender they identify with.
4 Cisnormative refers to a culture that privileges non-transgender person as 'normal'. Hence, transgender persons within a cisnormative society are viewed as 'deviant'.
5 A person assigned male at birth whose gender identity is female. The label of transgender woman is not always interchangeable with that of transsexual woman, although the two labels are often used in this way.
6 Cisgender refers to an individual's experience of their own gender matching the sex they were assigned at birth; therefore, a person who is not transgender. In a transphobic culture, cisgender persons have unearned privilege. Cisgender privilege speaks to how perceived gender/sex alignment means not having to think or address topics that transgender people have to deal with, often on a daily basis.
7 These liberatory conversations we have with our clients are complicated and nuanced. For some transgender clients, liberation means having the space to challenge the sex they were assigned and live the gender that they feel they authentically are (in some ways an essentialist view of gender that may reinforce the binary). For others liberation may include challenging the notion of a fixed gender binary all together and embracing a third or other-gendered identity, or without a gender (often a term used to describe such persons is genderqueer).

References

Afuape, T. (2011). *Power, resistance and liberation in therapy with survivors of trauma: To have our hearts broken*. New York: Routledge.

Alexander, M. (2010). *The new Jim Crow: Mass incarceration in the age of colorblindness*. New York: The New Press.

Beck, P.A. (2013). *PREA data collection activities, 2013*. Washington, DC: US Department of Justice.

Butler, J. (1999). *Gender trouble*. New York: Routledge.

Montero, M., & Sonn, C.C. (Eds) (2009). *Psychology and liberation: Theory and applications*. New York: Springer.

Nylund, D. (2007). Reading Harry Potter: Popular culture, queer theory, and the fashioning of youth identity. *Journal of Systemic Therapies, 26*(2), 13–24.

Peek, C. (2004). Breaking out of the prison hierarchy: Transgender prisoners, rape, and the Eighth Amendment. *Santa Clara Law Review, 44*, 1212–48.

Prison Rape Elimination Act. (2014, 30 March). Retrieved from www.prearesourcecenter.org/about/prison-rape-elimination-act.

Rosenblum, D. (2000). Trapped in Sing Sing: Transgendered prisoners caught in the gender binarism. *Michigan Journal of Gender and Law, 6*, 499–530.

White, M., & Epston, D. (1990). *Narrative means to therapeutic ends*. New York: W.W. Norton.

PART IV
Teaching and practice within wider systems

12

HARD TO REACH SERVICES?

Liberating ourselves from the constraints of our practice

Gillian Hughes and Nsimire Aimee Bisimwa

Gillian and Nsimire are colleagues, both working in the Child and Family Refugee Service based at the Tavistock Centre, part of a National Health Service Trust in Central London. Gillian is the team leader and is trained as a clinical psychologist and systemic psychotherapist. The context of her journey to liberation ideas is described in Chapter 1. Nsimire is a qualified medical doctor from the Democratic Republic of the Congo (DRC), and is currently training to be a family therapist and is working as a community mental health practitioner.

Nsimire: my Congolese cultural background and upbringing has a huge influence on the way I relate to others and, most importantly, on my approach when working with families. Education has played an immense role in my life; my parents were both teachers when I was very young and, as a family we valued education very much. In fact, I was brought up with a belief that education was a powerful liberation tool. My parents taught me to be kind, caring, compassionate, and humble. Moreover, we strongly believed in social justice, which led me to go into exile in my early adulthood. Resistance and protest were quite dominant in my childhood as people were opposing the political dictatorship in Zaire; Zairians wanted to have a voice, they wanted to be liberated and establish social justice. I joined the students union to contribute and fight for this noble cause but unfortunately the oppression was so strong that I ended up in hiding before leaving the country. Furthermore, my experience of war and migration has contributed a great deal to shaping my personality and my relationships in all areas of my life. I know from experience how much raising awareness and developing sensitivity among professionals can make a difference in people's lives (Hardy & Laszloffy, 1994).

Introduction

Mental health services have long grappled with the issue of how to serve the needs of marginalised communities who are described as 'hard to reach' while also recognised as some of the people most in need of support. This issue is brought into sharp focus for us – Nsimire and Gillian – where we work in the Child and Family Refugee Service. Refugee families are often very reluctant to use mental health services, and we hear too many stories of people having experienced misunderstanding and disqualification, verging on abuse, when they have sought help. For many people, mental health services are viewed as stigmatising and too culturally different to be accessible. Attempts by services to reach out are often viewed as unhelpful surveillance from the authorities, and an intrusion into personal life. These relationships hold echoes from a history of colonisation and are rooted in experiences of discrimination of Black and minority ethnic communities by our institutions in the UK. Tensions are magnified for refugee communities who have experienced persecution from authoritarian regimes from where they have fled, creating a profound distrust of state institutions.

We argue here that if we are to offer services consistent with a liberation agenda, or even a basic ethical agenda, we need to start turning the spotlight on our own practices. We should be asking ourselves what it is that makes *our services* hard to reach, and how are our relationships with service users are being shaped by social structures that serve to oppress some and favour others. How can we, as service providers working within the state system, liberate ourselves from some of the oppressive practices that we inevitably become part of, and to what degree is this possible?

In this chapter we will describe how we have attempted to start addressing these issues in our work in the Refugee Service, drawing particularly on our experience with the Congolese community. Although work around emotional wellbeing with refugee communities offers some unique challenges, we believe that the themes we discuss here are relevant to any marginalised community.

We begin by setting out our understanding of the limitations of current mental health services, and how histories of colonisation, combined with the agenda of individualistic modernist science, has led us as mental health practitioners to take an expert view on what wellbeing is and intervene according to our professional theories and agendas. Within these practices, ideas of self-determination, resistance and liberation get lost. We explain how we have responded in the Tavistock Child and Family Refugee Service – by positioning ourselves in ways that allow our professional practices to be questioned, to guard against colonisation of those who consult us. We have also set out some of the liberation principles that have guided us. We draw on the model of Coordinated Management of Meaning (CMM) developed by communication theorists Barnett Pearce and Vernon Cronen (Cronen & Pearce, 1985; Pearce, 1994), which offers a framework to address the liberation agenda at different levels of context. We argue that we need to attend to relationships of power at multiple points within a system if we are to provide services that avoid individualising practices.

Limitations of current concepts of mental health and wellbeing

Most of our psychological theories have been developed in North America and Europe within cultures that privilege individualism over collectivism. As Waldegrave (2003; p. 151) points out, 'destiny, responsibility, legitimacy and even human rights are seen to be essentially individual concepts'. Our therapies are largely focused on conversations with individuals with the aim of changing their ideas about their world and their individual responses to it. This is firmly rooted in the conception of people as distinct and independent individuals, with little reference to the social contexts of people's lives. This individualistic view is culturally bound and does not fit with the more communally orientated perspectives of many of the families we are working with. If we uncritically apply our individualistic theories in our work with these families, we risk entering into colonising practices. We also risk inviting people into believing their distress is a consequence of personal failure unless we help them make connections between their social/historical circumstances and the impact on their wellbeing.

Similarly, mental health services in Europe and North America have developed within and from the perspective of imperialist countries. As Martín Baró (1994) describes, dominant ideology and associated discourses structure our society and govern social relationships, which are then assumed to be the 'natural' and correct way of doing things. Unless, as service providers, we have a critical perspective on our practices, we will be drawn into behaving in ways that are congruent with this imperialist thinking. In addition, modernist scientific discourses predominate, where mental wellbeing is considered measurable against normative standards. Combined with our imperialistic trajectory, it is easy to see how people who are functioning outside of these cultural discourses and standards can feel marginalised and disqualified when they come into contact with our social institutions.

We therefore have to ask ourselves: is it helpful to see wellbeing as a universal concept? And how is wellbeing connected to culture, social contexts, personal preferences and values of the people using our services? Some recent work with a Congolese family highlighted differences in how praise was seen as related to wellbeing and motivation. The father chose not to praise his sixteen-year-old son because he believed that this would encourage his son to feel content with what he had already achieved and not push himself to reach his full potential. We as practitioners believed that praise was important to encouraging motivation, and we were tempted to persuade this father to change his approach. However, we realised that we needed to work from within the belief system of this family, holding our ideas lightly, and not attempting to colonise them with our beliefs. If we are to liberate our practices from the constraints of our professional tradition, we need to re-construct our practices from the perspective of the people we are attempting to help. In the words of Martín Baró (1994; p. 25), 'to achieve a psychology of liberation demands first that psychology be liberated'.

In the Refugee Service, two guiding principles have helped us with this.

1. Creating opportunities for *dialogue* with those using our services and others who are close to their experience. We are interested in what Freire (1993) describes as 'true dialogue', which is a generative process capable of transforming reality. Dialogue involves an exchange between people engaged in the process of naming, or describing the world. Oppression and abuse occurs when one person is denied the right to engage in this process. When we talk with people, we do so with the intention that they will influence and change our practices. By having Nsimire as a community practitioner working alongside us, we have also brought dialogues into the heart of our team about how to work ethically with the Congolese community. Through these dialogues, we are able to constantly review our practices, examine our relationships with respect to power, evaluate the stories that we are giving voice to in our work (and those that remain unspoken), and strive for accountability to those using our services. These forms of dialogue also help us to come alongside people we are working with and reconstruct our practices from their perspective.
2. Another guiding principle involves putting *context* at the heart of our theories and practices, to avoid individualising distress. We use the framework offered by CMM (Cronen & Pearce, 1985; Pearce, 1994) to help uncover the contexts which are governing people's lives and relationships, and understand their distress in relation to their social conditions, rather than as a fault within themselves. We also draw on narrative therapy which offers a wealth of methods for deconstructing social narratives and the contexts in which these are created. In this way, we invite people to move into what Martín Baró (1994) describes as positions of critical consciousness where they can appreciate the systemic nature of oppression in their lives. These practices also serve to connect us as practitioners with the reality of power and oppression in the lives of the people we meet.

How we have created opportunities for dialogue

We have created staff posts for mental health practitioners from the Somali and Congolese communities, as these are two of the biggest refugee communities in our area. These colleagues, Nsimire Bisimwa and Fadumo Ahmed, have been invaluable in bringing different voices into the team, generating dialogues which enable us to challenge our Eurocentric practices and ideas. They have helped us to engage more effectively with families, offering 'cultural translation', and have enabled us to build trust and credibility in the community. As there are so few qualified mental health practitioners from refugee communities, we employed people pre-qualification and are supporting them to do therapy training. We also work with interpreters so that people are always able to use their first language when they meet with us.

Nsimire's experience: I have lived and worked in Camden, with the local authority and Tavistock Centre, for almost ten years. I am part of the local Congolese community and my children attend local schools in Camden. I understand how people are living their lives in the shadow of ongoing trauma in the DRC. I know how hard it is for people to trust services here, and even to trust each other. It needs a lot of patience and time to build trust. For example, I was stopped in the street by a mother who had heard about me from someone in the community. She wanted to know if I could help her, so we made a time to talk after dropping the children at school the next day. She was surprised when I turned up as she believed that Congolese people were not interested in helping each other. She had a history of trauma in DRC and was bringing up two autistic children on her own. I asked if she had a social worker and she said that she only wanted help from me, because other Congolese ladies told her that I could help her. She needed help with her children's disability and schooling. I explained what services were available for her and sources of financial help (Disability Living Allowance or Family Fund for children). She said that she had previously refused this help from her social worker because '*When people start doing forms, you don't know what they are going to get on to, they bring trouble.*' She asked me how she could get the forms. I offered to get them for her and asked if she needed help filling them in but she said she wanted to try on her own. I gave her my number, but she didn't call. Three weeks later, I saw her at a local market and she then asked me if I could help her fill her forms in. I told her about the refugee service at the Tavistock Centre and the Congolese group we run there, and she came. It took me about three months to build this trust. Experience from the past can affect people's confidence and ability to trust services. This example illustrates what stepping into the world of our families might mean. If we do not make these efforts, then we will not be serving the needs of those who are most outside of mainstream social structures, and whose positions of disempowerment make it hardest for them to access services.

This example illustrates what stepping into the world of our families might mean. We find it helpful to think about our first meetings with families as them offering us 'gracious invitations' (Lang & McAdam, 1996) to meet with them. Taking this position helps us to listen more respectfully to what people are hoping for from us. We call families when first making contact, so they can ask us questions and we can negotiate how and where to first meet. We use mobile phones so they can see our number, as we have found people usually don't respond to an unknown call. First meetings often take place in schools, a children's centre or home, with us going to families rather than inviting them to us. We talk about what we can offer without assuming this is what is wanted, and may give a leaflet about our service, which we have available in a number of languages. Sometimes, people approach Nsimire if they meet her in the community to ask more about our service before they decide to meet with us. We do not register people on our computer system until we feel they have properly understood and consented to this. We accept self-referrals because we find that sometimes if we have helped a family, word spreads and others in the community approach us for help. People also learn about us, and build trust in our team, through our community work, which is another avenue for self-referrals. Our awareness of the history for refugee communities, of persecution by oppressive regimes, has made us particularly attentive to the many small ways in which we can help people have more power and choice in their relationships with us.

Nsimire: This ground work is important because most of our families are referred to us when someone else has identified the problem. They haven't chosen our service and don't know what we offer. I talk with people about why they might need to think about their emotional wellbeing. This is a new concept for many families and we need to explain the rationale of therapy and see if it fits for them. People are used to consulting medical doctors for their physical health and come home with a prescription to fix it, and don't understand how things can be fixed by talking. I often need to find an analogy in our culture to make sense of how therapy might help. It is not just a matter of a language barrier, but the whole system and the therapeutic framework needs translating. I have the privilege of having a wide knowledge of the diverse Congolese cultures and values as I lived in different parts of DRC in my youth. I can therefore explain concepts in forms that people can understand. For instance, in DRC, problems are sorted out within the family and with elders or very close friends, which can be compared to therapy.

I worked with a refugee mother who had previously not engaged with mental health services. She was very isolated, didn't speak English and was struggling with parenting her son. I first arranged to meet with her at a local library as she didn't want us to meet at our workplace or in her home. She said that she was not 'mad' and didn't want to attend a mental health clinic, and was suspicious of me coming to her house looking for trouble. I later understood that she was very suspicious of any professional coming to her house because she associated them with 'the authorities' and being arrested at her home in her country of origin. She told me that the language barrier was the most challenging thing for her as being unable to express herself limited her in everything she attempted to do, a finding echoed by Baylav (2003). I thought about the time when I was newly arrived in the United Kingdom with very little English. I could remember how excluded and powerless I felt. I specifically thought about the frustration I felt when I could not join in with conversations around me or get my voice heard, and how difficult it was to build relationships (Holder, 2004). This led me to wonder how this could affect this mother's inclusion and her relationships in this country (Burck, 2005). I therefore helped her get library membership, and was also able to attend an ESOL class through the library service. I also connected her with a local children centre, where she joined a mother and children group and met other parents. Although she was still struggling with her asylum case, I could see a big difference after a few weeks of working with her. I could see a confident mother who had become more responsible in her parenting. Most importantly, she had gained a sense of belonging. Having found this safe space, she felt ready to engage with therapeutic work.

Nsimire's position means that she has access to experiences and conversations with families that others in the team do not, so she can help us open our eyes to contexts of oppression which are hard to voice in therapy. As Nsimire shares the experience of migration, culture, and being a refugee, families talk with her differently.

With Gillian, they tend to speak the language of 'the system', adjusting to what they believe is acceptable to say.

Through our dialogue with families, we have learnt that we need to let go of rigid ideas about what constitutes therapy. If people come to a meeting and they have heard bad news from back home, they may need to talk about this first before the agreed focus of therapy. Similarly, problems with legal status, employment or housing may need to be addressed and connections made with agencies that can help, before people are ready or able to talk about their emotional needs.

Nsimire: Families test us to find out if we really want to help. Are we listening? We must prove ourselves to be trustworthy before they can share the more hidden issues with us. For example, a Congolese mother, Marie, focused on housing and child problems at school before she felt able to talk about domestic violence. Time is needed for this, but therapy is almost set up so that our clients have to pass the test – can they come on time? Can they come regularly for appointments? Can they do their 'homework' between sessions? The squeeze on public resources means that time with each family is increasingly being rationed.

Putting context at the heart of our liberation practices

We draw on the CMM (Cronen & Pearce, 1985; Pearce, 1994), as a framework for both inviting critical consciousness, and to consider the effects of our interventions in different parts of the system. We are using the understanding of critical consciousness defined by Martín Baró (1994) as being the dialectical process through which people decode their world and grasp the mechanisms of oppression, which enables them to gain a new understanding of themselves and their social identity. The CMM model is based on the idea that meaning given to any communication is dependent on the context in which it occurs, and that there are always multiple contexts operating at any one time. Some of these contexts may offer opportunities for empowerment, and others may limit choices for action. CMM can be used to help people attain critical consciousness by offering a way to evaluate the multiple meanings and stories being generated in the different contexts within which they are living. By evaluating how the social structures in which they are embedded are shaping their social relationships, people can begin to see what choices they have about how to act in relation to the different contexts.

For example, Figure 12.1 illustrates how we used CMM (with addition from Afuape, 2011)[1] to map a conversation which involved the developing critical consciousness of a group of Congolese women.

The discussion began with someone talking about a friend who had just fled a violent relationship, and led to talk about how domestic violence is widely prevalent in the Congolese community. The majority of the women present had direct experience of violence, although this was the first time they felt able to share their experiences. Together, we examined the different contexts that support this situation at the level of family, community, culture and wider society – a process that facilitated critical consciousness. We discussed how interpersonal relationships (such as those

POWER*
Contextual force:
The effect different levels of context have on experience.

Society – history of colonisation, refugees seen as a drain on resources, oppressed status

Culture – violence and oppression is the norm, at least people are safe in the UK

Community – ideas about role of women: should tolerate violence, role of 'witchcraft'

Family – a single-parent who has brought shame on the wider family

Interpersonal relationships – women in the group who trust each other to support and maintain confidentiality

Identity/life script – a violated woman who can resist (narrative practices identify resources)

Episode – discussion about domestic violence and prevalence in the Congolese community

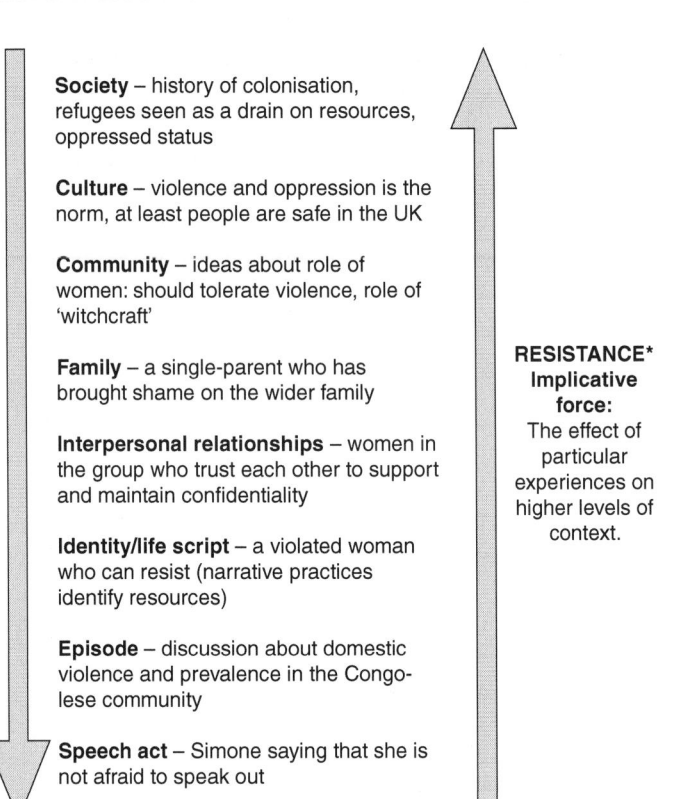

Speech act – Simone saying that she is not afraid to speak out

RESISTANCE*
Implicative force:
The effect of particular experiences on higher levels of context.

FIGURE 12.1 Use of CMM (with addition from Afuape, 2011) to map a conversation which involved the developing critical consciousness of a group of Congolese women.

supported by the group), and personal life stories could contribute to resisting abuse. We had already worked together, using narrative practices to identify stories in the women's cultural and social histories that they could draw on as sources of strength. Then one woman, Simone, in a deeply moving gesture, given the enormous stigma associated with being a victim of domestic violence, asserted that she was not afraid to speak out about her experiences of abuse. This led the group to think about the various ways that it was possible to resist domestic abuse in their community.

This conversation highlights what Burton (2004) names the importance of bringing people together so that suffering can become a social, shared experience rather than a secret distress. It also illustrates what Martín Baró (1994) described as 'the recovery of historical memory', where collective memory can function as a political and social resource, and can enable people to work together to voice alternative realities.

The meeting concluded with the group agreeing to invite representatives from local domestic violence services to visit them in order to make connections, learn more about what support is available, and for them to share their knowledge of the Congolese community so that services could be more responsive. They had shifted to viewing themselves as having valuable knowledge to share, rather than simply being the receivers of knowledge. The women also decided they would organise a conference in the community to make the issue of domestic violence more public.

As CMM describes, social interactions within each context have a reciprocal influence on other contexts. An intervention may have a ripple effect, encouraging other parts of the system to function in less oppressive ways, or it may fall on stony ground if other contexts of oppression override its effects. For example, a mother who experiences her work with us as liberating, may influence our team with the feedback she gives through our evaluation systems, and other professionals if we use her example in teaching, or she may influence her family, or her community, in how our service is viewed. Therefore, if we are to make significant changes in addressing power and liberation, we propose that we need to address change at multiple levels. In the example above, the effects of one piece of anti-oppressive work may remain localised if the wider contexts (agency and beyond) are not receptive to change in practices that marginalise particular communities. We therefore focus our interventions at different levels of context to address multiple potential sites for liberation. For example:

Context of personal life scripts: we work with individuals, families and groups using narrative practices such as the 'Tree of Life' (see Chapter 7). These methods can help people recover identities that are liberating rather than constraining, and a pride of belonging through an exploration of their social histories (Martín Baró's 'recovery of historical memory'). Through this, possibilities are opened up for new ways of being in the world which can position people to transform their social reality.

Context of community: we bring people together through groups to share common concerns, support each other and draw on shared cultural/community resources. The Congolese parents group is an example, as is the Richmond park project (see Chapter 7).

Context of Refugee Service: we have built-in structures to invite our own critical consciousness: employing community practitioners; making space to discuss the impact of wider structures such as the immigration system; and running workshops to discuss community-specific issues led by members of those communities.

Context of NHS services: we use our voice to shape other services through teaching, consultation, joint work and conversations with service commissioners. We use our positions of power to ensure that the voices of the refugee communities we work with get heard. This work is also about helping clinicians feel more competent in their work with oppressed minorities so that they are likely to approach it with more tenacity and commitment.

Context of government and society: we use opportunities to influence policy and social attitudes where we can; for example, through our writing, contributing to government select committees and reviews, and through our projects that create a platform for those using our services to get their voices heard. The 'What's Our Story?' project (see Chapter 5) is an example of this.

As CMM proposes, new ideas or information introduced in any of these contexts has the potential to influence other contexts, whether at micro or macro levels (represented in CMM as implicative or contextual forces). For example, how we organise our staff team, where we centralise joint work and sharing of ideas, shapes our interactions with children and families and the process by which we engage with communities. What we learn from our community projects is brought into our work with families, and all of this experience feeds our teaching and consultations with policy makers. Whereas Sue Holland's (1992) social action psychotherapy model describes how she helps people move from individual psychotherapy through to group work and social action, we find that our work may begin at any point. Although we often begin with a family who is referred to us, our first contact with people may be through social action (such as Somali mothers attending a meeting to discuss sex education in schools), which then becomes a group to discuss parenting of teenagers. Personal relationships and trust built up gradually in these contexts and often lead to individual parents asking for help from us on an individual family basis. We therefore propose that liberation needs to be attended to within the whole range of levels of contexts if it is to have lasting and profound influences.

Conclusion

We have attempted to set out our understanding of how social structures pull us, as mental health practitioners, towards ways of working that serve the interests of the dominant and privileged. We are inevitably influenced by the dominant discourses about what emotional wellbeing is, how we understand the causes of distress, and how we should apply our professional practices to address this. We propose that in order to avoid colonising the people who consult us with our Eurocentric views, we need to constantly strive towards our own critical consciousness – our awareness of our position in the social hierarchy and the discourses that we are attending to in our work, in an attempt to liberate ourselves from the constraints of our professional practice. We have set out ways that we have attempted to do this in the Tavistock Refugee Service through interventions at multiple levels of context, and have described how our interactions with people in multiple contexts shape our work in every domain.

It is a constant struggle for us being part of the social system that so many of our families feel disempowered by, and at times we ask whether we can truly liberate ourselves as practitioners while we continue to work within the confines of the system. We will always hold positions of power in relation to our families, and they will always view us as representing the establishment. However, through striving for ongoing dialogue with people and constantly holding the different contexts in mind, we hope to at least remain open to adapting our practices to fit the needs of the communities we serve. It is an exciting journey we are on, and we are aware we still have a long way to go.

Note

1 Afuape (2011) proposed that contextual force can be likened to power, and implicative forces, forms of resistance.

References

Afuape, T. (2011). *Power, resistance and liberation in therapy with survivors of trauma: To have our hearts broken*. London and New York: Routledge.

Baylav, A (2003). Issues of language provision in health care services. In: R. Tribe & T. Brunner Raval (Eds), *Working with interpreters in mental Health*. Hove and New York: Routledge.

Burck, C. (2005). *Multilingual living: Explorations of language and subjectivity. Language use and family relationships*. London: Palgrave Macmillan.

Burton, M. (2004). Liberation social psychology: Learning from the Latin American experience. *Clinical Psychology, 38*, 32–7.

Cronen, V., & Pearce, W.B. (1985). Towards an explanation of how the Milan Method works: An invitation to a systemic epistemology and the evolution of family systems. In: D. Campbell & R. Draper (Eds), *Applications of systemic family therapy: The Milan approach* (pp. 69–86). London: Grune & Stratton.

Freire, P. (1993). *Pedagogy of the oppressed*. New York: Continuum.

Hardy, K.V., & Laszloffy, T.A. (1994). Deconstructing race in family therapy. *Journal of Feminist Family Therapy, 5*, 3–4.

Holder, R. (2004). Impact on psychotherapy of working with asylum seekers and refugees across languages. Paper presented at BPS Conference, London.

Holland, S. (1992). From social abuse to social action: A neighbourhood psychotherapy and social action project for women. In: J.M. Ussher & P. Nicholson (Eds), *Gender issues in clinical psychology* (pp. 68–77). London: Routledge.

Lang, P., & McAdam, E. (1996) Referrals, referrers and the system of concern. Unpublished manuscript, Kensington Consultation Centre. Retrieved 20 April 2014 from www.taosinstitute.net/Websites/taos/Images/ResourcesManuscripts/McAdam-Lang.

Martín Baró, I. (1994). *Writings for a liberation psychology: Essays, 1985–1989*, ed. A. Aron & S. Corne. Cambridge, MA: Harvard University Press.

Pearce, W.B. (1994). *Interpersonal communication: Making social worlds*. New York: Harper Collins.

Waldegrave, C. (2003). The challenges of culture to psychology and postmodern thinking. In: C. Waldegrave, K. Tamasese, F. Tuhaka & W. Campbell (Eds). *Just therapy: A journey*. Adelaide: Dulwich Centre Publications.

13

TEACHING LIBERATION PSYCHOLOGY

Maria Castro Romero and Taiwo Afuape

Introduction

We have known each other personally for over a decade and although we were developing our praxis in similar directions, we connected professionally at the Eighth European Congress of Community Psychology. Maria was leading a roundtable discussion with Mark Burton, Raquel Guzzo, Steve Melluish and clinical psychology trainees, on what European community psychology can learn from Latin America, where Taiwo was participating. This was the starting point of conversations and Maria inviting Taiwo to teach liberation psychology together.

This chapter is based on our experience of joint teaching on a London-based Professional Doctorate in Clinical Psychology course since 2011 (brief excerpts from the tapes of our teaching session in October 2013 appear in quotation marks and italics), and recorded dialogues between us taking place over meetings between November 2013 and February 2014. This chapter has offered us the opportunity to reflect and build on this shared teaching journey and to share our praxis. We start the chapter by introducing our relationship to emancipatory education before contextualising our teaching with respect to the workings of oppression and liberation in educational and professional contexts. We then describe key ideas based on Freire (1972, 1974), Martín Baró (1994) and our joint experience[1] of teaching liberation psychology.

Positioning ourselves in relation to emancipatory education

Taiwo: In my youth, a lot of my learning happened in non-school settings; at home, debate and critical discussion were always around and involved me; my older siblings took me to see life-changing films (for example, *Biko*, *Cry Freedom*, *In the name of the Father* and *Malcolm X*) and attend community-run conferences, seminars and

workshops on social issues that shaped my view of the world. Co[...]
and the audience were passionate and engaged; bursting out in s[...]
reading out powerful poetry and suspending the distinctions bet[...]
listener, service-user and service-provider, knower and known. [...]
challenged the notion of listening passively to an authority as a means of jo[...]
professional class, and presented education as a creative and alive 'practice of freedom' (hooks, 1994).

Maria: My mother embodied the student revolution of the 1960s; she had a strong liberatory voice, which she was not meant to have as a married woman with children in the conventional context in which I grew up, under a fascist dictatorship in Spain. Running counter to and challenging the status quo, she educated me in expressing my own voice and standing up for social justice from a very early age. My connection with Cuba and the ideals of the Cuban Revolution – although acknowledging flaws – are also part of this, particularly, in that I have experienced a very different (in my insider view, freer) society. The narrative framework (White & Epston, 1990) and critical education (e.g. Freire, 1974; hooks, 1994) led my pursuit for a dialogical method of mutual learning in higher education.

The workings of oppression

Oppression operates as long as oppressive social conditions (such as prejudice and poverty) continue. With an awareness of macro-cultural and historical factors in service of oppression, it can be difficult not to assign blame to oppressors/abusers versus the oppressed/victims. However, we rarely, if ever, belong discretely to one or other category, given that in different contexts we could be either. Further, oppression is best understood as originating outside of people (rather than resulting from individual personalities) and dehumanising us all (Freire, 1972), as it disrupts the potential for social equality, justice and wellbeing.

Oppression within an educational context

Education and knowledge are not neutral, but are culturally, socially and politically situated. Therefore, education can uphold the interests of domination and oppression or act to challenge them. Dominant ideas inform what is considered intelligence, the way we learn, the content of what we learn, and the manner in which we are taught. The structure of higher education in Britain can be said to pose a number of blocks to the realisation of the type of radical praxis (theory, action and reflection combined) advocated by Freire, hooks, Martín Baró and other critical thinkers. Obstacles relate to both proximal (university) and wider (societal) contexts, which draw on and reinforce dominant beliefs about teaching and learning based on what Freire referred to as the *banking concept of education*, which sees students as passive recipients of expert teachers who deposit knowledge. In addition, bureaucratic and administrative demands upon educators can constrain possibilities to join for thoughtful dialogue. If we apply to the context of education the idea that processes impact on subsequent results or outcomes, it is unlikely that the traditional banking system of education will be able to educate for critical consciousness or *'conscientização'* (conscientization)[2] (Freire, 1972), given the lack of dialogue between 'learner' and 'teacher'.

Particular educational structures might also reinforce the divide between learners and teachers. For example, Maria is both an educator and evaluator (course tutor), with inherent power to pass or fail trainees. Conventional assessment methods continue to create this divide, which can be at odds with the aims and ethos of critical education. To embody a liberatory praxis, education needs to be dialogical; what hooks (1994) called *engaged pedagogy*, 'to share in the intellectual and spiritual growth of our students [and] to teach in a manner that respects and cares for [their] souls' (p. 13). Although we are unable to radically change conventional assessment methods, we are able to facilitate, from the very beginning of training, critical thinking that engages trainees in dialogue and challenges normative ideas about psychology. As a result, questions are posed, such as: What gives more voice to some ideas and silences others? Who is doing the asking and who is the subject of scrutiny? Who benefits? Having critique based on collective praxis as a primary element of education is congruent with our aim of co-education with trainee psychologists towards critical thinking and liberation praxis.

Oppressive professional discourses and identities

Teaching liberation psychology happens within the context of wider professional discourses that shape our roles, how we understand distress and what we do to *ameliorate* it. Dominant discourses contribute to the construction of particular professional identities and constrain alternatives (Madsen, 2006). These professional discourses have embedded within them unspoken values and taken-for-granted assumptions that shape professional legitimacy and lead to unexamined daily practices. Generally, psychologists work within institutions and institutional practices that privilege professional expertise and knowledge, and *responsibility for* people defined by deficit and the need for protection; over curiosity, collaboration and *accountability to* people viewed as resourceful agents (Madsen, 2006), with the need for *transformation* of social conditions at the roots of distress largely ignored. Teaching liberation praxis challenges dominant ideas within psychology, such as psychologists as scientist-practitioners, and the importance of practice that has a 'scientific' evidence base over other forms of evidence. From our liberatory ethos, we consider the common concepts *boundaries* and *neutrality* bad shortcuts in negotiating the complexity of therapeutic relationships, and positioning the therapist in relation to the other in ways that reinforce the power of the psychologist. Rather than bringing these issues into the conversation so the other person can take part in thinking about them, psychologists traditionally come into the conversation with a set of established ideas that may not fit with the other person. It may also be easier to draw on the notion of neutrality than reflect with the other person about how we achieve transparent and genuine engagement while maintaining them at the centre of the conversation. Furthermore, these bad shortcuts may not encourage us to critically reflect on what we are doing. By unquestioningly accepting the well-worn corset of boundaries (read Tomm's 2013 online article listed in the references for a critical perspective), and viewing therapist disclosure as problematic instead of reflecting on what might be important to share, the profession may avoid fully immersing itself in the world of others.

The challenge for trainees is that while assumptions and practices that fit within dominant discourses gain institutional support, ways of working that fall outside dominant discourses and do not fit are often de-legitimised. This marginalising and disorienting process can impact on the wellbeing of trainees and make them question the sustainability of liberation praxis in the real world – as explored by them in a reflecting practice (Freedman & Combs, 1996) we describe below.[3]

The workings of liberation

Liberation, resulting from the transformative process of *conscientização*, is dialectical, dialogical, relational and co-created; therefore, no one person does the *liberating*. The development of critical consciousness is liberatory because it creates space to reflect on how we are shaped by our realities, and to see new possibilities for being creative '*actors in our lives*' (Maria), rather than passive subjects. This process is regarded as humanising and leads to wellbeing. 'Humanising' requires 'an opening against all closure, flexibility against everything fixed, elasticity against rigidity, a readiness to act against all stagnation' (Martín Baró, 1994; p. 183). Liberation is thus not an end point but a point of departure and a dialogical process of transformation and humanisation of all those who participate.

Well-being in the context of education

Given that our identities are relational (Gergen, 2009), so too is the experience of wellbeing, which does not take place in our minds, but in our relationships (Afuape, 2014). When we teach (a form of human interaction) in ways that are disconnected from the lives of people and the lives of learners, we risk encouraging confusion, alienation and frustration. Teaching that does not humanise learners can impact negatively on their wellbeing. hooks (2003) argues that teaching should enrich life 'in its entirety' (hooks, 2003; p. 42) and quotes educator/activist Parker Palmer as saying: teaching and learning 'is not just about getting information or getting a job. Education is about healing and wholeness ... empowerment, liberation, transcendence, about renewing the vitality of life' (hooks, 2003; p. 43).

Key ideas in teaching liberation psychology

Educating towards liberation requires a new language. Traditionally, clinical psychology training makes 'theory–practice links', which implies that theory is separate from practice and, thus, needs to be linked. However, theory is not empty, as there is an action and effect in the world that comes out of it and there is no action without implicit ideas and values. We propose instead the concept of *praxis*, which is action and reflection combined (Freire, 1972). In teaching liberatory praxis we are grounded in the following key ideas:

The place of dialogue and conscientização (conscientization)

A dialogical approach to teaching where all participants engage openly and critically is essential to education as a form of social action and conscientization. This involves creating a space to really hear learners from their perspective, in their words, with respect to their preferences, which does not set them in any particular direction except that of critical reflection. We are aware of the danger of trainees feeling overpowered by our passion for liberation psychology, and so we encourage them to engage in an active way, rather than passively accept our ideas. At the start, we ask trainees to consider what fits and what does not fit for them in relation to *their* values, while reflecting on where these values come from. It has been important for us to think about our audience (including those reading us right now), who may not have feelings or thoughts that fit with ours, and what we can do to allow for all positions to be acceptable. One way has been for us to own our positions and their limitations, and be open to being changed by learners as co-educators. While this is an ongoing process that does not necessarily lead to resolution of different positions, in *true* dialogue (Freire, 1972) each person is moved and changed.

Ethical commitment to social justice: siding with people

We have personal responses to the stories we hear, however, the profession's emphasis on *neutrality* can make it difficult to feel free to be responsive. More congruent with liberation psychology's commitment to social justice is taking an ethical position alongside the oppressed and marginalised. Getting inside oppressed peoples' perspectives is perhaps more of a 'true' *empathy* than generally understood in psychology, in that perceiving the world from another's standpoint and feeling from that position is possible only when immersing oneself in that person's *context* and practising *alongside*, rather than *for* them. Even if we cannot do so through lived experience, we can go some way with 'true' dialogue and engagement of the heart (see below). Being a full person in dialogue brings coherence and integrity to living, working and educating as an ethical act (Castro, 2014; Freire, 1974). We do this by embodying our particular contexts, set of values and principles for living, and 'personalising' our ideas and knowledge (rather than these being abstract, all-powerful theories).

The process of teaching liberation psychology

We bring ourselves, as full persons, by starting our teaching with briefly introducing who we are, in a dialogue in front of trainees, '*so we can position ourselves in our context*' (Taiwo). We share our preference for learning communities (White & Denborough, 2005) where everyone learns from each other. We talk about discourses and, as we speak, invite trainees to reflect on their '*own personal-professional contexts and how these inform their values, ethics and intentions*' (Taiwo). We unpack discourses that have influenced psychology, asking trainees to reflect on current discourses and their own vision for psychology. We introduce our interest in liberation psychology and why we feel that it might enable us to go '*from the known and the familiar to something very different*' and '*look to other horizons for inspiration*' (Maria). This process of context setting allows us to respond to questions by first inquiring about values and assumptions within the question and then contextualising our response within our own principles and beliefs, leading to a mutual examination of ideas that underlie our work. We attempt to encourage critical thinking (*concientización*), by reflecting on three tasks: *de-ideologising the everyday experience, utilising the virtues* and *recovering the historical memory* of trainees (Martín Baró, 1994).

De-ideologising everyday reality: reflecting on the taken-for-granted

We try to get students to reflect on the taken-for-granted assumptions about what counts as professional behaviour, how these relate to wider professional discourses, whose agenda these discourses serve, and the effects of these ideas on therapeutic relationships. Our aim is to unpick epistemologies, ideologies, and frameworks in psychology with respect to how they perpetuate injustice and oppression and diminish well-being; for example:

- Maria shared her interest in the idea of turning things upside-down and inverting things in order to see something previously not seen, or to see the familiar differently. Maria presented a reversed map of Latin America, '*which for a long time has been influenced by the West – the US, and European theories and practices*'. The map, by Uruguayan artist Joaquin Torres, proposes that Latin Americans need to stop seeing North America as their North, '*as the direction to guide ourselves towards ... we need to be our own guide, so he turned the map of Latin America upside-down ... he said our North, our direction, should be our South; should be South America*'. One student commented at the end of the session: '*one of the things I will take away with me was when the map got switched upside down, and I haven't been able to stop thinking about it since ... how do we support service user's voices? ... it's really opened my mind to think about things differently and I'm still thinking about that now.*'

Utilising trainees' values: building on trainees' best intentions

Given that praxis combines theory–reflection–practice, social, cultural and political understandings of people's emotional distress call for particular forms of action. We ask trainees to reflect on what is required of them following a critical, contextual assessment of the difficulties people face. Our assumption is that trainees are ethical persons who care about what they do, so it is important to reflect on what they are already doing to embed their work in the experiences, values and wishes of people they work with, despite professional and organisational constraints. We did this by asking trainees to bring themselves and their context into the session and *'reflect on what we have been talking about together, in relation to your* **own** *vision; that is important to you. How do you see the future of psychology? What do you think is missing from the current discourse? And how do you hope to be practising when you qualify?'* (Taiwo). In a reflecting practice, we invited trainees to think about the ideas discussed in relation to who they are, their values, ethics, beliefs, and so on. We asked them to be critical of us, to *'ask challenging questions, any burning questions or make comments not made so far'* (Taiwo), inviting their reflections *'***particularly*** if they are different'* (Maria) to what makes sense for us *'because it is important that all points of views are heard'* (Taiwo).

Changing the context

Although challenging established discourses can be energising, in that it opens up new avenues for action, it can also cause confusion and frustration among trainees, who may feel that the point of their education is to train them to *become* something other than what they are (professionals in the established order). We try to acknowledge the reality of dominant discourses that pervade the profession while asking trainees to reflect on what alternatives might look and feel like, using methods that expand their understanding rather than disrupt it; for example:

- Taiwo showed a YouTube clip of young homeless people engaged in a theatre project facilitated by Cardboard Citizens[4] based on 'theatre of the oppressed'[5] in which one participant said the project was about 'opening our eyes, letting ourselves see things, rather than what we've already decided to see'. This seemed to beautifully articulate the idea of developing critical consciousness or, as we referred to it, *'deconstructing an assumed reality'* (Taiwo). One trainee commented that she was imagining *'what the very articulate and thoughtful young people in the clip would have seemed like, to others and themselves, sitting on a street corner'*. She reflected that by virtue of being in a different context (performing a play at the National Theatre), they were able to share insights, aspirations, dreams and ways of expressing themselves. Taiwo talked about Freire's concept of dialogue being a *'mutual interchange'*, so that *'the quality of someone's voice is intricately related to the quality of someone else's listening [...] So how we listen and the kinds of contexts that we create can help to shape someone's voice ... then they have opportunities to reflect on their lives'* which *'can have a transformative effect'*.

The aim of this teaching is not to replace one set of professional discourses with another, but to expand the options that are available to trainees to define what they regard as effective interventions, by using various ways of *'getting into dialogue with our reality*' (Maria). For example, rather than replicating the expertise versus non-expertise debate, we critically reflect on the opportunities and constraints of both positions. Dialogue helps us move out of the dichotomy altogether. Rather than defending one position against another, the focus becomes what is most liberating for the people with whom we work.

Implications of liberation psychology teaching

The more we engage with different experiences and voices, the richer our perspectives and knowledges, opening possibilities that were not obvious before. But what can we do in the real world with newly learnt ideas?

Working with differences in worldview

The kinds of questions we ask shape our learning. Asking questions and not taking ideas for granted is a counter-practice to powerful established discourses, such as within the NHS. Trainees often describe the challenges of being expected to engage in interventions on their placements that focus on the internal world of people they work with, while being faced with the realities of the person's relational, social and economic experience. Placing such challenges in the context of wider professional discourses can allow trainees to step back from the immediacy of their experience. By *externalising*[6] (White, 2007) discourses, trainees are supported in being 'critical of assumptions rather than individuals' (Madsen, 2006; p. 53), seeing how we are all in an ongoing and changeable relationship with discourses and reflecting together on the complex dilemmas various positions pose. Given that if we are not fully aware of something we may be 'naïve' to it (Freire, 1972), any critique might be empty if not accompanied by deep understanding and appreciation of that which is critiqued. Without suspending their ethical position, trainees can endeavour to really learn what they are expected to learn on placement, and discuss conflicts with their ethical position in supervision and learning communities. By fully knowing the theory they are critical of, trainees can develop a critical consciousness about the impact on them and the other person of what they are doing together.

Ongoing dialogue

An important aspect of liberation praxis is shaping how trainees approach the profession and think for themselves about the professional they want to be. This shift from 'right versus wrong' to shared examination of values and assumptions often results in powerfully transformative conversations. Dialogue leads to meaningful action because as a living process it, and we, 'cannot remain static' (Anderson, 2012; p. 11). By relinquishing the idea of being experts who have the final word, we highlight our capacities for listening and questioning. By facilitating the creation of learning communities, we demonstrate that we want to learn from and alongside trainees, so that we all come to mutually trust the process of dialogue.

Centralising dialogue in the teaching session experientially demonstrates the role it has in liberation and well-being.

We end our session by getting trainees to engage in a reflective practice, to talk to and listen to each other. Trainees come to understand more fully how dialogue allows us to jointly examine the potentially positive and negative effects of our practice. Rather than responding with certainty, dialogue is particularly needed, given that what constitutes liberatory or oppressive practice is not uncomplicated, but subject to varying views and positions. An example of dialogue between trainees follows:

SPEAKER 1: As a minority I can relate to the ideas and concepts ... but I'm struggling as a trainee to make sense of how we translate this to practice and how much difference we can make.

SPEAKER 2: It's making me think about the importance of doing no harm.

SPEAKER 3: It resonates with me about how we translate this into practice.... I was thinking about what Taiwo was saying about having the space to talk about it, having a dialogue. It is quite easy to get caught up with the idea of doing things on a societal level straight away but actually opening up conversations in the teams we are going into can have an accumulative effect, and that person may go and have a similar conversation with someone else ... so it might be the start of something, rather than being seen as only happening once and therefore trivial.

SPEAKER 4: I'm struck by the similarity between Maria's and Taiwo's background in being supported to have a voice. I too have had a similar background. I was wondering what might facilitate having a voice for people who have not had those experiences, for clients who may not have those role models.

SPEAKER 5: My understanding of what our role could be is that just by purely giving the option that there are other ways of thinking about something, that might be liberating in itself for clients.

SPEAKER 6: What we do and what we don't do can feed into their oppression, for example, clients not coming to appointments then being discharged.... There are so many levels of oppression outside, which makes it difficult to come to our session ... so maybe we are also oppressing them.

SPEAKER 7: that comes down to questioning and not just accepting something as the norm and I think that's quite a hard thing to do. I was quite inspired by the idea of acting as collaborator ... accepting there can be difference of opinion, acknowledging difference and working with it.

The group outside this conversation, in the listener role, then reflected on what the first group had said:

SPEAKER 8: I was hearing a kind of heightened awareness of how our theories shape how we as professionals and as people might work or respond, and I am very struck by the things we may not notice we are doing, that clients communicate to us are oppressive ... the possibilities of becoming part of the mechanisms of oppression just by not noticing the impact of the theories we are subscribing to.

SPEAKER 9: Makes me think about alternative ways of doing things. So in relation to the point about people missing appointments ... why is it that people have to leave their homes and come to an out-patient appointment?... it's all part of that system of thinking that we provide a service on someone and actually there are other ways of doing things.

In dialogue about our practice, we have realised the importance of explicitly *recovering historical memory* and *eliciting a community of support* to validate the liberatory ethics that trainees may embrace. Introducing the use of 're-membering practices'[7] (White, 2007) is one way Taiwo has done this in her own teaching. Allies, both actual and evoked in the 're-membering' process, can be powerful buffers against institutional constraints and professional ideologies that pull trainees into practices that are dishonouring of what is most important to them and the people with whom they work. Creating a community of support helps to sustain our invitation to trainees to keep dialoguing, beyond the teaching, in their personal and professional lives and even with the reading they do, '*so that they keep going over, digesting, critically reflecting on and savouring the text*' (Maria). The hope is that trainees can *savour*[8] the joy of opening, evolving and expanding their ideas.

Engaging the heart

We make things explicit when dialoguing in ways that we do not when we think on our own; and come to know new things about others and ourselves because dialogue requires an ability to tolerate deepening our awareness and opening ourselves to others. For this reason we view '*true* dialogue', as a loving process that engages the heart. Engaging the heart in this way is potentially exposing, but can also ignite an adventurous desire (taking new journeys to unknown destinations), and a joy for constant learning. Love might seem irrelevant in traditional psychology or teaching, but it is pivotal in any liberation praxis. For example, systemic therapist Karl Tomm (1998) wrote about therapy as a labour of love; Ché Guevara said that 'the true revolutionary is guided by great feelings of love'; and Paulo Freire stated 'if I do not love life – if I do not love people – I cannot enter into dialogue' (1972; p. 90). In our own dialogue we noted that being able to name these issues out loud has been an enriching process, as putting the words *heart* and *love* in writing can give us permission to own them. Strangely, heart seems to have been '*taken out of psychology discourse*' (Maria) somewhere, as we can only assume that '*it must have been there at some point, because psychology started as a human endeavour and love is central to being human*' (Maria). Being called to be a real and whole person by the people we work with, and by trainees, is extremely liberating for us. We hope that owning this position encourages trainees to notice what for them most connects their hearts to what they do and stimulate ongoing reflections on the ways in which we can liberate the heart of psychology.

Notes

1 This experience includes learning from trainees.
2 The 'power to perceive critically *the way* [*we*] *exist* in the world *with which* and *in which* [we] find [ourselves]; [we] come to see the world not as a static reality, but as reality in process, in transformation' (Freire, 1972; p. 64).
3 Trainees were split into two groups with an inner and outer circle. The group in the inner circle first discussed ideas that had emerged from the teaching session, while the outer circle were invited to listen to this discussion until the designated time was over and the speakers and listeners were reversed.
4 http://cardboardcitizens.org.uk/what-we-do.
5 Theatre of the Oppressed (TO) is a liberation approach which challenges the commonplace view of theatre as only a performance on a stage, with performers and spectators and rehearsal as a means to an end – i.e. the performance. In the TO the process is the end in itself. Augusto Boal (16 March 1931–2 May 2009) was a Brazilian theatre director, writer, Marxist politician and founder of TO. Like Freire, Boal used liberation approaches to eradicate illiteracy by engaging people in theatre as a pedagogical tool, such that audiences were transformed into active participants in the theatrical experience. Boal argued that traditional theatre is oppressive since spectators usually do not get a chance to express themselves, and that collaboration between both parties, in contrast, allows spectators to perform actions that are socially liberating. Boal attempted to break down the divisions between spectator and actor and came up with the term 'spect-actor'. TO believe that every human being is theatre, and Boal argued that every human being is theatre and capable of acting, (given that every human being is capable of seeing a given situation and seeing themselves *in* the situation) and theatre is necessarily political.
6 By separating out who people are and the ideas they have, we can examine whatever is externalised (objectified) as separate from people. This is done to recover people's identities as separate to problems, or discourses, but also regarding skills, resources, and so on, to allow a fuller, larger story as foundation to solutions.
7 This involves 'purposive reengagements with the history of one's relationships with significant figures and with the identities of one's present life and projected future' (White, 2007; p. 129).
8 Savouring implies an appreciation of taste and aesthetics.

References

Afuape, T. (2014). The significance of dialogue to well-being: Learning from social constructionist couple therapy. In: K. Partridge & S. McNab (Eds), *Outside in/inside out: Creative positions in adult mental health* (pp. 187–204). London: Karnac.

Anderson, H. (2012). Collaborative relationships and dialogic conversations: Ideas for a relationally responsive practice. *Family Process, 51,* 8–24.

Castro, M. (2014). Teaching ethics for professional practice. In: R. Tribe & J. Morrissey (Eds), *Handbook of Professional and Ethical Practice for Psychologists, Counsellors and Psychotherapists* (pp. 291–302). London: Routledge.

Freedman, J., & Combs, G. (1996). *Narrative therapy: The social construction of preferred realities.* London: W.W. Norton.

Freire, P. (1972). *Pedagogy of the oppressed.* Harmondsworth: Penguin.

Freire, P. (1974). *Education for critical consciousness.* New York: Continuum.

Gergen, K.J. (2009). *Relational being: Beyond self and community.* New York: Oxford University Press.

hooks, b. (1994). *Teaching to transgress: Education as the practice of freedom.* New York: Routledge.

hooks, b. (2003). *Teaching community. A pedagogy of hope.* New York: Routledge.
Madsen, W.C. (2006). Teaching across discourses to sustain collaborative clinical practice. *Journal of Systemic Therapies, 25*(4), 44–58.
Martín Baró, I. (1994). *Writings for a liberation psychology.* New York: Harvard University Press.
Tomm, K. (1998). Co-constructing responsibility. In: S. McNamee & K. Gergen (Eds), *Relational responsibility* (pp. 129–38). Thousand Oaks, CA: Sage.
Tomm, K. (2013) The ethics of dual relationships. Retrieved 12 February 2013 from www.familytherapy.org/documents/EthicsDual.PDF.
White, C., & Denborough, D. (2005). *A community of ideas: Behind the scenes.* Adelaide: Dulwich Centre Publications.
White, M. (2007). *Maps of narrative practice.* New York: W.W. Norton.
White, M., & Epston, D. (1990). *Narrative means to therapeutic ends.* New York: W.W. Norton.

14

A STORY OF POLITICAL CONSCIOUSNESS AND STRUGGLE ACROSS TIME AND PLACE

Cristian Peña and Leopoldo Garcia

In 2012 my former manager recommended me to Redress, a London-based human rights legal organisation, which was working on a case involving a Chilean survivor of torture taking the state of Chile to the Inter-American Human Rights Court. Mr Garcia, a seventy-nine-year-old Chilean man, was fighting for reparation and justice for the torture he endured in Chile in 1973 under General Pinochet's regime.

This is the story of how I, Cristian Peña, the son of Chilean exiles, now a clinical psychologist working at University College Hospital and Founding Director of the multilingual Londres Psychology Practice, after decades, came face to face with the same state that forced my family into exile, the state that under the dictatorship of General Pinochet tortured thousands of Chileans, including a member of my own family, and killed more than 3,000 people.

For nearly ten years Redress' legal team had been working on Mr Garcia's case, which was finally going to be heard in March 2013 at the Inter-American Human Rights Court – the equivalent of the European Court of Human Rights in Strasbourg. I was asked by Redress to prepare Mr Garcia psychologically for the hearing in Medellin, Colombia, and prevent re-traumatisation. Another psychologist had already tried to work with Mr Garcia in the past, but this had not worked out. The prospect of working with a Chilean exile inevitably shook me and took me back to my own childhood.

Chile during the 1970s and 1980s

When the dictatorship of Pinochet took hold in 1973 it put an end to the democratically elected leftist government of Salvador Allende. At the age of thirteen, my family and I fled Chile and sought asylum in Sweden. My childhood, however, was shaped by those years in Chile, when the whole country was trying to live a normal life under the control of a dictatorship. TV portrayed a country that had no resemblance to reality: Telenovellas and colourful shows narrating the new capitalist agenda, perpetuating myths about consumerism and happiness. At school it was nationalism, not democracy, on the agenda. We 'learnt' about the heroic deeds of General Pinochet and his junta – namely getting rid of Marxists, and democracy for that matter. This enforced narrative, set up by the state and the media, created a dual reality in Chile – the reality endorsed by Pinochet and the everyday reality of people trying to live under the pressures of terror and economic turmoil (Memoria Chilena, 2014).

During those years, houses were raided and family members disappeared, never to be seen again. These disappearances provoked a collective and widespread fear. People were tortured in camps and thrown out of planes into the sea; mutilated bodies were buried in mass graves in the desert; people had to flee the country to seek safety and an opportunity to live with dignity elsewhere. Pinochet's freemarket policies subjected the country to two major depressions in one decade, resulting in 40 per cent of the population living in poverty (Bello, 2013). I recall seeing daily on my way to school homeless families with children living in cardboard boxes under bridges. A miasma of mutual mistrust and suspicion reigned. People avoided talking about what they were witnessing. This silence, this pretend-game, left an entire population in a surreal state. To Martín Baró, trauma was a collective experience rooted in the distortions of social relations and the disruptions of community life (Mishler in Martín Baró, 1994). In Chile, no one wanted to risk talking to the wrong person, to a *momio* or a *sapo*.[1] Making new friends and showing your true colours was too risky. Many Chileans were afraid and demoralised, and thought that the safest thing to do was to adapt to this enforced reality and hope for the best. Some Chileans found this impossible and collective action for human rights took place. Organisations such as the Vicaria de la Solidaridad, groups of family members of those affected by the terror, tried their best to fight for social justice (Sahyoun Bowie, 2012). Protests resisting the dictatorship were frequent, despite the risks involved, and were always followed by violent crackdowns. I remember the protests by the people and the shots being fired in our neighbourhood throughout the night by police. Through curfews, intimidation and terror, the junta tried to silence any resistance. As a child, night shots seemed normal to me; as soon as my father would hear shots, he would run outside to close the big, metal doors that protected our wooden house from the bullets that showered the neighbourhood. There was daily fear of saying something in school that could jeopardise the safety of my family.

On reflection, if I had to think of one thing that kept my parents sane in such an insane reality, it was their political awareness (critical consciousness). My parents had heated debates about what had happened in Chile with trusted friends and involved us in all their political conversations from an early age; they always offered us a narrative that helped us understand what was going on. Early on, I learned how Chile was one of many countries subjected to US hegemony: the victory of the Cuban Revolution, the growing appeal of its ideals (for some people) and the onset of the Cold War was sufficient justification for the USA to support Pinochet and his authoritarian government; a government based on the Chicago Business School capitalist doctrines, the same ideals supported and closely followed by Reagan and Thatcher. Chile became a laboratory for right-wing forces. On reflection, my parents' dinner conversations helped me make sense of the madness experienced in Chile and helped me realise early on that we were not the insane ones for failing to be enchanted by the promises of capitalism. Our failure to conform to the narrative enforced by the state was our blessing.

This political awareness is far from unique to my family. Political consciousness and activism have a long tradition in Latin America. Liberation theology and liberation psychology were influenced by the intellectual and social movements that developed in 1960s and 1970s Latin America, including Paulo Freire's popular education for the poor, simultaneously developing literacy and consciousness about the social conditions that keep people poor (Marlo & Osorlo, 2009), and Fals Borda, who believed that the duty of a sociologist was not just to examine social reality, but to try to remedy the grave injustices that research uncovered (Gott, 2008). It was under this unique Latin American context of critical thought that Allende, the world's first Marxist ever elected in an open and democratic election, became president of Chile in 1970, until Pinochet's coup d'état in 1973.

London, UK, 2013

I called Mr Garcia to make our first appointment. He sounded very hesitant, telling me that the lawyers at Redress thought it would be beneficial but that the psychologist he had seen in the past had not been helpful as they had tried to '*psychologise*' him rather than listen to what he had to say. Mr Garcia agreed to see me once and then decide what to do.

Bearing in mind that Mr Garcia was a survivor of torture, my plan for the initial assessment was to establish rapport, map Mr Garcia's social network and further explore his relationship to help (Reder & Fredman, 1996). Little did I know that it was not Mr Garcia who was going to be assessed that day, but I.

Mr Garcia invited me into his house on a cold and rainy winter's day. As soon as I sat down, he asked '*Why are you here? Where are you from?*' When I told him that I was from Chile, he immediately asked me who my parents were, and my political affiliations. I felt that using some of the classical answers psychologists use to avoid answering personal questions from clients was misplaced in this situation. In fact, considering what Mr Garcia had been through I felt that his questions were not only relevant and appropriate but also essential. His questions were perhaps his way of protecting himself from a world that had not been kind to him, or his way of resisting being labelled as mentally ill. After all, our profession has a tendency to offer diagnostic labels that are at times of little help to our clients.

I answered most of his questions in the knowledge that I was revealing perhaps more than I normally would about myself. At the end of our appointment I was unsure how the session had gone. I did not know whether Mr Garcia would engage with me or not. Before leaving his house, he looked out of the window and saw the rain, handing me a woollen hat and telling me: '*Put this on chap, so you don't catch a cold. I need you to stay healthy to help me with this case.*'

The following week, Mr Garcia's wife opened the door and greeted me with a kiss on the chin, the customary Chilean greeting. As soon as I sat down she served me tea and sandwiches and asked me about my background, not in a suspicious way, but more as a way of finding common ground. We soon started talking about Chile. I promptly realised that our relationship was going to be very special. Without forgetting the aim of my work, I immersed myself in this new encounter.

Mrs Garcia described having had a very fulfilling life in Chile. Both of them had well-paid jobs, they enjoyed the cultural life that the Chilean capital offered, and socialised with their many friends and relatives on a weekly basis. In exile, they experienced racism in the UK and remained quite isolated. Mrs Garcia revealed the impact this experience had on her entire family, on her as a mother, as a wife and as a woman.

Mr Garcia was less open. It took several sessions before he could really trust me, but once a rapport was established he talked to me about his political activism and his relationship with President Allende. He described being arrested by dozens of policemen in the city centre of Santiago days after the coup in 1973. He was blindfolded, his arm was smashed into several pieces by a blow from a rifle, and most of his teeth were knocked out. He was beaten badly around the head. For nearly two years he was detained and mistreated, before eventually being deported to the UK in 1975. Mr Garcia explained that he used to have a lot of vitality and was very social, but now he felt like a shadow of his former self. He described himself repeatedly as '*dead inside*' following the torture, unable to feel any joy or hope for the future and having to experience the physical and psychological consequences of the torture on a daily basis.

Mr Garcia did indeed present with many symptoms of post-traumatic stress and depression. However, the aim of our work was to help him move away from being reduced to a categorisation of symptoms, and allow instead a space for his unique experience to be given a voice. A space in which he could feel safe to speak the unspeakable horror; as well as a space to explore alternative stories that were less told, about his courage, his humanity, his power and his love – all the things that the torture and years of exile had not taken from him. I drew on narrative therapy (White & Epston, 1990; Epston & White, 1992; White, 2004) and liberation psychology with the aim of co-creating new stories, strengthening his identity as a survivor, and taking into account Mr Garcia's social, cultural and political context, within a human rights focus. During our sessions some of his difficulties such as intrusive memories, his 'inability' to forget, his frustration, his perseverance, were framed as signs of resistance, fuelling his struggle for justice and reparation.

I kept in mind the principles of a human rights approach to rehabilitation, addressing the impact of torture within the survivor's social, cultural and historical context, validating the survivors' dignity and challenging injustice (Smith, Patel, &

MacMillan, 2010). Our sessions involved lively political discussions about what went on in Chile during the 1970s, the reasons behind the dictatorship, his role as a political activist and what the state of Chile wanted to achieve with the torture. I reflected with Mr Garcia on how torture is used as an instrument of political and social control, intended to rob its victims of their voice and their agency, disable political activism, damage their mental, emotional, spiritual and physical integrity, and bring them as close as possible to annihilation (Gorman, 2001; Gurr & Quiroga, 2001; Hárdi, Király, Kovács & Heffernan, 2010; Physicians for Human Rights, 2010). We talked about how torture induces a sense of terror in the population as a whole, serving as a warning to comply and not to challenge oppression, and how this fear and subordination maintains the status quo (Fanon, 1963). For Mr Garcia to know that his legal case could help other torture survivors gave him a sense of meaning and reconnected him to the political activist he once was. Through this experience, Mr Garcia felt that he was giving a voice to the millions of survivors of torture who were never given the chance to voice their experiences in a court of justice. The intention of torture is to destroy a person's trust in others (Gurr & Quiroga, 2001) and to break the person's connections to meaningful and significant relationships (Herman, 1997). This is true for Mr Garcia. Conscious of the importance and the power of communities from a narrative perspective (Denborough, 2008), I decided to help Mr Garcia reconnect to meaningful relationships. I started emphasising and mirroring the language he used to speak about his experience. He would often speak about the torture he and his *'compañeros'* endured in a collective way. Some of Mr Garcia's worst memories were related to the suffering of others, to hearing the rifle fire that signalled the execution of his *compañeros*. Mr Garcia told me how he used to attend meetings held by a group of Chilean exiles and torture survivors in East London, but that he had gradually stopped attending. I suggested he attend one of these meetings with me. I told him I wanted to connect to the Chilean community. He told me that he would do it for me. The following week we went to a meeting and met old friends that he had not seen for many years. The meeting was informal and the debate, on this occasion, about the need for reform of the Chilean constitution to make it inclusive and democratic. For me it was a privilege to meet a generation of Chileans who continued to work towards a better Chile. After the meeting, Mr Garcia was invited to the pub and he accepted. He also received a couple of dinner invitations. I, myself, invited Mr Garcia and his wife to a Latin American poetry event. By chance, or synchronicity, one of the men performing was an old friend of Mr Garcia whom he had met in one of the detention camps in Chile. It was an emotional encounter, and one which helped Mr Garcia in the process of reconnecting with his past and his community.

Medellin, Colombia, 2013

When we arrived at the court, we could see that there was a long queue. The hearing was taking place in a convention centre in the middle of the city, Medellin. Mr Garcia would have to give his testimony in front of seven judges, the representatives of the state of Chile, around 500 spectators, and journalists who were broadcasting the event live.

Moments before taking to the podium, I asked Mr Garcia how he was feeling. He smiled and replied: '*I've been waiting for more than forty years for this moment . . . to give my testimony. The time has finally come.*'

I was to sit next to him while he was giving his testimony. His lawyers advised me to ask for a break from the judges whenever I thought Mr Garcia needed one, if the court process was becoming too emotionally overwhelming for him. Once in the podium, Mr Garcia was asked by the judges to give his name. He gave them the one that President Allende had given him first, '*Filistoque*'. Recalling his activist name seemed to give Mr Garcia strength, a reminder of how and why he was there. When the cross-examination by the Chilean side began, Mr Garcia became very emotional and told the representatives of Chile off. His voice became louder and he talked about the crimes these 'gentlemen' were now trying to diminish or defend. Mr Garcia took the opportunity to speak on behalf of the thousands of people that had been tortured and murdered; some of whom had their bodies thrown into the sea, never to be found. One of the Redress lawyers looked at me, as if to imply that I should consider giving Mr Garcia a break to calm down. I considered it for a moment, but then remembered what Mr Garcia had said before taking to the podium. He had waited forty years to voice his story, to speak his mind and I did not want to interrupt him. Mr Garcia seemed empowered on the podium. He had been transported to a position of strength. Yes, he was angry, he was emotional, he was loud, but his anger was more than justifiable.

London, UK, 2014

In one of the many conversations that we had on our return to the UK, I asked Mr Garcia about his political activism during the late 1960s and early 1970s and the importance political awareness and *conscietización* held for him. In response Mr Garcia gave me a glimpse into the events that had come to impact my life, as well as the lives of all Chileans, up until this day, events that have shaped my view of the relationship between liberation and wellbeing, and the role of mental health practitioners.

Mr Garcia:

> Allende wanted to conscientize people and transform the country. The poor and the workers were always his priority. Allende was always in dialogue with the people, speaking the language of the people.
>
> Before the 1970 election, the right wing parties had most of the media on their side. El Mercurio (the biggest newspaper in Chile) hated Allende and worked fiercely against him from the beginning. The Right were well financed; they received money from the CIA who wanted to make sure that American interests were not jeopardised by a socialist presidential candidate like Allende. In the Left we had no finance. The only thing we could do was

to instigate critical thinking and help them formulate their own reality. Allende was a democrat and had no intention of gaining power through an armed revolution. The aim was a revolution of the minds.

I had the opportunity to attend a couple of meetings in which Allende spoke to students in schools and universities in San Antonio and Valparaiso. I was truly impressed by his ability to engage people. Allende explained things so clearly. People could understand it. He could improvise, engage in heated conversations and at the same time listen to what the people had to say, to their worries, their reality. In my view, Allende won the 1970 election thanks to his ability to conscientize people.

You see, a lot of people are never given the opportunity to acquire the knowledge they need to transform their lives. It is not that they are ignorant or slow, but poor people, working class people are always put in the dark. To conscientize to me is what Allende did, to guide people, to make them aware of 'where the shoe is tightening'. It was done in a natural manner, not by telling lies, not through propaganda, but by explaining the truth. The idea is not to make people think like you, but to make them think. It is to communicate what you see, what you know, what you feel, and to listen to what they have to say about it.

I give you an example: after Allende won the elections he decided to nationalise the copper industry. Before doing that, he initiated a vast campaign of awareness explaining the pros and cons of taking what, to some, was a very radical move. I remember the debates and all the posters everywhere explaining the most basic equation of why it was in the interest of the whole country that the copper industry and its profits should belong to all the Chileans and not to one American owner. According to Allende's ideology, the natural resources of a country should belong to the people of the country. People soon realised the truth of that. Even the Right were eventually convinced, understanding that what Allende was doing was for the benefit of everyone, including them. The Right never returned the copper industry to foreign private hands, even when they regained power by force. Until this day it has remained in the hands of the state. Allende was a champion.

Critical thinking is a powerful thing and the Right knew that, that is why they had no other way than to destroy us through a coup d'état. They began to torture and kill because they knew that the Left was dangerous, that it could easily gain power again by making people aware of why they were poor, of why things were the way they were and how this knowledge could help them do something about it. They had to destroy us. That's why the dictatorship happened.

The Right will always be concerned about people who think for themselves. That is why in Chile today, the access to education is restricted and expensive. Those in power just don't want to instigate thinkers. But students are not stupid, they read things, they know. That's why at this time students from different walks of life are marching together in massive protests, trying to change the status quo, demanding free and quality education for all.

On the morning of the 11th of September 1973, as the Chilean presidential palace was being attacked by Pinochet's military forces, Allende's last presidential speech to the people was broadcast live through the radio. Allende said: 'I am certain that the seed which we have planted in the good conscience of thousands and thousands of Chileans will not be shrivelled forever.... Go forward knowing that, sooner rather than later, the great avenues will open again where free men will walk to build a better society' (Memoria Chilena, 2014). You see, once you plant those seeds of critical consciousness, anything can happen.

After hearing Mr Garcia's stories from Chile, I could not help but think of the many similarities to the current situation in the UK: the debate about university fees and public schools, the quality of education in state schools, the stealth privatisation of the National Health Service, the vast inequality giving rise to youth unemployment and the debate, or lack of it, resulting from the August 2011 riots, and therefore why it is important for us practitioners to apply the principles of liberation psychology in our work. Our role is to help our clients explore and formulate (in the words of Mr Garcia) '*where the shoe is tightening*'. We should always contextualise our clients' experience of distress, thinking about the wider historical, cultural, socioeconomic and political context and not succumb to the temptation to simply individualise and psychologise a problem. We should not be afraid of linking mental health problems to the vast inequalities produced by the current political context in the UK (well documented by epidemiologists such as Wilkinson & Pickett, 2010). Not only have I seen the relationship between mental health problems and social injustice when working with refugees, but also through my day-to-day role both as an NHS and private practitioner – for example, in adolescents from deprived communities presenting with self-harm and psychosis, and in Black and ethnic minorities, LGBT and female clients experiencing discrimination because of their race, gender or sexual orientation.

As Martín Baró (1994) warned us, we need to avoid becoming passive observers who reinforce the status quo dictated by those in power. Freire (1973) pointed out that the key to social change is through dialogue and conscientization so as to enable marginalised people to critically analyse their situation and organise action to improve their reality. It is our role as psychologists to help our clients scrutinise the existing values, ideas and stories that dominate our society, incorporating insights about power and inequality, highlighting the link between distress and social injustice. It is our duty to encourage social action, help our clients to search out alternative stories that strengthen them so they can transform their lives, help them to challenge oppression rather than simply helping them adapt to it. Only then will clients be able to truly liberate themselves and achieve individual, relational, collective and social wellbeing.

I am aware that I have pushed many of the boundaries of what traditional therapy should be in my encounter with Mr Garcia. My objective was to create a genuine encounter with him, taking a non-expert position, consistently seeking feedback from him about our work together, following some of the guiding principles of liberation psychology. Latin American sociologist Fals Borda summarised some of these principles when describing participatory action research:

> Do not monopolise your knowledge nor impose arrogantly your techniques, but respect and combine your skills with the knowledge of the researched or grassroots communities, taking them as full partners and co-researchers. Do not trust elitist versions of history and science which respond to dominant interests, but be receptive to counter-narratives and try to recapture them. Do not depend solely on your culture to interpret facts, but recover local values, traits, beliefs, and arts for action by and with the research organisations. Do not impose your own ponderous scientific style for communicating results, but diffuse and share what you have learned together with the people, in a manner that is wholly understandable and even literary and pleasant, for science should not be necessarily a mystery nor a monopoly of experts and intellectuals.
>
> *(Fals Borda, 1995, p. 27 in Chevalier & Buckles, 1993)*

Mr Garcia's case highlights the relationship between justice, reparation, and wellbeing. It highlights the need to enter into dialogue with our clients, with our colleagues across professions and others in order to co-create stories about how to transform our realities and achieve liberation. Only together can we develop a new way of existing; only together can we resist and break the shackles of injustice.

Little did I know that this case was going to be so poignant for me. That it would put me in touch with my Chilean past, my UK present and future, by reinforcing the direction that we all ought to take, not only as practitioners but as human beings. It is the responsibility of all of us to help co-create a different world, a better world. Liberation psychology offers us some tools to fulfil this aim, and as this story reveals, these are powerful tools that can not only help one man find his voice, with a profound impact on his wellbeing, but can also change the fate of an entire country.

London, 2013

In November 2013, after an eleven-year quest for justice, the Inter-American Human Rights Court ruled in favour of Mr Garcia against the state of Chile, ordering Chile to compensate Mr Garcia and initiate a criminal investigation into what happened to him in detainment. This case has become a landmark judgment and sets a precedent for victims of military dictatorships across the world (Bowcott, 2013; Redress, 2013).

Acknowledgements

I would like to thank Nimisha Patel for recommending me to Redress; Sara Portnoy for supporting me throughout this case; and Taiwo Afuape for hearing our story and suggesting we be invited to tell it here. I would also like to thank Sebastian Peña, Gonzalo Peña and Marcela Peña for all their support, Matthew Zimmer and Alexandra Koren for their encouragement throughout this journey, and finally, I want to thank my parents for conscientizing me from very early on.

Note: Mr Garcia has given permission for this chapter, has seen a copy of it and wishes to be named.

Note

1 Momio: a mummy – a person so conservative (right-wing) and resistant to change that he might as well be a mummy (Garcia-Marquez, 1987). Sapo: an undercover police officer or police informer.

References

Bello, W. (2013). Short-lived legacy: Margaret Thatcher, neoliberalism and the global south. Retrieved 4 July 2014 from www.theguardian.com/global-development/poverty-matters/2013/apr/16/legacy-margaret-thatcher-neoliberalism.

Bowcott, O. (2013). Chile ordered to pay £20,000 to compensate Pinochet torture victim. *Guardian*. Retrieved 1 July 2014 from www.theguardian.com/world/2013/nov/04/chile-ordered-compensation-pinochet-torture-victim.

Chevalier, J.M., & Buckles, D.J. (1993). *Participatory action research: Theory and methods for engaged inquiry*. London: Routledge.

Denborough, D. (2008). *Collective narrative practice: Responding to individuals, groups and communities who have experienced trauma*. Adelaide: Dulwich Centre Publications.

Epston, D., & White, M. (1992). *Experience, contradiction, narrative and imagination: Selected papers of David Epston & Michael White, 1989–1991*. Adelaide: Dulwich Centre Publications.

Fanon, F (1963). *The wretched of the earth*. New York: Grove Press.

Freire, P. (1973). *Pedagogy of the oppressed*. New York: The Seabury Press.

García Márquez, G. (1987) *Clandestine in Chile: The Adventures of Miguel Littin*. New York: Henry Holt.

Gorman, W. (2001). Refugee survivors of torture: Trauma and treatment. *Professional Psychology: Research and Practice, 32*(5), 443–51.

Gott, R. (2008). Orlando Fals Borda sociologist and activist who defined peasant politics in Colombia. *Guardian*. Retrieved 1 July 2014 from www.theguardian.com/world/2008/aug/26/colombia.sociology.

Gurr, R., & Quiroga, J. (2001). Approaches to torture rehabilitation: A desk study covering effects, cost-effectiveness, participation and sustainability. *Torture, 11*(1a), 3–35.

Hárdi, L., Király, G., Kovács, E., & Heffernan, K. (2010). *Torture and survivors: Manual for experts in refugee care*. Budapest: Cordelia Foundation for the Rehabilitation of Torture Victims.

Herman, J.L. (1997). *Trauma and recovery: The aftermath of violence from domestic abuse to political terror*. New York: Basic Books.

Marlo, J., & Osorlo, F. (2009). Praxis and liberation in the context of Latin American theory. In M. Montero, C. Sonn (Eds), *Psychology of liberation: Theory and applications* (pp. 73–92). New York: Springer.

Martín Baró, I. (1994). *Writings for a liberation psychology: Essays, 1985–1989*, ed. A. Aron & S. Corne. Cambridge, MA: Harvard University Press.

Memoria Chilena (2014). *La transformación económica chilena entre 1973–2003*. Retrieved 1 July 2014 from www.memoriachilena.cl.

Physicians for Human Rights (2010). *PHR toolkits: Physicians for Human Rights tools & resources*. International Rehabilitation Council for Torture Victims. Retrieved 26 August 2014 from http://phrtoolkits.org.

Reder, P., & Fredman, G. (1996). The relationship to help: Interacting beliefs about the treatment process. *Clinical Child Psychology and Psychiatry, 1*(3), 457–67.

Redress (2013). Inter-American Court upholds the right to justice and reparation for exiled Pinochet-era torture survivor. Retrieved 26 August 2014 from www.redress.org.

Sahyoun Bowie, N. (2012). *Between sharing and silencing: The role of mental health professionals in human rights movements for Los Desaparecidos*. San Diego, CA: Department of Spanish and Portuguese & Centre for Latin American Studies, San Diego State University.

Smith, E., Patel, N., & MacMillan, L. (2010) A remedy for torture survivors in international law: Interpreting rehabilitation. Discussion Paper, Medical Foundation for the Care of Victims of Torture.

White, M. (2004). Working with people who are suffering the consequences of multiple trauma: A narrative perspective. *The International Journal of Narrative Therapy and Community Work, 1*, 45–76.

White, M., & Epston, D. (1990). *Narrative means to therapeutic ends*. New York: W.W. Norton.

Wilkinson, R., & Pickett, K. (2010). *The spirit level: Why equality is better for everyone*. London: Penguin Books.

PART V
Issues and dilemmas

15

IS IT POSSIBLE TO TAKE A LIBERATION APPROACH AS A CLINICAL PSYCHOLOGY TRAINEE?

Dzifa Afonu, Katarina Kovacova and Abbie Unwin

We approached the question 'Is it possible to take a liberation approach as a clinical psychology trainee?' through a series of dialogues. We began by thinking about our own connection to liberation approaches and how this links with wellbeing, before considering some of the constraints that hinder us when attempting to practise in this way and how we try to address these, while continuing to grow a sustainable liberation practice.

Who are we?

We are (Abbie and Dzifa) and were (Kat) clinical psychology trainees at a university that has historically promoted critical approaches[1] to psychology. As part of our training we were introduced to liberation psychology, and this brief encounter led us to want to find out more. We recognise that what liberation means to us is influenced by our contexts and experiences.

As a person with multiple, fluid and intersecting identities – Black, Muslim, queer,[2] disabled – I (Dzifa) have throughout my life experienced limitations on my liberty due to oppression. This has made me particularly interested in resistance against systems of oppression and cultural imperialism.

I (Abbie) am a White British heterosexual woman with no religious affiliation. I grew up in the north of England in a family environment where mutual support was reinforced and the importance of a fairer society was instilled in me. These values arose through a family history of manual work and trade unionism, while I was further influenced by my parents' involvement with cooperatives and the caring professions.

I (Kat) see my 'identity' as not easy to categorise; however, to situate myself I could be described as a White, non-conformist woman in a heterosexual relationship. I grew up in Czechoslovakia in the political context of forced single-party politics. I was part of a working-class family that resisted the regime and strongly held values of pluralism and critical thinking, despite the resulting loss of privileges. I have learnt from that historical memory, and later engagement with alternative cultures, about the importance of staying true to my values and striving to liberate myself and the people I work with from dominant discourses, if these feel oppressive.

Our personal histories and values have led us to develop an awareness of the ways that wider social and political structures contribute to people's distress, creating a foundation for our connection to liberation approaches.

What a liberation approach means to us

We recognise that 'liberation' can hold different meanings for different people and must be defined by people in the context of their lives. Liberation is not a fixed event that takes place at a particular moment; rather, it is 'a movement and a series of processes' (Burton, 2004; p. 585) that cannot be given to people (Montero, 2009). As Martín Baró (1994) stated, a liberation approach must be co-constructed alongside the people we work with; hence, there are multiple 'psychologies of liberation' (Watkins & Schulman, 2008). Further drawing on Martín Baró's (1994) ideas, we feel that it is important to highlight the connections between the sociopolitical contexts and power inequities in people's lives and their distress. In this regard, we are greatly influenced by Smail's (2005) theory of social materialism and his critique of the naïve concept of willpower, which expects people to gain insight and take individual responsibility to address their difficulties, irrespective of wider contextual factors. As psychologists, we have a responsibility to listen out for opportunities to ask questions about contextual factors and to acknowledge their impact. We recognise that 'wellness cannot be conceived out of context' and without a consideration of power (Prilleltensky, Nelson & Peirson, 2001; p. 147); hence we regard a liberation approach and wellbeing as being inextricably linked.

We are influenced by Wade's (1997) writings on everyday acts of resistance, and his belief that people will find creative and determined ways to resist in situations in which they are oppressed. While such responses may be subtle, for example a facial expression or remaining silent, they are often accompanied by the threat of reprisal and their significance cannot be underestimated. Wade (1997) described the 'health-inducing' impact of such resistance, as people begin to conceive of a stronger sense of self, able to respond in the face of violence and oppression. Hence, we believe we have a responsibility to recognise and honour such acts of resistance. We also see a liberation psychology approach as a process through which we raise our awareness of social realities through critical analysis, reflection and action, based on Freire's (1970) concept of 'conscientization' or 'critical consciousness'. In outlining our liberation approach we recognise that while some aspects may be more easily incorporated into our work as trainees, others may prove more difficult.

Obstacles to a liberation approach

There are constraints imposed on us both within the context of training and more broadly within the National Health Service (NHS), where the medical model dominates and people's distress is regarded as 'mental illness', and thus as individual pathology. As psychologists we are required to use 'evidence-based' models and approaches that perpetuate a narrow, individualistic, Western notion of psychology, often resulting in little attention being paid to wider contextual factors and people's choices or preferences. This has a significant impact on the degree to which we can centralise people's voices if they differ from this dominant notion of psychology, while it also has implications for what is taught during clinical psychology training. As trainees we are required to fulfil specific competencies set by our training regulatory bodies in order to fit the 'mould' of what is required to become a psychologist; for example, each trainee must become 'competent' in using cognitive behavioural therapy (CBT). Such restrictions can act as a barrier when we are trying to be responsive to people's needs.

I (Kat) met with a client who told me about his housing difficulties. During supervision, I was asked to formulate what might have been maintaining his difficulties. When I suggested that it appeared to be social factors, I was told that this is not part of a CBT 'hot-cross bun' model and therefore out of the equation. I was told to remember that psychologists have a clear and boundaried role, which does not involve dealing with social issues. While this example highlights the difficulties we can face when trying to be responsive to people's understandings of their distress, it also touches on the inherent power imbalance in the supervisory relationship (Muratoi, 2001). A supervisor is required to judge trainees' performance, essentially acting as a gatekeeper to the profession through their ability to 'fail' the supervisee (Holloway & Wolleat, 1994). Concerns have been raised that this dynamic may stifle critical thinking and reflective practice (Newnes, Hagan & Cox, 2000) and hence, a liberation approach.

'Even when you feel like you're trapped in a box, you can still make holes in it'

Despite the constraints placed on us as trainees, we feel that it is possible for us to take a liberation approach and to work with people in ways that are consistent with our values. We regard the small and perhaps subtle things we do to be as important as more overt forms of resistance, as we shall now describe.

Reflecting on our power

We recognise that power is a complex concept that is socially, culturally and historically situated (Patel, 2012). While we may feel disempowered at times, we are in a privileged position and have a degree of power within society by virtue of being clinical psychology trainees. For example, we have secure employment, receive continued education and we have access to critical reading materials and physical resources. The label of trainee also affords us a degree of power by placing us in a position of 'learner', allowing us to ask questions from a stance of supposed curiosity at times when we may disagree with what is being said.

When considering our power within the supervisory relationship, we reflected that the sharing of ideas is a two-way process. Supervisors have commented that they learn from trainees whose questions, ideas and knowledge keep them connected to new approaches and ways of thinking. Through sharing our ideas we may also find allies who can help our liberation praxis to grow. Where supervisory relationships do not support our values, however, there are subtle ways to resist. For example, when I (Dzifa) hear a supervisor talk uncritically in a way that individualises someone's distress when the person has expressed that they are struggling with practical or economic issues, even if I cannot say that I disagree at least I can refuse to nod along as may be expected of me.

Remaining aware of our power is crucial within restrictive contexts, whether this means acknowledging the impact of wider contextual factors or simply connecting with someone on a human level. For example, I (Kat) was working with a Black man in his forties who was referred for gambling difficulties using a structured CBT programme. In our second meeting he shared with me that he had been feeling suicidal and described feeling angry with himself for not earning enough to support his family. This opened up an opportunity for us to talk about his early life experiences of being disadvantaged by a severely deprived social environment. We reflected on how little power he had to access the resources available to his peers. I remember how he commented on my young age and the privileges that come with it, and how we used it to think about different levels of social injustice he faced. These conversations helped him to move away from self-blame and freed him to make plans for his future. I feel that not having these conversations, which were outside of the therapeutic model, could have led to his 'disengagement from therapy',[3] as had historically been the case.

Our values and ethics underpin our work; hence, liberation comes in the relationships we form with people, witnessing and appreciating their stories and honouring their acts of resistance. I (Dzifa) can remember times when just sitting next to someone who was crying on an inpatient ward and listening to them when no one else seemed to be responding felt like it was going against the prevailing culture. Opening our hearts (Afuape, 2011), staying connected with our emotions on a human and moral level, and continuing to ask questions helps us resist the risk of colluding with potentially oppressive practices and institutional structures.

Placement opportunities

As we are able to request placements in our third year, we have all actively sought and been assigned placements that have allowed us to take a liberation and community psychology approach. On my placement I (Abbie) have had the privilege of being invited as a participant to join a 'walk and talk' group, inspired by the work of Guy Holmes (2010), a clinical psychologist in Shropshire who organises walks for people in the local community to support access to the countryside and to facilitate the development of relationships. The 'walk and talk' group that I join sees Holmes' idea transferred to the urban multicultural context of Hackney in East London (Peddie *et al.*, 2014), and involves a weekly walk around parts of London, ending with a visit to a café. The group members are long-term users of mental health services who have a shared interest in walking. While the group was initially started by a trainee clinical psychologist and a community development worker, it has developed and is now led by two members who have transformed it to meet the interests of the group. For example, the group now creates their own guided tours and 'memory walks'.[4]

The group engages in conversations covering a diverse range of topics including racism, the gentrification of the local area, colonialism and people's experiences of mental health services; dialogues which have helped to develop my critical consciousness. The group members have described the importance of the group's welcoming environment, which allowed them to feel energised and to develop valued relationships (Peddie *et al.*, 2014), thus enabling a collective, supportive identity of a 'family', in contrast to the stigmatising identities often imposed on people by mental health services. I asked some of the members about their experiences of the group:[5]

> I think it's a fantastic group. You get exercise, you get fresh air, it gets you out of your flat and you get a nice meal at the end.
>
> *(Michael)*

> A good thing about this group is we all look out for each other. I find kindness in the group and it's bringing me out of my shell.
>
> *(Gordon)*

> We all care about each other. People don't care about each other enough in society today. When someone doesn't come for a couple of weeks we make a concerted effort to ring them to see how they are. This is a lifeline for a lot of people who otherwise might be isolated and lonely.
>
> *(Janet)*

Being welcomed into this group has provided me with a unique opportunity to form relationships with people while walking alongside them as a member of the group. When talking to one of the members about my role within the group he replied *'you need us so that you can learn'*. I have enjoyed the challenge of taking the position of learner and the uncertainty this brings, allowing a reconstruction of psychology from the perspective of the group (Martín Baró, 1994).

Our research

Our third-year theses enabled us to carry out research that was connected to our interests and values. Below we describe how we utilised this opportunity to explore what a liberation approach might look like in our practice.

Dzifa

I did a participatory action research project with a group of young adults (aged thirteen to thirty-five) and musicians who worked with me as co-researchers. The project explored UK hip-hop and grime culture and its connection to sociopolitical issues and the wellbeing of young people in inner London. It also aimed to explore what clinical psychology can learn from the UK hip-hop and grime community and the ways that young people engage with it. As a young person I took part in a participatory youth project, which had a massive impact on me and influenced the following ten years of my life working in the charity sector, doing work in which youth participation was central. I am also a fan of UK hip-hop and grime and have found it to be really important to my wellbeing, due to its political content, the many ways it connects me to community and the ways that it gives voice to the experiences of marginalised people.

I found that the values and methods of participatory action research clashed with the regulations and requirements of the thesis as part of the doctoral training; for example, the expectation of taking a 'scientific' approach that is expert-led. I wanted to be completely led by the co-researchers, but I had to balance this with what was required of me.[6] Despite this, I felt honoured to be able to listen to what the co-researchers wanted to focus on.

There can be a desire to make young people fit into certain methods of working, such as having meetings and speaking in a professional language. It is important to allow young people to communicate in creative ways that feel more connected to their ways of being in the world. For example, the young people wanted to be able to perform a rap for the people in the forum. Although this stepped outside of what would be expected for a research focus group, it allowed the young people to take a central place in the discussions in their own way. Here Josh[7] (aged fifteen) freestyles a rap following a group discussion about the impact of UK hip-hop on young people:

> You can grow and expand like seeds in the earth, I can help you with raps and peace with these words. It's usually the hardest that are feeling the hurt that goes deeper than words emotions are blurred, so they seem to be heard on the road to the curbs, but you grow so you learn. To grow you have to go deeper in earth. See what the freedom is worth to the deans that are hurt. Look deep into the system submerged in delusion. Hypocrisies honestly the main cause of confusion. Controls a generation of druggies and slags, drugs, sex and alcohol are not seen as bad. Weed grows wild in this concrete jungle, young kids on rocks don't stumble. Live progressive, stay humbled, believe you'll succeed. Still, it's easy to crumble. And they say that we are living in democracy, the government lies on the rise of hypocrisy, bending the truth, warping our minds, honestly. It's got me feeling deep when I'm deep in philosophy.
>
> *(Josh)*

Building relationships and finding ways to talk about important issues in a way that is accessible and fun is important in a liberation practice that seeks to centre the voices and experiences of young people:

> We had fun, so it was not boring, just copying what ... what it was ... a good experience.
>
> *(Josh)*

Abbie

My research looked at young people's's[8] stories of their stay on a residential care farm,[9] which aims to facilitate their re-engagement with school and education, while supporting their overall wellbeing. I initially became interested in green care[10] approaches after hearing of Guy Holmes' (2010) 'walk and talk' group (as previously discussed) and the value that people placed on having access to the countryside and green space. Green spaces offer an alternative to people's daily 'toxic mental environments' (Holmes, 2010; p. 143), including those in which people typically access mental health services. The approach taken by the farm with which I collaborated is based on a 'farming, family and therapy' model, avoiding the use of labels and placing an emphasis on positive feedback, self-discovery, mutual support and inclusive activities. I was interested to see how the young people experienced their time on the farm and the implications this might have for a liberation approach and for service development.

Aspects of the farm model were experienced by the young people as liberating, supporting the emergence of alternative and positive stories of self. While the farm model offered an alternative way of nurturing wellbeing, the young people also revealed that they found their lack of voice and choice with regard to timetabled activities oppressive. I kept my interquestions broad so as not to restrict their responses. The young people's stories introduced narratives of school, London and society more generally, and of the oppression, fear and judgement they experience within these contexts. I explored and elaborated on their experiences of oppression during my research interviews, the process of which became an intervention in itself, drawing on Freire's (1970) ideas about conscientization. All of the young people talked about their experiences of feeling oppressed within the school context and many contrasted school with the farm where they could 'talk freely':

> Like, [teachers] either raise their voice or they tre-, treat us like little children. And thinkin' like, I'm at the age where, I can't be treated like that.
>
> *(Claire)*

> cos at school you're, it's the teacher–student, and you work. And, when you're, cos you're away from school you can act different and talk and speak freely.
>
> *(Cook)*

The young people's stories of school highlighted the potentially oppressive nature of what Freire (1970) described as the 'banking' system of education, which requires young people to suppress their beliefs and opinions in order to conform, and to store and memorise deposits of information to be reproduced during exams. Some of the young people also described the judgement they experience in London:

> you can be with a group of friends in London, and people will just think you're a gang. So, you could just be walking along the street and people, you, you might even get stopped by the police ... one time, no word of a lie, [the police] did me three times in one day.
>
> *(Archer)*

Listening to the young people's stories, I was inspired by the creative and subtle ways they found to resist when they felt oppressed, particularly given the lack of voice and power afforded to young people. Their determination was especially striking when I reflected on my own experience of being a young person, when I was keen to follow the rules and do what was expected. I felt it was important to recognise and honour their acts of resistance when sharing my analysis with them. Their stories gave me a sense of hope, reminding me of the importance of connecting with our power as trainees, and of not giving up in the face of restrictive and oppressive systems.

Kat

My research used discursive psychology[11] to explore how clinical psychologists talk about practices which, from a critical point of view, are seen as potentially problematic. I believe that using discursive psychology in research can be viewed as a social and political action in itself because of its potential to reveal obscured mechanisms of power, oppression and discrimination by detailed analysis of language.

My study showed that as psychologists we can inadvertently justify the use of the medical model in devising individualising interventions, while at the same time orient to them as morally problematic practices. For example, psychologists in the study raised concerns about the potential negative impact of labelling children with diagnoses, on their identities and future, while also attempting to 'diagnose in safer ways', such as assigning a less specific DSM code of an unspecified diagnosis, by rendering diagnosing as a necessary administrative task or by not disclosing the diagnosis to clients. While this could be seen as a form of resistance within the institutional structures, these 'safer' ways can be viewed as maintaining the status quo by not challenging the mechanisms of power that maintain the use of diagnosis. In addition, psychologists might construct diagnosing as democratic and talk about client choice. Lastly, the research suggested that psychologists talk in terms of common sense by emphasising the practical limitations on their work ('*You have to be practical*' or '*You have to accept the limitations of what you as a psychologist can do*'), which seem to function as self-sufficient arguments that require little elaboration due to their taken-for-granted quality. Despite seeming reasonable, these ideas might provide a warrant for not dealing with social circumstances impacting on our clients' lives.

The findings highlighted the need for psychologists themselves, and the profession as a whole, to engage in a process of critical consciousness (Freire, 1970) in order to reflect on our professional interests, use of language and the social structures within which we practise, in order to avoid creating and maintaining situations of injustice. I believe that in order to be able to work according to our moral values and liberation principles, we need to start turning the critical lens on ourselves and embrace a collectively supported critique of psychological discourses, concepts and interventions in order to use them for human liberation and wellbeing of us all.

Growing and sustaining liberation approaches

Part of growing a liberation approach as trainees means reading outside the course texts to broaden our understanding of critical and liberation approaches; for example, by drawing ideas from sociology, music or poetry from around the world. We continue to learn by engaging in conversation with clients, colleagues, friends and people outside of work, helping us to raise our critical awareness by considering multiple perspectives on liberation and wellbeing. We recognise the importance of ongoing critical self-reflection in order to consider issues such as difference and our own personal privilege and power. For example, I (Abbie) found reading McIntosh's (1998) paper 'White privilege: Unpacking the invisible knapsack' raised my awareness of the privilege that I have due to my skin colour, and the impact this has on my experience within society. We have valued exercises during training which have helped us to reflect on our positions and those of the people we work with. For example, being asked to recall a time when we felt powerless helped us to tap into our own feelings of anger, frustration and hopelessness, which aided our reflection on how people we work with might feel in similar situations.

We reflected that there is much to be learnt while on challenging placements which require us to work in ways that are contradictory to a liberation approach. Our reactions to these restrictive placements can feed into our energy of wanting to find ways to work alongside people in order to centralise their experiences and honour their preferences, rather than trying to fit people into pre-existing models.

Dzifa

When I was working on an acute ward, I was crying after each ward round because of what I felt was a lack of human connection between clinicians and clients. There was little I could do to change the dominant medical culture as a trainee; I felt powerless. I spoke to a colleague who said that he survived training by seeing himself as a spy. He saw his role as someone going in to see how it works; collecting data that you hold on to for when you're qualified. I started to see my role a bit differently; I was actually getting this experience as a privilege in a way, because it meant that I could use it to inform my future practice. However hard it was, however much I cried, the other people there had little control over when they could leave, with some being held under section. The fact that I could leave meant that I could manage to be there.

We acknowledge that taking a liberation approach can sometimes mean sticking our necks out and disrupting the status quo, with the risk of resistance from the system. Therefore, we try to nurture alternative ways of looking after ourselves by forming alliances, networking and maintaining contact with people who aspire to work in this way. I (Dzifa) am greatly influenced by Audrey Lorde's (1988) idea that self-care and collective self-care is political. I share Lorde's assertion that survival and self-belief, when in an oppressive environment, is in itself an act of resistance. I try to practise collective self-care through my involvement with a group of queer artists and activists. I see collective self-care as resistance and activism, such as some of my political work which involves writing about the experiences of marginalised groups, organising events and spaces for reflection and development, attending conferences and staying informed about political issues.

Our liberation approaches connect to our personal values and therefore impact on our ways of being in the world, which do not stop when we leave work. For example, Dzifa and Abbie go on marches against cuts to government services, recognising the importance of standing alongside others in solidarity and gaining strength from their collective voice. We have also written letters to authorities and supported campaigns around issues related to the asylum system, giving emotional and practical support to individuals, groups and global organisations. We regard solidarity and connectedness as crucial components of a liberation approach; hence, we recognise the importance of witnessing and appreciating the work of our clients and colleagues, and of standing alongside them in order to sustain a liberation approach (Reynolds, 2009).

Final reflections

The writing of this chapter has taken us on a journey; learning from each other through our dialogues, and helping our liberation approaches to grow. We reflected on the subtle differences and emphases of our liberation approaches which are perhaps related to our backgrounds and our values. Ongoing dialogue with others, continued reading and placement and research opportunities during training have allowed us to conceive of a liberation approach that is possible as trainees. Part of our role is to be critical of psychological discourses and practices that can inhibit collective wellbeing and the reconstruction of psychology from the perspective of the people we work with (Martín Baró, 1994). This involves critical self-reflection, recognising the ways in which we might perpetuate potentially oppressive discourses, and being transparent about the limited and restrictive nature of psychological theories and practices. We endeavour to have influence at higher political and legislative levels, but we appreciate that liberation can also be found in the relationships we form with people and the position we take in our work.

We continue to grow through witnessing and appreciating the ways in which both our clients and colleagues oppose social injustice. We draw inspiration from the stories we hear of determined and creative resistance, acknowledging our responsibility to recognise and honour these, while maintaining a commitment to our values. These stories touch us on a human level, as human beings trying to support other human beings, where psychology is simply another tool (Patel, 2011). We have been left with a sense of hope when considering the many ways that we can connect with our power, and the subtle everyday acts of resistance (Wade, 1997) that are possible in spite of the potential constraints to our practice as trainees. We look forward to continuing our journey towards liberating ourselves and the people we work with.

Notes

1 Critical approaches challenge mainstream psychology that tends to explain people's distress and behaviour at the level of the individual, instead endeavouring to acknowledge the impact of multiple layers of context.
2 Queer is a term I (Dzifa) use to describe my gender and sexuality as being undefined and deviating from the dominant constructions of gender and sexuality; it marks a deviation also from the LGBT labels, and connects me to a political community of people who embody non-normative gender and sexual orientations.
3 This is not to suggest that people need to engage in 'therapy' in order to get the support they need.
4 Group members take it in turns to lead the group around an area that has personal meaning for them, sharing their memories and stories.
5 I would like to extend my thanks to the group members who agreed to let me use their comments in this chapter.
6 I had to collect data in conventional ways using just forum groups when as a group we had wanted to create a film or magazine using interviews and drama.
7 I use a pseudonym here to keep the identity of the participants and co-researchers who were part of the project anonymous.
8 The young people were aged fourteen to seventeen years old, and each chose their own pseudonym.
9 Care farming has been defined as 'the use of commercial farms and agricultural landscapes as a base for promoting mental and physical health, through normal farming activity' (Sempik, Hine & Wilcox, 2010; p. 37).
10 Green care activities use nature as a setting for a range of interventions, in the hope of improving health and wellbeing.
11 Discursive psychology is a form of discourse analysis that focuses on how psychology is used by people in everyday and institutional settings (Potter, 2006).

References

Afuape, T. (2011). *Power resistance and liberation in therapy with survivors of trauma: To have our hearts broken*. London: Routledge.
Burton, M. (2004). Viva nacho! Liberating psychology in Latin America. *The Psychologist*, 17(10), 584–7.
Freire, P. (1970). *Pedagogy of the oppressed*. London: Penguin.

Holloway, E.L., & Wolleat, P.L. (1994). Supervision: The pragmatics of empowerment. *Journal of Educational and Psychological Consultation, 5*, 23–43.

Holmes, G. (2010). *Psychology in the real world: Community based groupwork.* Ross-on-Wye: PCCS Books Ltd.

Lorde, A. (1988). *A burst of light: Essays.* Ann Arbor, MI: Firebrand Books.

Martín Baró, I. (1994). *Writings for a liberation psychology: Essays, 1985–1989*, ed. A. Aron & S. Corne. Cambridge, MA: Harvard University Press.

McIntosh, P. (1998). 'White privilege: Unpacking the invisible knapsack'. In: M. McGoldrick (Ed.), *Re-visioning family therapy.* New York: Guildford Press.

Montero, M. (2009). Methods for liberation: Critical consciousness in action. In: M. Montero & C.C. Sonn (Eds), *Psychology of liberation: Theory and applications* (pp. 73–92). New York: Springer.

Muratoi, M.C. (2001). Examining supervisor impairment from the counselor trainee's perspective. *Counselor Education and Supervision, 41*(1), 41–56.

Newnes, C., Hagan, T. & Cox, R. (2000). Fostering critical reflection in psychological practice. *Clinical Psychology Forum, 139*, 21–4.

Patel, N. (2011). The psychologisation of torture. In: M. Rapley, J. Moncrieff & J. Dillon (Eds), *De-medicalising misery: Psychiatry, psychology and the human condition* (pp. 96–117). London: PalMacmillan,

Patel, N. (2012). Difference and power in supervision: The case of culture and racism. In: I. Fleming & L. Steen (Eds), *Supervision and clinical psychology* (pp. 239–55). London: Taylor & Francis.

Peddie et al. (2014). In prep. *Understanding 'Walk and Talk' in an urban, multicultural environment.*

Potter, J. (2006). Discursive psychology. In V.E. Jupp (Ed.), *The Sage dictionary of social research* (pp. 77–79). London: Sage.

Prilleltensky, I., Nelson, G. & Peirson, L. (2001). The role of power and control in children's lives: An ecological analysis of pathways toward wellness, resilience and problems. *Journal of Community & Applied Social Psychology, 11*, 143–58.

Reynolds, V. (2009). Collective ethics as a path to resisting burnout. *Insights: The Clinical Counsellor's Magazine & News*, December, 6–7.

Sempik, J., Hine, R. & Wilcox, D. (2010). *Green care: A conceptual framework.* Loughborough: Loughborough University Centre for Child and Family Research.

Smail, D. (2005). *Power, interest and psychology.* Ross-on-Wye: PCCS Books Ltd.

Wade, A. (1997). Small acts of living: Everyday resistance to violence and other forms of oppression. *Contemporary Family Therapy, 19*(1), 23–39.

Watkins, M., & Shulman, H. (2008). *Toward psychologies of liberation.* New York: Palgrave Macmillan.

16

IS PSYCHOANALYSIS A LIBERATION APPROACH?

African sisters in dialogue

Taiwo Afuape and Tayo Afuape

Introduction

In this chapter, Black African sisters Tayo and Taiwo dialogue about the extent to which psychoanalysis can be regarded as a liberation approach. Tayo is a child and adolescent psychoanalytic psychotherapist who originally trained as a teacher and educational psychologist; Taiwo is a clinical psychologist and systemic psychotherapist. The aim of this chapter is not to conflate their views into a single-voiced text, but to highlight the differences in their voices and the ways in which dialogue itself becomes a third entity that holds difference, without watering it down or smudging it together. Rather than reiterating some of the many established critiques of psychoanalysis, this chapter explores the ideas that emerged from this dialogue.

Psychoanalysis and liberation

Taiwo

As with others (e.g. Prilleltensky & Nelson, 2002; Wetherall, 2003), I was critical of what appeared to be psychoanalysis' blaming, expert-driven and individualising tendencies. At the same time, I had interesting conversations with my eldest sister Tayo, who seemed to be doing something quite different in her work. Although I could not relate to her language ('transference', 'projection'), I found her approach to connecting with clients, in a range of ways (viewing therapy as 'a relationship of humility, humanity and love'), fascinating. Tayo has a deep sense of social justice and equality. Despite our many conversations about racism, misogyny, homophobia and classism, somehow I did not connect her two passions – psychoanalysis and challenging oppression. Embarking on this dialogical journey with my sister has been insightful, as I have been able to turn my critique of the apparent invisibility of social context in psychoanalytic formulation and intervention, into a desire to look further into the social, political and historical contexts of Freudian psychoanalysis previously unseen by me. Before exploring this further, I will briefly reflect on what liberation praxis means to me.

Liberation praxis is based on critical reflection and action that transforms the social structures and ideas that reproduce inequality and oppression. Liberation psychologist Ignacio Martín Baró argued that considering psychological problems as primarily individual means 'obscuring the relationship between personal estrangement and social oppression, presenting the pathology of persons as if it were something removed from history and society' (Martín Baró, 1994; p. 27). Instead, liberation psychology connects people's wellbeing with the social, cultural, economic, political and ecological contexts in which they live; what Martín Baró called *critical consciousness* or *concientización*. In my dialogue with Tayo I shared my view that if psychoanalysis simply affirms that injustice and oppression happen in people's lives but does nothing tangible to challenge this oppression, other than an attempt to ameliorate personal problems, it does not serve the interests of liberation, but upholds the status quo. As Martín Baró (1994; p. 40) puts it: 'concientización does not consist of a simple change of opinion about reality, a change of individual subjectivity that leaves that objective situation intact.'

TAYO: What does deprivation, unemployment, family discord do ... to the psyche? ... One person might fight for the rights of people to have knowledge about how the system oppresses them. Another person ... [might be] concerned with ... the consequences that stem from that oppression ... so one is dealing with the more socially contextual aspects and one is dealing with the individual needs of the person.

TAIWO: But ... you can't do one without the other.

TAYO: But my point is exactly the same ... people are conditioned to accept certain systems ... and we don't even realise it. Institutionalised through education, ... the legal system, ... the social security system, ... the medical system.

TAIWO: Including psychology and psychotherapy ... we also help to institutionalise people.

Tayo

Like Martín Baró, Sigmund Freud (6 May 1856–23 September 1939) was an observer of the human condition and human behaviour as influenced by one's political, historical, cultural and religious context. Set in the context of the First World War, Freud's 1930 book, *Civilization and its Discontents*, de-ideologised everyday experience by proposing that society inhibited people's natural instincts and controlled their behaviour, including their murderous tendencies (Freud, 2010). Not only did Freud highlight the importance of one's sense of self as separate from (but still part of) our mother, father, family and community, he argued that society is maintained by a collective consciousness or conscience which seems to be the antithesis of Martín Baró's concientización. Whereas Martín Baró argued that critical consciousness was an awareness of the link between social oppression and emotional distress, for Freud collective consciousness not only restrained critical awareness but punished the individual for having thoughts contrary to social norms, or inconsistent with the masses. Freud argued that the way society is set up creates individuals who have to restrain their instinctive nature. Liberation, therefore, is about creating space around these restraints.

It is ironic given Freud's background that he is considered anything other than a liberation psychologist, as he wanted to free himself and others from the social oppression he had encountered all his life. He risked his own sanity, used unorthodox methods (meditation, drugs, self-analysis and analysis of his daughter) and was relentlessly fearless in his exploration of the unknown territories of our mind.

Freud: 'White but not quite'

Taiwo

Given that Tayo and I seemed to be coming from such different places with respect to 'liberation' it seemed important for me to try to understand where Freud may have been coming from in order to proceed in the dialogue. A number of times Tayo highlighted Freud's Jewishness and linked this to why liberation of the *mind/soul* was so important to him.

TAYO: Remember Freud was a Jew and he grew up in a very oppressive, repressive society ... he couldn't free himself physically, he couldn't free himself from what was happening to Jews socially and politically, but he could free his mind and that's why he experimented with drugs; he wanted to reach, experience and understand a more instinctive, intuitive and primal aspect of himself. That's why he was fascinated by African societies, shamanism. That's why he wrote 'Totem and Taboo' ... because he wanted to get away from the repressiveness of Western society ...

When I [was doing my psychoanalytic training] ... I thought the point was to give a critical analysis. As a psychologist I was taught to do this [but] the format and the structure [of psychoanalytic training] was not about criticising Freud; you had to learn about Freud, his context, his influences, his passions. So I changed my thinking.... The first book I read which I latched onto was 'What Freud did Wrong'. Then I read a book by Peter Gay called 'Freud: A Life for Our Time' ... it was absolutely fascinating. Freud's theories came from his interest in Greek mythology; from his passion for and loathing of the Jewish faith; his own self-analysis, how he felt about being in a society of anti-Semitism and his own conflicts about wanting acceptance but also needing to be ground breaking and polemical. Hitler was saying that Jews were inferior and dirty people; that they were the cause of the recession and their mass extermination was a taboo subject, even amongst the Jews. Psychoanalysis came from that.

Gaztambide (2010) argues that *recovering the historical memory* of psychoanalysis means understanding Freud as a Jewish man growing up in nineteenth- and twentieth-century Nazi Europe, and the chronic poverty that resulted from sustained socioeconomic oppression (Salberg, 2007). Although he was able to pursue higher education, Freud experienced venomous anti-Semitism throughout his life, as 'being Jewish meant being seen as different, as diseased, as culturally incomplete' (Gilman, 1993b; p. 16). Nineteenth-century medical anthropology regarded Jewish people as having an 'African character' (animal-like and primitive) and often referred to Jewish people as 'White negroes' (Aron & Starr, 2013; p. 241). Based on Cone's (1970) notion that 'Blackness' is both a physiological trait that comes up against structural racism and an ontological sign for all oppressed people, Gaztambide (2010) argues that Freud was a 'Black' man, in that, despite resembling the White hegemony with the Whiteness of his skin, he was 'nevertheless denigrated[1] and excluded because of what [he] "really" [was]' (Gaztambide, 2010; p. 4): 'White, but not quite' (Boyarin, 1997). According to Gilman (1993a), Freud viewed himself as closer to a 'Moor' than an Aryan (Gilman, 1993a; p. 55). Jacques Derrida (15 July 1930–9 October 2004), an Algerian-born French philosopher, came up with the term 'undecidables' to highlight this sort of complex identity. Being a Jewish man from Algiers, it is not surprising that Derrida, like Freud, experienced himself as on the margins, and developed the concept of deconstruction (the opening up of fixed and oppositional realities) and undecidability (that which does not fit neatly into a category and highlights 'the dualities of presence and absence'). Being Jewish was also an asset that allowed Freud to critique mainstream ideas. In a letter to the Jewish humanitarian organisation B'nai B'rith he wrote: 'as a Jew I was prepared to be in the opposition and to renounce agreement with the "compact majority"' (Freud, 1961; p. 368).

Gaztambide (2010) argues that Freud developed a theory and practice that universalised the racist stereotypes associated with Jewishness (susceptibility to hysteria, aggression and sexual perversion), and turned them into the pathology of humanity projected onto Jewish (or any oppressed) people.

Tayo

Freud was a member of an ethnic group that had been demonised and dehumanised since medieval times. Surrounded by the annihilation of Jewish people, and his own daughter Anna being interviewed by the Gestapo, Freud must have experienced his own 'nameless dread', described by Bion (1962) as a vacuous, hostile space of catastrophic anxiety and fear. I imagine he felt powerless to change the tide of hatred that plagued Europe as well as the growing possibility of his and his family's destruction. He might have felt that the mental domain was his only retreat and salvation, so he sought to liberate the individual from the inside out rather than the outside in. Freud's focus on internal dynamics was to the detriment of focusing on the impact of external reality; including the possibility that, if galvanised, our shared experience can challenge the tide of oppression bringing about social change and justice. Working with looked after children I know only too well how important it is to observe, acknowledge and manage the interaction between the child's interpersonal, family, social and cultural context and their distress.

However, the chicken-and-egg argument is more convoluted in light of the unique and diverse needs of clients, even within their shared social context. To highlight the need for both an 'inside out' and 'outside in' approach I wish to bring into the equation a transgender young person that I have worked with for some time. For some trans-individuals, but not all, the disconnection between mind and body can cause great angst, and society's dismissal of this profound conflict can further exaggerate this dilemma. Although I would argue that Western society's prejudice and intolerance of the 'Other' is of central importance, for some trans-individuals, as long as they are in the wrong body, the disconnection between mind and body and the angst it causes, prevails. My client, for example, experienced a feeling as he called it of being 'encased' in a skin he could not call his own and his sense of isolation from others in this 'alien skin' made him feel hopeless, helpless and at times suicidal. This experience was powerfully conveyed in my counter-transference (the connection between us at times so intense that it was as if we were one mind and body). His 'you get me' comment seemed to be an appreciation and acknowledgement of my ability to get (inside this skin with) him and reflect his angst back to him and significant others.

Political psychoanalysts

Taiwo

The more I learnt about Freud the more I came to see him as both an upholder of oppressive values and a staunch critic of them.

TAYO: Freud grew up in Edwardian times, a time of being 'proper' and doing things properly – 'this is what proper ladies do', 'this is what proper men do' – and there was a social structure that determined how proper people behaved and how they thought. And he radicalised that, by saying that men *and* women had sexual fantasies. He talked about the penis and breasts at a time when women were not supposed to show, talk or think about any aspect of their bodies. Maybe now we recognise his oppressive opinions that were misogynistic and racist, but there were also a lot of things he was doing that were revolutionary.

TAIWO: But that's an interesting point about the context and how it shaped the *ways* in which he was radical and also the constraints to [his] radicalness; which is a different way of thinking about it than he was just reinforcing the status quo. But then that begs the question of how to bring psychoanalysis into the era we are in now, so that it is radical with respect to the contexts we are in now.

Dialogue with radical thinkers seemed key to Freud developing radical roots. In a letter to Carl Jung (26 July 1875–6 June 1961), Freud called on psychoanalysis to 'combat the authority of State and Church where they commit palpable injustice' (cited in Zaretsky, 2004; p. 85). Freud's friend and training analysand Anton Von Freund convinced Freud to open free psychoanalytic clinics for the poor (Danto, 2005). Freud's colleague Sándor Ferenczi (7 July 1873–22 May 1933), a Jewish man raised in a progressive household and forerunner of relational psychoanalysis and short-term psychodynamic therapy, was like Freud both 'embedded in cultural streams of patriarchy and misogyny, and no less likely to repeat its ideologies' (Gaztambide, 2012; p. 144), *and* committed to challenging and critiquing them. In 1903 Ferenczi presented a paper advocating for better wages and working conditions for exploited medical workers (Sziklai, 2012). In 1908 he advocated for supporting the rights of gay people, urging his analytic colleagues to 'take sides against' oppression aimed at people who are gay. He also urged the medical community to challenge the pathologisation and dehumanisation of gay people (cited in Rachman, 1993; p. 84). In 1911, Ferenczi described the social causes of alcoholism, which required addressing its social aetiology.

Ferenczi encouraged a lesbian analysand, 'Rosa K', who was persecuted, harassed, rejected and subjected to various forms of violence, to write an autobiography so he could connect more fully to her experience. He not only used his emotional connection to her to directly challenge homophobia but to 'redefine psychoanalysis into a transformative relational encounter' grounded in empathy and mutuality (Gaztambide, 2012; p. 145). Similarly, in our dialogue, Tayo argued that truly listening to clients and truly empathising should lead to advocating on their behalf and challenging oppression; as true empathy calls us to act in the world.

TAYO: Psychoanalysis has become part of the restrained society that Freud talked about ... some psychoanalysts have restrained their instinct to move towards resistance and liberation and conform to the status quo.... They take up the aspect of Freud who sat at the end of the couch listening to the privileged ... but not essentially the spirit of Freud, who challenged the status quo and put his head on the line many, many times.... Psychoanalysis can be very oppressive or it can be very liberating, depending on the analyst's approach to oppression. If they want you to just go along with the status quo then its oppressive ... but if it's about truly understanding your experience then it is very liberating.

In 1910 Ferenczi attempted to dissuade Freud from his belief in the inherent destructiveness of human beings by arguing for the role of social factors in human suffering, drawing parallels between anti-Semitic and anti-Black racism (Gaztambide, 2012). In 1918 Freud gave a keynote speech at the Budapest Congress, referring to 'psychotherapy for the people' in free clinics adapted to the 'new conditions' psychoanalysts encountered (Freud, 1955; p. 167). He further argued that for treatment to be successful, it should '[combine] mental assistance with some material support' (Freud, 1955; p. 167).

Other psychoanalysts, such as Otto Fenichel, Edith Jacobson and Annie Reich, took an overtly political stance. In the 1950s Robert Lindner, a Baltimore analyst, wrote a series of books about rebellion: *Rebel Without a Cause*, *Prescription for Rebellion* and *Must you Conform?* In 1970s Latin America Marie Langer 'called for a psychoanalysis whose theory would embrace a Marxist conceptualisation of class society in order to shed light on the inevitable psychological suffering that was the product of a social order composed of inherently exploitative relations' (Hollander, 1997; p. 8). Her condemnation of the repressive Argentine government provoked right wing death squad Argentine Anti-Communist Alliance (Triple A) to put her name on the death list in 1974, forcing her into exile for the second time in her life.

Becoming medical and Americanised

In our dialogue I asked Tayo the question '*Given its radical history, nature and potential . . . why doesn't modern psychoanalysis comment more on the social aspects of oppression and have a more radical stance on the social context of distress?*' Similarly, Jacoby (1983) argued that 'the political Freudians sank into the [European] psychoanalytic unconscious. When they are remembered, they are only half-remembered' (Jacoby, 1983; p. x). European psychoanalysis became insular, medical and clinical with the rise of Fascism (leading to the exile of many 'political' Freudians), and professionalisation and Americanisation (which encouraged analysts to become mainstream supporters of the status quo). Jacoby (1983) argued that 'Once incorporated into medical schools, psychoanalysis came to attract those who find security in conformity and propriety', '[turning] "legitimate and respectable" as well as "sluggish and smug"', such that 'it is no longer apparent that psychoanalysis was ever rebellious' (p. ix).

But what drove politics from the consciousness of twenty-first-century British psychoanalysis? Whereas Tayo viewed the answer as lying in the lack of diversity on training courses, such that people who have intimate understanding of oppression are not present to shape it, I thought the lack of critique of Freud was also a factor. Whereas Tayo felt that self-analysis, analysis and reflectivity were the main critiques needed, I felt that they were not enough.

TAYO: Child psychotherapists are by nature reflective practitioners and self-critical of our practice. We use intensive personal analysis, supervision, multi-professional team discussion and case management to review our practice. We facilitate our clients' sense of agency and when this is not possible act as their advocates. As revolutionary scientists we work on the premise that paradigms are not static and set but part of a kaleidoscopic landscape. We are constantly viewing and reviewing our thoughts and theories depending on the client's internal and external contact. . . . It's about critiquing yourself, your psyche, your experiences, how your experiences determine how you relate to other people – [interruption]

TAIWO: It's not enough to just be aware of your thinking.... What about reflecting on power, challenging the social ideas that influence your thinking?... Sometimes there is a tendency to think that just by creating awareness that's enough. But it's not always linked to power and difference.

In addition, Tayo described a tension in psychoanalysis between the desire to be responsive and a preference for a 'pure' approach.

TAIWO: If you really are about liberating people and being in their experience then why not do it outside in the community?

TAYO: Exactly! Nine years ago ... if you weren't working at the clinic ... in consulting rooms, then 'that's not therapy'. Then it moved to working in schools, working in the community, even going into people's homes.... But we have a conflict ... there is a belief that when you apply [psychoanalysis] in its pure form [it is] most effective ... so then there's the challenge as to how to get this knowledge to the masses and keep it pure – [interruption]

TAIWO: But why keep it pure?

TAYO: Exactly. The answer is we can't keep it pure. We have to adapt it and improvise.... It's about using psychoanalytic thinking to impact on people's lives, not just in terms of us doing things with people, but in terms of people themselves having a language that enables them to talk about what is going on for them; so it becomes one possible way we all use of explaining our experience and challenging it ... and it's a good question: How do we do that? Maybe it's about changing the language.

These tensions seemed to mirror Freud's own conflict between his conservative desire-to-conform and his progressive desire-to-disrupt. Although Freud encouraged the development of interventions that were tailored to meet the needs of a greater range of people, and argued that psychoanalysis should be demystified so clients were active participants in it, he also rendered any 'other' psychodynamic approach 'subservient to his "classical" approach'. Despite a history of analysts who believed in addressing social problems directly, Freud's belief that the 'real ingredients of change would be analytic interpretations' (Gaztambide, 2012; p. 148), seems to have persisted in the psychoanalytic field, more than the tendency to get involved in social causes. It is this belief, that the analysand's difficulties can be resolved within the boundaries of therapy without addressing their social, political, cultural and ecological context, that has been so heavily criticised.

Ways forward: using psychoanalysis against itself

The tautological nature of some of the dialogue between Tayo and I highlighted the ways in which we were talking about different sides of the same coin rather than talking at cross purposes. Understanding Tayo's view of psyche helped shift me from a stuck oppositional position, as she argued that *'psyche means soul ... the organisation has a psyche, a system has a psyche, a family has a psyche'*.

TAYO: The psyche is organisational ... the psyche is social. It's not just individual ... the [place where Tayo trained] was often seen as being in an ivory tower and then ... [it] had to become part of the NHS so had to fulfil certain conditions.... It had to be less classist basically.... Myself [and others], would talk about the institutional psyche, and how the institution in which we were being trained was re-enacting some of the defensive positions that they identified in their clients, such as repression and denial etc.... So 'it's not my problem, it's all the people-out-there's problem'. We used the same ideology to say to them 'but this is what you're doing'.

TAIWO: So psychoanalysis can actually be used as a liberatory practice, if it uses its own theories against itself.

Concluding reflections

Taiwo

In my 2011 book about power, resistance and liberation in therapy, I critiqued the ways liberation psychology seemed to draw on psychoanalytic ideas, without really understanding this link. Through dialogue with my sister I have come to understand why it is that psychoanalysis is regarded by some as not just a theory of clinical practice, but a theory to challenge oppression and advocate for social justice. When psychoanalytic and liberation psychology ideas are in dialogue with each other, there is the potential for an unearthing of hidden gems, uncovering of repressed histories and a critique of some mainstream psychoanalytic ideas. This can lead to a reformulation, expansion or even discarding of ideas that do not serve the needs of people, and an introduction of ones that have been left out of the analytic canon and better serve a liberatory agenda (for example, those of Frantz Fanon, Albert Memmi and Marie Langer).

Historically psychoanalysis developed a socially conscious radical ethic and Freud's own racial identity played a role in that. This does not take away from challenging many of his sexist and racist ideas or the fact that Freud's Whiteness (along with his maleness) afforded him many privileges. It does, however, highlight that his 'non-Whiteness' also afforded him a personal understanding of 'otherness' and oppression. Recovering the historical memory of radical psychoanalysis might help move it towards a progressive vision of it.

Any approach is oppressive if it relies more on the 'truth' of its own concepts than on mutuality. It is still unclear to me if 'blaming, certainty and individualising' come from a type of reading of psychoanalysis or are embedded in the theory itself. Perhaps it is the many contradictions in Freud's approach to liberation that poses both a challenge and an opportunity to twenty-first-century psychoanalysis.

In trying to pursue ideas we feel passionate about it is not uncommon to revert to monological descriptions of reality competing with other versions of reality, and produce an *'expert' single-voiced text*, arguing about the oppressive nature of *'expert' single-voiced texts*. By highlighting our dialogue the reader can make up their own minds about where they stand and we have demonstrated how people can discover new ways of understanding not only their position but also the position they had previously considered opposite to their own. We did not strive for consensus, having discovered tensions *within* our various positions, as much as *between* them. We also discovered that our differences are important because possibilities, as well as challenges, can arise from them, if we fully engage with each other.

Tayo

Taiwo's book, *Power, Resistance and Liberation*, might have been a fitting title for Freud's autobiography, had he written one. My sense of Freud was that he struggled with power and authority; he was compelled to challenge the medical and political regime despite being fully cognisant of the consequences and despite his profound desire to be accepted by them. His conflicts, struggles and overwhelming contradictions are to my mind his strengths, what made him fearless, great and quintessentially human.

As a teacher and educational psychologist I was unable to find a language that conveyed my practice and expressed what was at the interface of my relationship with my clients that made a difference to their wellbeing. My difference, as a Black woman, was often, initially, met with negative assumptions about my competence, knowledge, experience and professionalism. As a child psychotherapist my difference has become a metaphoric skin, which works as a canvas for my clients to project on and then identify with their own sense of difference. My skin colour and colourful attire set me apart from other clinicians and yet I am a full-fledged member of the team. I am aware that my otherness can at times confirm the negative aspects of clients' sense of difference but more often I become a mirror to their aspiration of being unique but also an integrated and accepted part of a whole. I believe this is because I am 'the Other' but also proud to be my authentic self. I believe this was part of the reason the transgender young person felt that I got him after the first session.

This edifying dialogue with my sister takes me back to Freud's interest in what he called primitive societies, but what I wish to refer to as more spiritually sophisticated, attuned and enlightened communities. The native peoples of the Americas, from Alaska to Chile, and of Siberia and many parts of Central and South East Asia, held intersex, androgynous people (feminine males and masculine females) in high respect. The Native Americans called transgender individuals 'two-spirit' people. Androgynous males were commonly married to a masculine man, or had sex with men, and masculine females had feminine women as wives; but rather than emphasising the sexuality of these persons, Native Americans focused on their spiritual gifts. Being endowed with a feminine and masculine spirit meant that they were often given the status of spiritual teacher or leader. Learning about this reminded me of a much earlier discussion with my sister Taiwo about a paper I wrote on transgender identity. While I was trying to deeply connect to the feelings, based on fixed views about gender, of the young people I was seeing, which could be understood as being about their 'encasement in a societal skin' of intolerance and prejudice, Taiwo proposed that I had missed a fundamental point. That being/feeling both male and female was in itself a legitimate gender status. This perspective offered a range of possibilities, from effeminate males or masculine females, to androgynous or transgender persons, to those who cross-dress and act as the 'other' gender. I did not see this possibility as I was very connected with my clients' sense of self as being/having a different sex to their biological sex. In order to see other possibilities, I had to reflect on how social stories, discourses and narratives influence how I might maintain the status quo that gender is only binary.

Whoever determines what constitutes oppression and liberation does so from their way of seeing the world based on social stories and narratives. There is a paradox in focusing on collective action for social change while being mindful of and responsive to the voice of the individual; what might be liberating to one can be oppressive to another. The proviso for liberation, no matter how well intended or humanitarian, is that it is always open to exploitation, contamination and abuse. The tensions, contradictions and conflicts highlighted in this chapter are just as much a part of our authenticity as human beings, as us striving for reparation, freedom and justice.

Note

1 In a world where Blackness is associated with badness, denigrate literally means 'to blacken'.

References

Afuape, T. (2011). *Power, resistance and liberation in therapy with survivors of trauma: To have our hearts broken.* London: Routledge.

Aron, L., & Starr, K. (2013). *A psychotherapy for the people: Towards a progressive psychoanalysis.* London: Routledge.

Bion, W.R. (1962). A theory of thinking (reprinted). In: E. Bott Spillius (1988) (Ed.) *Melanie Klein today: Developments in theory and practice. Volume 1: mainly theory* (pp. 178–81). London: Routledge.

Boyarin, D. (1997). *Unheroic conduct: The rise of heterosexuality and the invention of the Jewish man.* Berkeley, CA: University of California Press.

Cone, J.H. (1970). *A black theology of liberation.* New York: Orbis Books.

Danto, E.A. (2005). *Freud's free clinics: Psychoanalysis and social justice, 1918–1938.* New York: Columbia University Press.

Freud, S. (1955 [1919]). Lines of advance in psychoanalytic therapy. In: *The standard edition of the complete psychological works of Sigmund Freud* (ed. and trans. L. Strachey; pp. 157–68). London: Hogarth Press.

Freud, S. (1961). *Letters of Sigmund Freud 1873–1939* (edited by E. Freud). London: Hogarth Press.

Freud, S. (2010 [1930]) *Civilization and its discontents.* Eastford, CT: Martino Publishing.

Gaztambide, D.J. (2010). A preferential option for the repressed: Freud and Liberation Theology. Unpublished manuscript, read 21 July 2013.

Gaztambide, D.J. (2012). 'A psychotherapy for the people': Freud, Ferenczi, and psychoanalytic work with the underprivileged. *Contemporary Psychoanalysis, 48*(2), 141–65.

Gilman, S.L. (1993a). *The case of Sigmund Freud: Medicine and identity at the fin de siècle*. London: John Hopkins University Press.

Gilman, S.L. (1993b). *Freud, race and gender*. Princeton, NJ: Princeton University Press.

Hollander, N.C. (1997). *Love in a time of hate: Liberation psychology in Latin America*. New Brunswick, NJ: Rutgers University Press.

Jacoby, R. (1983). *The repression of psychoanalysis: Otto Fenichel and the political Freudians*. New York: Basic Books.

Martín Baró, I. (1994). *Writings for a liberation psychology: Essays, 1985–1989*, edited by A. Aron & S. Corne. Cambridge, MA: Harvard University Press.

Prilleltensky, I., & Nelson, G. (2002). *Doing psychology critically: Making a difference in diverse settings*. London: Palgrave.

Rachman, A.W. (1993). Ferenczi and sexuality. In L. Aron & A. Harris (Eds), *The legacy of Sándor Ferenczi* (pp. 81–100). Hillsdale, NJ: Analytic Press.

Salberg, J. (2007). In plain sight: Freud's Jewish identity revisited. *Psychoanalytic Dialogues, 17*(2), 197–217.

Sziklai, A. (2009). *The Jewish theme in the relationship of Sigmund Freud and Sándor Ferenczi: Between the state and the public sphere*. Working paper 84-2009 of the European Forum at the Hebrew University, Jerusalem, Centre for Austrian Studies. Retrieved 31 August 2013, from www.ef.huji.ac.il/publications/working.shtml.

Wetherall, M. (2003). Paranoia, ambivalence and discursive practices: Concepts of position and positioning in psychoanalytic and discursive psychology. In: R. Harré & F. Moghaddam (Eds), *The self and others: Positioning individuals and groups in personal, political and cultural contexts* (pp. 99–120). New York: Praeger/Greenwood Publishers.

Zaretsky, E. (2004) *Secrets of the soul: A social and cultural history of psychoanalysis*. New York: Random House.

17
TOWARDS AND BEYOND LIBERATION PSYCHOLOGY

Carolyn Kagan and Mark H. Burton

Introduction

What is the appeal of liberation psychology (LP) to people like us, two privileged, white intellectuals resident in one of the core countries of the global system of domination and exploitation? For this chapter we tried to explore the question via our separate but intertwined biographies, in the anticipation that it would provide clues as to how the approach might be communicated to others.

Previously, we have assessed some of those important distinguishing characteristics of LP that, taken together, make LP so innovative, from a perspective outside Latin America (Burton, 2004, 2013a, 2013b; Burton & Kagan, 2005, 2009).

From the vantage point of early 2014 we have redefined the list somewhat, as follows (the references we cite are to our own works that embody these principles):

1. Social justice and the social system: an approach that is orientated to action on the causes of social problems rather than their amelioration, but more than this, a resistance to the individualistic psychologisation of phenomena that are constituted socially and historically (Kagan & Burton, 2004).
2. Understanding and taking the perspective of the oppressed. This means the prioritisation of work with those in conditions of disadvantage and oppression and the taking of the perspective of the excluded, as a critical and corrective voice (Burton, 2013c; Burton & Flores Osorio, 2011; Edge *et al.*, 2004).
3. Becoming aware of social forces and relations and helping people to understand their situation so they can begin to change it (Burton & Kagan, 1996).
4. Going beyond appearances and questioning ideology: working towards a clear appreciation of the forces and relations that create oppression but are typically shrouded in an ideological mist that serves to obscure and misinterpret the mechanisms of oppression (Burton & Kagan, 2006).

5. Using (a diversity of) theory pragmatically, where theory supports good practice rather than determining it (what Martín Baró termed *realismo-crítico*[1]) (Kagan, Burton, Duckett, Lawthom & Siddiquee, 2011).
6. Using tools in creative and unorthodox ways: the creative use of methods (methodological eclecticism), dictated by the circumstances of inquiry and action rather than by a priori preference (Burton & Kagan, 1998; Kagan, Burton & Siddiquee, 2007).

This framework resonates with our reflections on our two distinct but linked journeys. We have assembled the material that follows through conversation and then working on the notes of those conversations, reflecting on how we became the people, and psychologists, that we are.

We have organised the material here in three cross-cutting themes: social justice (which relates to points 1, 2, 3 and 4), the edge (points 2, 5 and 6) and stewardship (points 1, 4 and 5).

We are writing in the third person as each of us is telling the story of the other. As we have lived together for thirty-seven years we are comfortable with this approach.

Social justice

Our work has social justice at its core, not as an end point but as a goal that is constantly shifting. We can see the origins of our commitment to social justice in a number of life experiences.

Throughout his childhood, both of Mark's parents were active in the Labour Party and, from its inception, in CND. Mark gradually learnt what it was like to be in a minority political movement, and some of the tensions of reformist politics. The issues brought into the household for critical discussion included the Vietnam War, the nuclear bomb and the hopes followed by disillusion for the Wilson government of 1964–1970. Carolyn's father was a family doctor and through his work came an early awareness of people's differing fortunes and circumstances. In post-war rural Britain there was poverty: children wore callipers from polio, not all houses had running water and electricity and there was overt hostility to encampments of travellers. Carolyn has always known how the National Health Service transformed people's lives through her parents' commitment to it. Her mother had a university education but, like many of her generation, did not work after marriage. The injustice of this stimulated Carolyn's interest in the fledgling women's liberation movement but it was not until much later that she was actively involved.

Mark's mother had a good friend who had escaped from Franco's advancing army in Spain, and the abomination of fascism was brought home to Mark very clearly. His mother discussed current affairs with him and during this period Mark had the dawning of awareness of a number of things that have stayed with him throughout his life. He became aware from within, of oppression and cruelties in schools (and later in other organisations and institutions). From his visits to his grandparents in Liverpool and from being told about it, he became aware of poverty, slums, squalor and different people's poverty of opportunity. He was moved by hearing about concentration camps and became aware of the terrible things that people can do to each other, and the system that enables it.

While still at school, Carolyn gained first-hand experience of postcolonial injustices. In the mid 1960s, Gravesend, the town in which she went to school, received a large number of Sikh families from East Africa – Kenya, Tanzania and later from Uganda. Rapidly the town became multicultural and through school projects she saw consequences of racism – personal and institutional. This understanding formed the basis of an interest in anti-racist action and work and contributed to her being involved in the anti-Nazi movement of the 1970s and 1980s, and to active involvement in writing anti-racist and multicultural policies in the university. She was a member of the Moss Side Enquiry panel, following the Manchester civil disturbances in 1981. Her role was one of bearing witness to the demands of local people for equal and fair treatment and to the ill treatment of (mostly Black) youth in the context of institutional and societally embedded racism.

When he was fourteen, Mark's family moved to Northern Ireland because his father had secured a job as an environmental studies adviser. There, Mark's awareness of poverty and exclusion grew as he was faced with the reality of life for travellers and for the Catholic minority in the province, as well as the consequences of the sectarian divide. At the same time, in the 1960s, there was a blooming of alternative cultural perspectives: the BBC, for example, broadcast the Wednesday Play (a weekly ration of socially relevant and experimental drama which included Ken Loach's groundbreaking *Cathy Come Home*, the first major treatment of homelessness); Mark became interested in world radio and listened to broadcasts from the USSR and China, and also Czechoslovakia and its experiment with 'socialism with a human face'. This stimulated his interest in communism, which to him seemed the logical conclusion of the reformist politics of his parents.

Awareness and understanding of institutional injustices came from both our school experiences and our early work experiences. We were victims of the Eleven Plus selection process to determine which kind of secondary school we went to. Mark passed and Carolyn failed: both were confronted with the social stigma and opportunities afforded by different schools. At work, Carolyn encountered the youth justice system and its gendered practices of locking up young women 'in need of care and protection'. Mark worked at All Saints Hospital with a remit of applying behavioural principles to ward organisation via a token economy, and concluded that token economies work because of structured social interactions (being more socially engaging than unstructured ones), not because of the tokens (Hall et al., 1977).

In 1977 Mark moved to Manchester to train as a clinical psychologist, and it was here that he and Carolyn met.

His course placements gave Mark more opportunities to implement applied behavioural analysis for change. Through working in a variety of settings, he found himself increasingly looking at the geography of the settings (ecology), rather than at interventions. He had many conversations with Carolyn that helped him loosen up his thinking and helped him let go of the behavioural approach and be open to other ideas. The limitations of what he was taught as a clinical psychologist were apparent.

Much of Carolyn's work in community psychology has been with people living in conditions of poverty and/or exclusion and this has been a constant source of outrage, motivation and commitment. A key has been working with activists as colleagues, accompanying their struggles, rather than intervening in their realities, but this has not meant abandoning the conceptual and practical resources that she has been privileged to acquire (Edge, Stewart, & Kagan, 2004; Kagan et al., 2004; Raschini, Stewart, & Kagan, 2005).

In addition to these formative encounters with difference, disadvantage and discrimination, we have both been influenced by work we have done and seen elsewhere in the world. In 1996 we both took some time off work, took the children out of school and spent time in Cuba, Venezuela and Australia. This experience broadened our horizons and radicalised us further. It was an opportunity to see how people maintained hope in difficult social circumstances (Cuba during the Special Period following the collapse of its trade with the socialist countries, Venezuelan shanty towns, Aboriginal Australia), but also to get to know something about other interventions and conceptual frameworks, most notably Latin American social psychology. It was from encounters in Venezuela that we came to understand how the work of Ignacio Martín Baró could be put into practice.

Working at, within and creating the edge

The idea of an 'ecological edge' has been a useful way of conceptualising and understanding much of our formative experiences and psychological practices.

All her life, Carolyn has lived at the edge of nationalities and identities. Her father's parents had come to England at the turn of the twentieth century, escaping the pogroms of Eastern Europe. Her mother's family was from the Scottish Highlands and Islands, some of the relatives Gaelic speaking. There wasn't an English accent to be heard among her relatives and her upbringing incorporated diverse cultural practices.

Moving to Northern Ireland as a teenager, Mark was abruptly cast into a different society with rigid, conservative ways of thinking, in contrast to the questioning he had grown up with among like-minded people in Worcestershire. Now he was the outsider. He had an English accent, held no religious belief and was not part of a local extended family or kinship network. He lived in the edge of two cultures as they coincided. Both of us, then, were confronted with different ways of being in the world from childhood.

Mark went to University College London and studied psychology, determined to change the world. He struggled to find the relevance of psychological thinking, but began to find behaviourism a useful tool for interrogating the rest of the curriculum with which he was dissatisfied. Behaviourism was action orientated and held that personal/social change is the central problem for psychology. In social psychology Mark was influenced by Peter Kelvin's work on order and value (Kelvin, 1971) and Rob Farr, who was becoming increasingly interested in continental currents in the subject. Their teaching was both interesting and often different from the mainstream, less empiricist and more conceptual.

Mark went on to do a PhD at Birmingham, to pursue his interests in behaviourism. This was a mistake. The department was not stimulating even though some of the students were (such as Alan Costall, e.g. Costall, 2006). However, other parts of the university were exciting and forging new, interdisciplinary thinking. Most important was Stuart Hall's Institute for Contemporary Cultural Studies. Mark was involved with the anarchist group but also developed an interest in Marxism and especially Gramsci (Gramsci, 1971) and the Frankfurt School. He read Freire, thanks to the Penguin Education Series (Freire, 1972a, 1972b), and tried to make sense of it, which was quite a struggle for him at the time. Via a public lecture he came across the work of Imre Lakatos (1970) on the historiography of science. These experiences helped form Mark's integrative approach to intellectual currents and work with diversity. From this time he believed that as long as ideas and concepts took one further and opened up new possibilities for knowledge, they were worthwhile – thus finessing the notion of 'truth'. This appraisal helped him thereafter to simultaneously use contradictory sets of ideas: he was awaking from his 'empiricist slumbers', to invert Kant.

At Birmingham, Mark got involved with a small group called Alternative Socialism (this included Keith Paton, a former member of the radical psychology Red Rat Collective, with an interest in social psychology who later took the name Keith Motherson in homage to feminism). This brought contact with radical feminism as another fundamental way of understanding oppression. Paton articulated an inclusive approach to political organisation; emphasised the commonalities between liberal and socialist approaches; and was interested in forming alliances. This was also the time when Chilean refugees were arriving in the UK, highlighting the capacity of the 'empire' to fight back, and the value of international solidarity.

Carolyn, too, encountered new thinking at the edge of the discipline as it interfaced with other ideas. She went to North East London Polytechnic (now University of East London) to study psychology, not to change the world but to see where the practising psychologists she had worked with got their crazy ideas. Social psychology was, for her, the most socially relevant part. Following this she went to Oxford to study for a DPhil with Michael Argyle (Kagan, 1984). This was the time of the 'Crisis in Social Psychology', a crisis brought about by the irrelevance of much social psychology and a challenge to the dominant positivist experimental paradigm. Rom Harré, a frequent visitor to the department, was a vociferous critic of mainstream social psychology, and the idea that social situations could be studied in meaningful units and episodes was gaining hold (Harré & Secord, 1972). Non-experimental work, as well as experimental work, was recognised – it was truly a methodological edge.

In 1979 we both spent a year in Australia at the University New South Wales. Here we got to know (and Carolyn to work with) Alex Carey, whose work on propaganda explored the manufacture of disinformation to 'take the risk out of democracy', that people might vote in their interests rather than those of the corporate power elite (Carey, 1997). He was very much a role model as scholar activist: for working at the edges between scholarship and activism, and university and social reality. In the University New South Wales, there were no women with tenured academic appointments. Against this machista culture, Carolyn gave a public lecture on the psychology of women, an interest which led to the first psychology of women course in the UK, which she delivered on her return.

Back in Manchester, Mark was fortunate to be funded to attend a PASS (Wolfensberger & Glenn, 1975) workshop for programme evaluation, and became very interested in the philosophy of normalisation (Wolfensberger, 1972): the whole experience reinforced the doubts he had about trying to reform institutions rather than replace them with community-based alternatives.

He had the opportunity to apply the systems design thinking derived from PASS to two large ambitious service design projects. The first was for a new community mental health project and the second led to the replacement of institutional long-stay psychiatric provision. In both of these projects he led participative planning sessions and saw the power of helping people think about aims and purposes of services in different ways – informed by an understanding of the experiences of people using the services.

This was also a period of getting insights into ways the system can fight back, in this case parts of the medical establishment, and enabled Mark to learn more about dynamics of democracy and leadership, and find ways of working in a principled way while being a functionary of the system.

We both wanted to work more closely together, so in the early 1980s we established the Blackley Leisure Integration Scheme (BLISS) – a leisure advocacy project linking intellectually disabled people with people living nearby for leisure pursuits. This project focused on finding different ways of helping people make connections with others – recognising that skills-based methods of empowerment did not work (Burton & Kagan, 1995). We learnt how to connect the projects to local politicians and engage them in the work. We also found ways of including people with learning difficulties in the management of the projects – something that was new at the time.

In the mid 1980s Carolyn was appointed on a part-time basis as a research and social work member of the North West Development Team for intellectual disability services. The small team worked in a multidisciplinary and highly collaborative way across the north-west of England. The brief was to facilitate the closure of the long-stay hospitals and development of high-quality community-based services, thereby working simultaneously across several boundaries – geographical, organisational and cultural – always conscious of creating new edges and maximising resources.

Over a ten-year period, we both worked on the closure of long-stay hospitals. At times we worked together, specifically on participative ways of enhancing the quality of services, predicated on an understanding of the challenges of social exclusion and vulnerability as a basis for an evolving understanding of quality in people's lives. We learnt about the nature of ambitious social reforms, about the limits of organisational change in social change projects and about how small resources can have big impacts under the right circumstances (Kagan, 2007). We both contributed ideas that we had taken and reworked from the social, political and environmental sciences, many of which later surfaced in our textbook (Kagan et al., 2011).

So in various ways we have constantly inhabited and traversed edges between cultures; between community, formal services and university; between the professions and management; between psychology and other disciplines. And we believe this has both necessitated a reconstruction of psychological theory and practice, and provided the sources for that.

Stewardship

Stewardship (taking care of things not owned but entrusted to one) is a value that underpins our work and that we have cherished from an early age.

We both had unfettered rural childhoods, free to roam and learning to respect animals and plants. We grew up in the austere 1950s, in the shadow of the Second World War. Our parents all grew their own vegetables, made, mended and re-used clothes, and lived well within their means. These childhoods instilled in us values of self-sufficiency and frugality and built the foundations for self-reliance and self-confidence.

Carolyn participated in a rather strange form of girl-guiding – little attention was paid to the national-monarchist elements or the gaining of badges, but instead a lot of time was spent in what would now be called wild living or survival activities – always in teams, tracking in the woods, building overnight shelters in remote places, cooking a whole meal in half a grapefruit, furnishing a tent with articles made of bamboo and string, and so on.

Mark's father trained first as a history and later rural studies teacher after being demobilised, and encouraged Mark to find out things for himself, to make things and to experiment. He nurtured a keen interest in history and science, particularly that of the natural world. The budding interest in ecology blossomed when Mark was a teenager. At university Mark started an ecology action group, inspired by the ecologist Frank Fraser Darling, who raised questions about man's [sic] responsibility for the environment in the 1969 Reith Lectures. He got involved with creative, direct action, drawing on workshops organised by the NUS environment officers. Some early green campaigns he was involved with included: the Friends of the Earth return of one-trip bottles to Schweppes, a supermarket protest over the introduction of plastic disposable milk bottles; dressing a woman up and 'undressing' her on 'over packaging day'; and having a funeral for the planet. He learnt some ways of getting the maximum impact from the efforts of a small group of activists.

This interest in ecology took another turn when, in his forties, Mark followed a course in permaculture design (see Mollinson, 1988). Here, he was introduced to or reminded of concepts that he would use in other settings, such as the ecological edge (see above), different aspects of the notion of environmental stewardship and the importance of working with existing energies and with minimal intervention.

An important aspect of stewardship is the nurturance of talents and other resources and the duty not to waste these resources. Carolyn encountered a distinct lack of stewardship when she left school and went to work as a volunteer at a residential ('approved') school for girls aged fifteen to eighteen, sent by the courts for being in need of care and protection. At only eighteen, she was responsible for young women of similar age but whose experiences of life had been, and still were, very different from her own. Their life stories were full of various kinds of aggression from family members and the social system itself. During this period she became interested in the possibilities of operating closed institutions through therapeutic community models (Wills, 1971); psychoanalytic ideas (from supervision sessions); social psychology (having been attracted by the interaction diagram on the front of Argyle's *Psychology of Interpersonal Behaviour*, 1967); the psychodrama of Moreno; and the philosophy of Homer Lane, whose thesis was that children behave better when they have control over their lives. She also observed psychology in practice through clinical and art therapy interventions with the young women. These influences took her into psychology, to find out more.

The nurturance of talent and the encouragement of others was a feature of both of our lives – Mark in the work he did to encourage staff to actively contribute to the learning disability services he managed in Manchester; Carolyn in the participative way she formed and ran the Research Institute for Health and Social Change at Manchester Metropolitan University. Both of us worked in different ways to acknowledge the life experiences of people who rely on services and research participants, and to encourage creative, collaborative ways of working.

Discussion and conclusions

We have not presented a linear narrative but rather told three overlapping stories of encounter and exploration in terms of three themes that are important to us. These themes are not isomorphic to LP as generally articulated, but nevertheless they point to some important characteristics of this way of thinking and doing psychology. We will summarise the connections of these three themes with LP and then briefly reflect on the nature of our relationship with both LP and psychology in general.

Social justice is the core, the pulse of LP. To practise LP requires the ability to see injustice and the anger to do something about it. That affective consciousness is social in nature – at its strongest when fed by the empathy and humility that comes from direct encounter with the oppressed other.

Inhabiting and working with the 'edge': LP must live uneasily on the edge of psychology and in the places where different worlds collide. It draws strength from life on the border, and the thinking and practice that surges there.

Stewardship: whether considering psychological resources, people's lives or the health of the ecosystem that supports our life, LP has to treat assets responsibly, neither exploiting nor squandering social and ecological capital.

It would be fair to say, however, that we do not simply adopt LP as a framework. First, that approach is situated spatially, in Latin America, and temporally, from the mid 1980s in Martín Baró's work, and then after a pause of some ten years in the work of a broad network across Latin America and beyond (Montero, Sonn & Burton, in press). We draw upon this body of work but are located differently. The similarity is that we take seriously both the idea of the 'preferential option for the oppressed [global] majority' and the 'analectical' (see Burton & Flores Osorio, 2011) imperative of subjecting theory, policy and practice, that comes from a privileged location, to the critique of Martín Baró's 'new interlocutor'. This is the direct or indirect interrogation from the standpoint of the oppressed as a check and corrective. It is a similarity, despite differences of geopolitical location, that led Mark to argue for 'a second psychology of liberation, valuing and moving beyond the Latin American' (Burton, 2013a).

Second, our approach, as can be seen above, draws upon other intellectual and practical frameworks that are not part of the LP canon. Rereading Martín Baró's two textbooks we are struck by how rooted they are in mainstream social psychology, while at the same time correcting and augmenting it from the standpoint of the oppressed other. For us, psychology has an indefinite boundary and we are not interested in trying to define or delimit it. When we talk of 'a really social psychology' or a 'critical community psychology' this is part of what we are trying to draw attention to. So, for instance, much of our textbook of community psychology (Kagan *et al.*, 2011) indeed comes from outside the discipline, and while the boundary of psychology interests us, we are also at home in the borderlands of other disciplines, including philosophy, economics, cultural studies and management – fields artificially separated in the modern university.

The above reflections we hope explain our title, and we wish readers well in their own travels in the borderlands of psychology and liberation psychology, where the destination is not mapped, although the compass is that of social justice combined with the openness and humility that comes from trying to stand in others' shoes.

Note

1 The obvious translation, 'critical realism' does not really work since in English that term is 'already taken' for the philosophical approach of critical realism initiated by Roy Bhaskar (e.g. 1998). That has a distinct meaning, although Bhaskar's approach to questions of knowledge and being is not inconsistent with that in LP.

References

Argyle, M. (1967). *The psychology of interpersonal behaviour*. Harmondsworth: Penguin.
Bhaskar, R. (1998). *The possibility of naturalism: A philosophical critique of the contemporary human sciences*. London: Routledge.
Burton, M. (2004). Viva Nacho! Liberating psychology in Latin America. *The Psychologist, 17*(10), 584–7.

Burton, M. (2013a). A second psychology of liberation? Valuing and moving beyond the Latin American. *The Journal of Critical Psychology, Counselling and Psychotherapy, 13*(2), 96–106.

Burton, M. (2013b). Liberation psychology: A constructive critical praxis. *Estudos de Psicologia (Campinas), 30* (2), 249–59.

Burton, M. (2013c). The analectic turn: Critical psychology and the new political context. *Les Cahiers de Psychologie Politique, 23*, online.

Burton, M., & Flores Osorio, J.M. (2011). Introducing Dussel: The philosophy of liberation and a really social psychology. *Psychology in Society, 11*, 20–39.

Burton, M., & Kagan, C. (1995). *Social skills for people with learning disabilities: A social capability approach*. London: Chapman & Hall.

Burton, M., & Kagan, C. (1996). Rethinking empowerment: Shared action against powerlessness. In I. Parker & R. Spears (Eds), *Psychology and society: Radical theory and practice* (pp. 197–208). London: Pluto Press.

Burton, M., & Kagan, C. (1998). Complementarism versus incommensurability in psychological research methodology. In M.C. Chung (Ed.), *Current trends in the history and philosophy of psychology* (pp. 80–6). Leicester: British Psychological Society.

Burton, M., & Kagan, C. (2005). Liberation social psychology: Learning from Latin America. *Journal of Community and Applied Social Psychology, 15*(1), 63–78.

Burton, M., & Kagan, C. (2006). Decoding valuing people. *Disability and Society, 21*(4), 299–313.

Burton, M., & Kagan, C. (2009). Towards a really social psychology: Liberation psychology beyond Latin America. In M. Montero & C. Sonn (Eds), *The psychology of liberation: Theory and application* (pp. 51–73). New York: Springer.

Carey, A. (1997). *Taking the risk out of democracy: Corporate propaganda versus freedom and liberty*, ed. A. Lowrey. Champaign, IL: University of Illinois Press.

Costall, A. (2006). 'Introspectionism' and the mythical origins of scientific psychology. *Consciousness and Cognition, 15*(4), 634–54.

Edge, I., Stewart, A., & Kagan, C. (2004). Living poverty: Surviving on the edge. *Clinical Psychology, 38*, 28–31.

Fraser Darling, F. (1969). *BBC Radio 4: The Reith Lectures, Frank Fraser Darling: Wilderness and Plenty: 1969*. Retrieved from www.bbc.co.uk/programmes/p00h3xk5. Accessed: 21/03/2014.

Freire, P. (1972a). *Cultural action for freedom*. Harmondsworth: Penguin.

Freire, P. (1972b). *Pedagogy of the oppressed*. Harmondsworth: Penguin.

Gramsci, A. (1971). *Selections from the prison notebooks*. London: Lawrence and Wishart.

Hall, J.N., Baker, R.D., & Hutchinson, K. (1977). A controlled evaluation of token economy procedures and with chronic schizophrenic patients. *Behaviour Research and Therapy, 15*(3), 261–83. London: Sage.

Harré, R., & Secord, P.F. (1972). *The explanation of social behaviour*. Oxford: Blackwell.

Kagan, C. (1984). Social problem solving and social skills training. *British Journal of Clinical Psychology, 23*(3), 161–73.

Kagan, C. (2007). Working at the 'edge': Making use of psychological resources through collaboration. *The Psychologist, 20*(4), 224–7.

Kagan, C., & Burton, M. (2004). Marginalization. In G. Nelson & I. Prilleltensky (Eds), *Community psychology: In pursuit of liberation and wellness* (pp. 293–308). London: Macmillan/Palgrave.

Kagan, C., Burton, M., Duckett, P., Lawthom, R. & Siddiquee, A. (2011). *Critical community psychology*. Chichester: Wiley.

Kagan, C., Burton, M. & Siddiquee, A. (2007). Action research. In C. Willig & W. Stainton-Rogers (Eds), *Handbook of qualitative research in psychology*. London: Sage.

Kagan, C., Evans, R., Knowles, K., Sixsmith, J., Burns, D., Burton, M., *et al.* (2004). Working with people who are marginalized by the social system: challenges for community psychological work. In A. Sánchez Vidal, A. Zambrano Constanzo & M. Palacín Lois (Eds), *Psicología Comunitaria Europea: Comunidad, Poder Ética y Valores/European Community Psychology: Community, Power, Ethics and Values: (Papers from the European Community Psychology Congress, Barcelona, November,2002)* (pp. 400–12). Barcelona: Publicacions Universitat de Barcelona.

Kelvin, P. (1971). *The bases of social behaviour: An approach in terms of order and value*. London: Holt, Rinehart & Winston.

Lakatos, I. (1970). Falsification and the methodology of scientific research programmes. In I. Lakatos & A. Musgrave (Eds), *Criticism and the growth of knowledge* (pp. 91–195). Cambridge: Cambridge University Press.

Mollinson, B. (1988). *Permaculture: A designer's manual*. Tyalgum, NSW: Tagari.

Montero, M., Sonn, C. & Burton, M. (in press). Community psychology and liberation psychology: Creative synergy for ethical and transformative praxis. In M. Bond & I. Serrano García (Eds), *Handbook of community psychology*. New York: Springer.

Raschini, S., Stewart, A., & Kagan, C. (2005). *Voices of community participation: Report of the Community Activists' Project*. Manchester: Manchester Metropolitan University: RIHSC.

Wills, W.D. (1971) *Spare the child: The story of an experimental approved school*. Harmondsworth: Penguin.

Wolfensberger, W. (1972). *The principle of normalization in human services*. Toronto: National Institute on Mental Retardation.

Wolfensberger, W., & Glenn, L. (1975). *Program Analysis of Service Systems (PASS): A method for the quantitative evaluation of human services*: (3rd ed.). Toronto: National Institute on Mental Retardation.

PART VI
Reflections on practice

18
A PASSION FOR CHANGE

Liberation practices and psychology

Geraldine Moane, with final reflections by Gillian Hughes and Taiwo Afuape

Introduction

Liberation is an exciting and inspiring word; it evokes freedom, choices, self-determination, social inclusion, human rights, equality and emancipation from oppressive social conditions such as violence, poverty and censorship. When it is combined with psychology, flourishing, thriving, belonging, wellbeing and relief from psychological conditioning and from repression and isolation are added. These are the responses to the phrase 'liberation psychology' given in workshops on liberation psychology that I have facilitated over fifteen years by students, trainees, lesbian, gay, bisexual and transgender people, women living in poverty, women who have experienced sexual assault and violence, and other groups.

The essays in this collection describe groundbreaking and inspiring examples of liberation practices in clinical and community psychology. They aim to expand traditional clinical practices to include the broader social context, and to engage clients in a participatory manner using a variety of creative techniques. The essays themselves are innovative, using a dialogical style that combines personal biography and reflection with the voices and experiences of participants. They are written in an accessible style, but are grounded in longstanding traditions of theory and research. They express the passion and vision of clinical psychologists aiming to improve the health and lived experiences of their clients, and to engage in social change.

The volume makes a vital contribution from clinical psychology to the growing international literature on liberation approaches that link psychology and social change (Aldarando, 2007; Rutherford, Capdevila, Undurti & Palmary, 2011; Johnston & Freedman, 2014). In the last decade, this literature has developed greatly in applied areas that include community (Orford, 2008), counselling (Goodman *et al.* 2004), health (Murray, 2014) and peace psychology (Dawes, 2001); additionally in social (Fine, 2006), developmental (Greene, 2004; Burman, 2008), research (Reason & Bradbury, 2008) and theoretical psychology (Teo, 2005); and also in counselling and psychotherapy studies (Gilbert & Orlans, 2010; Goodman & Gorski, 2015).

Psychologists have long recognised the psychological difficulties associated with social injustices such as poverty, deprivation, prejudice, violence and discrimination (Nelson & Prilleltensky, 2010). These were a focus of considerable research from the 1970s on, and were linked to the empowerment of minority and oppressed groups who had these experiences. These groups presented psychology with very strong critiques, in particular for its individualism – the focus on the individual in isolation from the larger social context – and ethnocentrism (Bulhan, 1985). A trend that has its roots at this time but only gained momentum in the late 1990s was to focus not just on oppression, but on empowerment, liberation and transformation. Psychologists in several fields set about developing and researching practices that would enhance wellbeing by working with people to transform the social circumstances that were at the root of their own psychological distress (Ruth, 2006; Rosado, 2007; Montero & Sonn, 2009; Lykes & Moane, 2009; Kagan, Burton, Duckett, Lawthom & Siddiquee, 2011).

A further aim of bringing about change in communities and society at large and attaining social justice emerged. This became relevant not only because individual contexts are embedded in community and society as a whole, but also because a growing body of research was demonstrating that wellbeing was linked to features of society as a whole – such as inequality, investment in education and health, institutionalised racism and sexism, and social mobility (Wilkinson & Pickett, 2009; World Health Organization, 2009; Ussher, 2014). Nelson and Prilleltensky (2010) capture the link between wellbeing, or wellness, and social justice: 'Wellness is a positive state of affairs brought about by the simultaneous satisfaction of personal, relational and collective needs' (p. 276).

Biographical background

Considering these trends in the context of my own personal history highlighted interesting parallels between developments in psychology and developments in my own life. I started with a complete separation of psychology and politics, moved through experiences and understandings of oppression, and then came to an integration of the psychological and the political through feminist and liberation psychology. Another biographical trend was to move out of the institutional setting of the university into communities, possibly the most challenging experience I have had.

Ireland in the 1960s and 1970s, where I grew up, was highly politicised, but psychology was newly emerging. Both of my parents had strong values of equality, and anti-colonial struggles were at the forefront, particularly at the time of the fiftieth anniversary of the 1916 rising (now facing its hundredth anniversary). Society was male and church dominated, with sexism (and other forms of prejudice and discrimination) embedded in all levels of society. I was drawn to psychology through reading the variety of works, from Freud to Eysenck, which were available in the 1970s. At the same time I was also reading feminists such as Simone de Beauvoir and Germaine Greer. At this time, I did not see the connections between the personal and the political. A dramatic experience in University College Dublin (UCD) changed this. A group of students were developing posters that included offensive images of women. I and another woman made some protest, but were effectively silenced. I did not have the language or the confidence, and felt angry and ashamed. The posters went up in the university restaurant. Suddenly, a group of twenty or so women appeared, with a leader who took a stand in front of the posters and protested strongly. The posters were taken down immediately. This was transformative for me. I became involved in the women's liberation (now feminist) movement, and have been active since. This illustrates what is for me a fundamental feature of liberation practice – the transformation of silence and powerlessness into solidarity and action.

In addition, the Tavistock Institute in London played a role in my development. A notable feature of my education in psychology at UCD was the influence of Eunice McCarthy. Eunice had qualified in psychology in UCD and then studied at the Tavistock Institute, where she was particularly influenced by systems theory. This perspective was embedded in her teaching in social psychology and became part of my social analysis. Eunice also encouraged innovative thinking and presented a challenge to the narrow experimental psychology and psychometrics that were dominant at that time.

I became increasingly dissatisfied with the narrow individualistic focus of psychology. Even the grand theories did not address people's embeddedness in society at large. This became particularly apparent when I studied clinical psychology during my doctoral training at University of California Berkeley. At the time, the focus was on assessment and diagnosis, and traditional approaches to treatment – medication and psychotherapy. At the same time, anti-psychiatry had a very strong presence, and social movements were developing analyses of society, oppression and internalised oppression. I was also influenced by the many written accounts by those who had experienced psychiatric hospitals and by the emerging critiques of psychotherapy.

While in Berkeley I had plenty of experiences of casual anti-Irish racism, but was also challenged to acknowledge White privilege. Additionally, I went through the process of coming out as lesbian. This brought the personal dimension of oppression into my life and experience.

When I returned to Ireland I took a position as an academic psychologist and aimed to make links between psychology and social justice issues in teaching and research. Placing gender, ethnicity, poverty and sexual orientation on the curriculum with undergraduate psychology students provoked enormous dialogue that ranged from challenging the relevance of social issues to seeking new ways of doing psychology. At the time, in the early 1990s, there was relatively little material in psychology that made these links. But through class dialogues, projects, essays, and even exam questions, many students showed their passion and interest in the broader social issues that were relevant to wellbeing.

At the same time, I had the opportunity to participate in the development of a women's studies programme in UCD. The programme was first established at the postgraduate level (away from impressionable undergraduates!), where I taught a module in feminist theory for five years which covered Marxist/socialist, radical, liberal and Black feminism, and was enormously helpful in expanding my social analysis. I developed a structural analysis of society as a system of domination with six modes of control – violence, political exclusion, economic exploitation, cultural control, control of sexuality and fragmentation (Moane, 1996; 2003).

In 1999 a Certificate in Women's Studies, in partnership with community-based women's groups, was developed and delivered in communities. The aim was to develop a course in psychology that would be relevant to women's lives and would use feminist pedagogical principles, especially ones of participation and experiential knowledge. I had long experience of activist groups, but did further training in community group work before setting out to facilitate my first course in a Women's Resource Centre in a deprived community in Dublin. The women there expected a participatory process, with a clear curriculum and assessment criteria – a combination of academic and community-based learning. The course started with a structural analysis that explored the six modes of control and their manifestations in the lived experience of participants. Psychological reactions to *oppression* were explored, and the similarities to psychological distress such as *depression* were noted. As a result, a systems view of change developed in these courses and workshops – that change can happen at all levels of society; that it can start in the immediate context of people's lives; and can accumulate over time. Feedback and evaluations of courses and workshops indicated that a clear analysis of social oppression was helpful to participants. They wrote that it named and analysed what they implicitly knew to be the case, placed their psychological experiences in a social context, relieved shame and self-doubt and motivated them to make changes in their lives (Moane, 2010; 2011).

My understanding of oppression and liberation evolved and developed over these years through dialogical and participatory practices in these community contexts, and with LGBT women and other groups. It was helpful and encouraging to also see the increasing amount of literature in psychology that engaged with social justice issues and with liberation practices. These ranged from Latin American liberation psychology (Martín Baró, 1994; Montero & Sonn, 2009), through feminist psychology (Lykes & Moane, 2009), community psychology (Watts & Serrano Garcia, 2003; Nelson & Prilleltensky, 2010; Kagan et al., 2011), to integrative and depth psychology (Rosado, 2007; Watkins & Shulman, 2008). However, many of these examples involved community and social psychologists, whereas students and trainees often wanted to know how to translate these ideas into clinical practice. This book provides invaluable insights into this question.

Elements of liberation practices

The table of contents highlights first the *diversity* of groups with whom the practitioners in this volume have worked. There is a range of ages, ethnic backgrounds, gender identities and contexts that intersect with each other in the complex lives and psychologies of clients. Contributions draw on experiences with refugees and asylum-seekers, transgender individuals, trainee clinical psychologists, young offenders, young people in marginalised and deprived communities and elders.

The experience of people seeking asylum epitomises many of the difficulties that clients from diverse backgrounds experience when engaging with psychological services, and conversely, presents mainstream clinical psychologists with enormous challenges. Although there are a variety of methods and approaches in clinical psychology, they share some features. For example, they are generally located in clinical or medical settings; the clients attend in these settings with one or more clinical psychologists, often in a one-to-one setting; verbal communication is the primary mode, usually in a seated dialogue; the client responds to the clinician, who maintains professional boundaries; many tests and techniques involve technical terms. Working with diverse groups highlights a second theme, namely the *limitations* of traditional approaches. One is with access and engagement – how can asylum-seekers actually make contact with, let alone visit, psychological services? How can the traditional methods of assessment and communication be used, relying as they do on literacy and capabilities for verbal self-expression? How do we form relationships with individuals from such different backgrounds and cultures from our own? Are traditional techniques helpful with this client group? How can psychologists recognise and work with extremely difficult social circumstances? The chapters written by Gillian Hughes, Sue Clayton, Angela Byrne, Jane Tungana and Nsimire Aimee Bisimwa describe these challenges vividly; illustrating the ways in which clinicians have developed innovative practices for engaging clients.

Yet if we replace asylum-seeker with young person, LGBT person, Black person, person living in poverty, the same issues arise. I have heard these difficulties presented to me repeatedly in community contexts. Research has demonstrated the difficulties posed for these groups, often associated with low participation and completion rates (Aldarando, 2007). The clinic can be a microcosm of society, reflecting the same issues of power, prejudice and social exclusion. Contributors such as Maria Castro Romero and Taiwo Afuape; Cristian Peña and Leopoldo Garcia; as well as Dzifa Afonu, Abbie Unwin and Katarina Kovacova, have written movingly about the dilemmas of professionalism (e.g. neutrality, non-disclosure), power and privilege, reflecting on the ways in which traditional practices can be oppressive to those with whom we work.

A third theme that I would consider vital is the need for *a social analysis*. A notable feature of the different chapters is the link between the authors' reflections on the role of oppression in their own lives and their ability and willingness to reflect on this relationship in the lives of their clients. We take it for granted in psychology that we need psychological theory and research to provide us with the knowledge and competence to work with clients, and indeed this collection considers a number of psychological frameworks. I would argue that we also need social theory, or a social analysis. We need to understand society as a whole, and a systems or structural analysis that clearly places domination, oppression and liberation at its core. Several contributors, such as Bernadette Wren, Sue Clayton and Gillian Hughes, David Nyland and Heather Waddle and Mark Burton and Carolyn Kagan, offer such analysis and make links to larger structural issues.

A fourth theme is the value of participation, or of *participatory processes*. Many have argued that participation is a cornerstone of liberation practices. This is partly because too often people from minority backgrounds and/or with less power have been excluded or subject to oppressive forces. By participatory practices, I mean consultation, partnership and dialogue. Maria Castro Romero, Ornette Clennon, Elisha, Taiwo Afuape and Ameila, Christian Peña and Mr Garcia, Angela Byrne and Jane Tungana describe the unpredictability of participatory practices and write in very insightful ways about how they have learned to recognise their own limitations and acknowledge the expertise of the clients. The *variety of methods* is a further striking feature of these contributions. It seems that activities involving creativity, or co-creativity, have the best chance of facilitating a participatory process; such as music, video and filmmaking, social media, group discussion, one-to-one dialogue, and writing. While there is an emphasis on creativity in the contributions, contributors also emphasise the importance of directly addressing social issues, such as legal status, unemployment and housing.

Finally, almost all of the liberation practices described in this volume involve the *community* in some form. There are a variety of reasons why community is central to liberation practices, and conversely, why taking people out of community can sometimes be harmful. These reasons are expressed most strongly in the voices of the clients in these contributions, particularly those of Gillian Hughes and Taiwo Afuape, Sue Clayton and Gillian Hughes, and Angela Byrne and Jane Tungana. Community provides recognition, comfort, solidarity, support, the means for self-expression, the context for relationship, culture and creativity. However, the difficulties of community are also evident – it can silence, threaten and undermine. And, of course, lack of community and isolation are also problematised.

Questions and future directions

The contributors write in moving and vivid ways about the realities of people's lives, and about their attempts to facilitate both psychological and social change. They show that acknowledging the realities of people's lives and making links between psychological and social issues has benefits for both the practitioner and the client. Moving beyond traditional professional practices and settings raises many questions and illustrates the need for further systematic analysis of psychological distress, its links to social injustices and the role of psychologists in bringing about change. The specific challenges for psychologists of acknowledging and engaging with social justice issues may vary, and can intersect with other identities and locations. For example, community and peace psychologists may be working with groups who have well-developed strategies for change, and who may not have the psychological vulnerabilities that clinical and counselling psychologists work with. However, questions about power and privilege, about perpetrating oppression, and about how to bring about social change are common themes.

I believe that understanding the interplay between psyche and society at large remains an enormous challenge to psychologists. Our psychological theories are too individualistic, and very often we lack the time and expertise to undertake a sophisticated social analysis. Combining liberation with psychology creates an in-between space where collective processes become central. I would suggest that collective processes are key elements of liberation practice at every level, from the individual to society at large. This focus on collective processes raises the following questions:

- How can we better understand collective emotions such as solidarity and compassion?
- How do we understand community from a liberation perspective?
- How can we understand the processes involved in collective action for change?
- What would a health service that incorporated liberation practices look like?

Taiwo Afuape and Gillian Hughes: final reflections

Understanding liberation

We cannot address social issues and human relationships without coming across complexity. In editing this book, we have come to realise that our guiding concepts are to some extent complex, contradictory, at times illusory and certainly open to critique; depending on our various positions, ethics and life experiences. *Liberation, justice, wellbeing, human rights, power, equality,* even *community,* are all contentious ideas; as well as being socially, historically, culturally and politically relative.

The term 'liberation' brings up different things for different people. For Geraldine Moane 'liberation is an exciting and inspiring word' that is linked to human rights and equality. Liberation combined with psychology evokes 'flourishing, thriving, belonging, wellbeing and relief from psychological conditioning and from repression and isolation'.

For Nimisha Patel 'liberation' risks being a 'grand and illusory' concept that neglects issues of power. She argues that both psychology and liberation are insufficient in ensuring the type of social change that leads to wellbeing, and that social change must include legal justice, policy change and reparation. Other contributors view liberation as a personal orientation and an emotional response. Tayo Afuape, in her dialogue with Taiwo Afuape, talks about the importance of being 'deeply connected' to the people who come to her for help; that liberation needs to attend to personal relationships. She argues that individual knowledge of how an oppressive system is affecting one's psyche is as much part of liberation practice as efforts to address social change on a collective level. Mark Burton and Carolyn Kagan view liberation psychology as 'an approach that is orientated to action on the causes of social problems', [and] 'a resistance to the individualistic psychologisation of phenomena that are constituted socially and historically'.

Bernadette Wren argues that while liberation psychology offers a political analysis of distress and 'resists the tendency to reduce complex social phenomena to individual psychological ills' it is equally important to 'acknowledge that some young people and families wish to live ordinary private lives without taking on the political issues of trans liberation'. In addition, with respect to the trans* community, it is possible that some distress may be experienced even in a more accepting social context.

Liberation practices can therefore operate at many different levels of context: in a relationship between two people in dialogue; in groups; with whole communities; or at a wider societal level through the shaping of social policy or law. Several contributors describe how their work has begun with individual relationships and has led them to influencing and changing social policies (for example, Bernadette Wren; David Nyland and Heather Waddle; Cristian Peña; Angela Byrne and Jane Tungana; Gillian Hughes and Sue Clayton).

The variety of different practices described in this book demonstrate how theories of liberation are shaped by multiple contexts, depending on the practitioners' social position, personal histories, work contexts and relationships with those they are attempting to help. For example, Bernadette Wren and Tayo Afuape in their two chapters reflect on the complexity of 'liberation' with respect to the trans* community, and Tayo and Taiwo when standing within different psychotherapeutic traditions (systemic and psychoanalytic).

Whatever position we choose to adopt, what is important is that we do not become too wedded to our ideas. As both Freire and Martín Baró urge, we must be led by those who come to us for support, such that interventions join people where they are and help them reach where they want to be; devoid of predetermined outcomes. To expect particular outcomes would be to 'turn the process of critical consciousness into indoctrination' (Afuape, 2011; p. 70). Similarly, we should not hold fixed ideas about what liberation or oppression look like. One person's experience and definition of liberation can be oppressive to another, as the debate about the wearing of headscarves by Muslim women shows. Where some see headscarves as a symbol of male domination, others experience the wearing of a headscarf as liberation from 'nagging consumer pressures and the constant, often sexual, scrutiny of women that is pervasive in Western society' (Grayson Perry, commentary on his screen-printed silk, *Who are You?* Exhibition, London, 2015).

However we understand liberation practices and the meaning of liberation, it is essential that we are able to critique our position if we are to truly remain accountable to those we are attempting to help. Indeed Ignacio Martín Baró emphasised the need for any praxis in professions that support people's wellbeing (including liberation praxis) to continually critique itself to ensure that it is grounded in the needs, wishes and experiences of those who are most oppressed in society. This is particularly important given that 'liberation' is a concept that is so open to misunderstanding and misuse. If liberation is regarded as an approach, that 'approach' is likely, in some contexts, at some time or other, to be irrelevant, inaccessible or too simplistic.

Towards wellbeing through dialogue

Just as Martín Baró (1994) challenged the tendency within psychology to offer individualistic solutions to socially produced problems while the social order is preserved, Nimisha Patel helps us to question whether our attempts to empower individuals, communities and societies is actually liberation 'when social policy remains intact, legal policy fails to protect oppressed and persecuted people and fails to ensure protection, reparation and justice.' In addition, Nimisha argues that the term liberation implies a linear one-way relationship that obscures power and that traditionally psychology has not been a useful 'tool' to '"liberate" people with psychological health difficulties rooted in pervasive social, economic and political injustices'.

This book is organised around the idea that dialogue is central to addressing power. Like 'liberation', 'dialogue' is a complex concept and process. Bernadette Wren highlights this when she both describes the importance of dialogue and the ways in which it can lead to 'sharp divisions' around an issue. For Freire, *true dialogue* was not necessarily a smooth process of agreement, but an ongoing and evolving process. From this perspective 'reflection' is always and inherently dialogical, and happens in interaction with others, not confined to the privacy of our individual thoughts and wishes; and to be transformative always comes from and leads to action. Freire argued that you cannot liberate others and yet no one is self-liberated (Freire, 1973). Liberation is what happens between people in a dialogical process. It would be impossible to know what (structures, laws, policies, behaviours, attitudes) needed to change, and in what direction, without *true dialogue*. This is why *dialogue* is important; not because liberation should (or even can) be confined to the level of human relationships. Contributors here demonstrate that when true dialogue happens, people move to positions where collaborative action becomes possible. The 'What's Our Story?' project described by Gillian Hughes and Taiwo Afuape is an example of how young people came together to challenge the stereotypes about their motivations and experiences, and initiated real changes in how adults in positions of power responded to them, and thought about their institutions and policies.

A number of other authors also describe how they have attempted and succeeded in influencing social policies (for example, Bernadette Wren; David Nyland and Heather Waddle; Cristian Peña; Angela Byrne and Jane Tungana). This book is also organised around the idea that concepts such as power and oppression are as complex and varied as 'liberation'. The chapters demonstrate the ways in which true dialogue addresses both 'traditional power', resulting from a dominant individual or group, and 'modern power' as it is enacted in everyday, seemingly innocuous, social practices, ideas, stories and 'truths' (Foucault, 1982). However, as Geraldine Moane (personal communication) points out, for true dialogue to take place, this requires the person in the position with more power to listen. Where the other person is expressing views which are habitually subjugated and marginalised, it takes effort to hear them. This is where participatory and creative methods of communication, such as film and performance, can be helpful, as they can position people differently in dialogue, therefore enabling marginalised narratives to become more central. True dialogue also makes possible the sorts of cross-profession working that Nimisha Patel described as central to 'social analysis, social awareness-raising and sustainable change'.

A (mental) health service based on liberation practices

Returning to Geraldine Moane's question, a health service incorporating liberation practices would not be based on the idea that something has gone wrong inside individuals. It would not involve moving away from the stark realities of people's lives, desensitising people to inequality, injustice and violence, and placing sole responsibility for recovery on individuals despite their social circumstances. Liberation approaches to wellbeing are radical in that they go *to the root* of distress, these roots being inherently social and political in nature; as well as the root of individual, relational and collective resources.

A mental health service based on liberation principles would therefore be shaped and run by those who are normally marginalised by social institutions and rarely have a voice; it would include a varied and creative array of approaches drawing on different frameworks, methods and theories that involve working across professions and disciplines; it would also involve professionals standing alongside people rather than 'assessing' and 'treating' them; it would function at different levels of context: within individual relationships, in groups, through whole-community interventions, and at the wider context level; it would support people in acting to influence social policy and law; it would draw on ideas from disciplines outside of psychology and psychotherapy, such as those from religion, social policy, sociology, political science and the arts; and it would enable people to have a voice through different creative media, such as social networking, music, art and theatre and film. It would join people together, breaking down the isolation that so often comes with distress, building solidarity and healing through sharing. Given these considerations, creativity and community seem central to a health service grounded in liberation praxis.

Creativity

What is always impressive is the ways in which people use diverse ways to challenge their objectification as passive victims. Ornette Clennon's work with young offenders, using music as a way to connect to their ethical selves and showcase their talents, reflected on the power of connecting to vulnerability, for young men, whose cultural experiences are dominated by hegemonic masculinity. However, his chapter also described implicit examples of resistance, such as A1 referring to 'keeping your head up'. The implicit and explicit forms of creativity highlighted the ways in which liberation approaches can support a young person to find non-criminal ways of challenging poverty. It also demonstrated something the editors have found time and time again; despite previous criminal/anti-social behaviour, young people can be ethical and these ethics are rarely as far from the surface as might be assumed by those around them. The music sessions seemed to act as a space for the young people's pre-existing ability to express themselves in creative rather than destructive or harmful ways.

More than simply using art as a form of expression, creativity is a powerful metaphor and powerful form of social action. As Sue Clayton explains, Bakhtin wrote about the carnivals and festivals of the Middle Ages and Renaissance as acts of 'rebellion, satire and playfulness'. While creativity directly challenged the status quo through deriding institutions, corporations and authorities, it also used joy and pleasure to challenge the 'hierarchy of the social order' (p. 178). Creativity, then, enables people to temporarily experience the fullness of life (Cohen, 2011).

Creativity can enable us to disrupt and invert the status quo. Gillian Hughes and Nsimire Bisimwa invert the notion of 'hard to reach' *communities* to reflect on challenging irrelevance, inaccessibility and inappropriateness of 'hard to reach' *services* shaped by oppressive postcolonial social structures. Similarly, Maria Castro, in her teaching of trainee clinical psychologists, presented an upside-down map of Latin America in order to invite the learning community to 'see the known and familiar in new ways'.

Creativity enables us to be responsive and improvisational in order to challenge established power relationships and dominant discourses. Gillian Hughes did this by going to Richmond Park with young refugee men, and handing hand-held video cameras over to them so that they could take ownership of what was recorded. One young person's comment, that '*They listened to us, showed us respect, they were prepared to get down on the floor* **with** *us. This never normally happens to us*', seemed a great metaphor for the ways in which we were alongside others, rather than, in Parker's (1999) words 'bending down' to pick them up.[1]

We respect the other person's agency when we recognise that we are the ones being assessed by them, as highlighted both by Nsimire Bisimwa when describing how 'families test us' to find out if we are really listening to them, and by Cristian Peña, who realised this during his 'assessment' of Mr Garcia.

Inverting the status quo also means challenging well-established and taken-for-granted ideas such as 'gender' and 'sex'. David Nylund and Heather Waddle highlight the impact of the gender binary (where there are two distinct genders, male and female), on the freedoms and wellbeing of US male-to-female (MTF) 'inmates'. Their chapter describes the ways that Western culture is informed by the conventional view that there is a link between biology and gender identity and transgender persons are oppressed because they disrupt this view.

Inverting the status quo requires *recovering the historical memory* of liberation approaches of the past that have been obscured by dominant systems and discourses, as illustrated by Tayo Afuape and Taiwo Afuape's chapter about psychoanalysis' history of radical discourse.

Community and solidarity

Geraldine Moane highlights the importance of developing a social analysis in a community, as well as the centrality of community to wellbeing. Angela Byrne and Jane Tungana's chapter movingly demonstrates the power of community; and as described by Amelia Horgan, the power of dialoguing with other women about our lives. All the chapters describe the importance of community, as resources are best nurtured by multiple people rather than a single voice, challenging the notion of the self-sufficient individual solely responsible for their wellbeing.

However, it could be argued that it is not *community* per se that is important; *community* is also where much abuse, violence and harm takes place, and where people can feel compelled to live by oppressive values. What seems to be enhancing of wellbeing is a dialogical community – one which supports different views and within which solidarity can be built.

It is clear from these chapters that wellbeing happens in our relationships, embedded in the different communities to which we belong, not in our minds. In Ornette's chapter OB started recording new lyrics based on 'love'; in this sense, 'holdin' on' seemed to both speak to *resistance* and 'holdin' on' *to someone else*. A common theme among the group of young offenders was that thinking about their families changed them from seeing themselves as reluctant victims of street violence to human agents 'able to make choices'. In the chapter by Gillian Hughes and Taiwo Afuape, young 'gang-affected' people talked about gangs, albeit at times dangerous, being 'like a family' that offered them opportunities, at times criminal, to challenge marginalisation. Rather than reinforcing stereotypes that young people need punishment, management or treatment, we followed their lead and drew on their creativity, and in the process they discovered a different type of family offering them opportunities to use a fuller, and more enabling, range of abilities and skills.

When Cristian Peña was asked by Redress to prepare Mr Garcia psychologically for the human rights hearing in Medellin, Colombia, and 'prevent re-traumatisation', his intervention was not intrapsychic but relational, collective and political; Cristian joined Mr Garcia in his outrage and protest, connected him to a responsive community and committed himself to being alongside him as he sought, and won, social justice.

Geraldine Moane asks what the role of solidarity and compassion is in liberation practices, and we (as editors) have come to realise how centrally important these ideas are. The solidarity between the women in the Re:Assure group, described in Angela Byrne and Jane Tungana's chapter, appeared to be extraordinarily powerful and uniting – for one woman, even stronger than family ties. The special relationship that Cristian Peña developed with Mr Garcia and his wife supported Mr Garcia in the international courts, after forty years of waiting. It is this solidarity and compassion that motivates Nsimire Bisimwa in her work with the Congolese community to answer calls at the weekend from families in distress, or meet people outside of work to talk about how services might be helpful to them. For all of us, it is solidarity and compassion that leads us to stretch the boundaries of our working day into evenings and weekends in order to fit with the schedules needed for effective work with communities. Although this work can be demanding at times, the solidarity we gain in turn from those we work with is the reward.

At times this work takes courage, to step out of the expected boundaries of our professional roles. We also have ethical responsibilities to ensure that we as practitioners are critically conscious of our positions, to ensure we are attending to our own 'conscientization'. The chapter by Dzifa Afonu, Katarina Kovacova and Abbie Unwin showed what was possible as trainee clinical psychologists on placement, despite the additional barriers facing them as trainees, when trying to take a liberation approach. They explored issues of power and the position of trainees in their training institutions, within the teams in which they work and within the profession as a whole. They suggest ways in which qualified psychologists and educators such as tutors and supervisors can act as gatekeepers to the profession and the development of liberation practices, as well as connecting to allies and embodying their own personal ethics. They demonstrate, what each chapter explores, that this work is certainly possible – whatever your place in an organisation.

This book suggests that perhaps we need a 'dialogical revolution', which not only centralises the significance of dialogue to wellbeing but extends our understanding of what constitutes 'politics', 'social action' and 'liberation' to include not just what happens in the abstract world of law and policy mediated by those who already have much social capital and power, but also what happens in the relationships and communities of everyday people's lives. This would shift the commonly held view of the political person and social actor, being an educated articulate (and often White and male) orator; to the 'youth', 'elder', the person who is stigmatised and voiced over, and who has experienced, survived and still suffers adversity. In her chapter about working with elders, Maria Castro highlights the ways that liberatory praxis unhelpfully gets associated with high levels of activity, activism and youth, which serves to both underestimate and overshadow the issues facing older people, and their abilities and responses in the face of oppression. In their chapter Gillian Hughes and Taiwo Afuape demonstrate the ways in which marginalised young people who are commonly viewed as either perpetrators or victims of their circumstances, often use creative ways of challenging oppression. A wider more inclusive view of 'liberation practices' helps us reflect on the people who we underestimate and often do not think of as 'activists'; those who make a difference and those we can be inspired by.

Note

1 Parker (1999) argues: 'the word "empowerment" betrays something of the position of the expert who thinks that they have been able to move an enlightened step beyond "helping" people but cannot give up the idea that it is possible to bend down to lift someone lesser than themselves up a step' (pp. 9–10).

References

Afuape, T. (2011). *Power, resistance and liberation in therapy with survivors of trauma: To have our hearts broken.* London: Routledge.

Aldarando, E. (Ed.) (2007). *Promoting social justice through mental health practice.* Florence, KY: Lawrence Erlbaum Associates.

Bulhan, H. (1985). *Frantz Fanon and the psychology of oppression.* New York: Plenum Press.

Burman, E. (2008). *Deconstructing developmental psychology* (revised 2nd ed.). London: Brunner-Routledge.

Cohen, L.E. (2011). Bakhtin's carnival and pretend role play: A comparison of social contexts. *American Journal of Play, 4*(2), 176–203.

Dawes, A. (2001). Psychologies for liberation: Views from elsewhere. In D.J. Christie, R.V. Wagner & D. Du Nann Winter (Eds), *Peace, conflict, and violence: Peace psychology for the 21st century* (pp. 295–306). Englewood Cliffs, NJ: Prentice-Hall.

Fine, M. (2006). Bearing witness: Methods for researching oppression and resistance. A textbook for critical research. *Social Justice Research, 19*(1), 83–108.

Foucault, M. (1982). The subject and power. In H. Dreyfus & P. Rabinow (Eds), *Michael Foucault: Beyond structuralism and hermeneutics* (pp. 208–228). New York: Harvester Wheatsheaf.

Freire, P. (1973). *Pedagogy of the oppressed.* New York: Seabury Press.

Gilbert, M., & Orlans, V. (2010). *Integrative psychotherapy: 100 key points and techniques.* London: Routledge.

Goodman, R.D., & Gorski, P.C. (2015). *Decolonizing 'multicultural' counseling through social justice.* New York: Springer.

Goodman, L.A., Liang, B., Helms, J., Latta, R., Sparks, E. & Weintraub, S. (2004). Training counseling psychologists as social justice agents: Feminist and multicultural principles in action. *The Counseling Psychologist, 32*, 793–837.

Greene, S. (2004). *The psychological development of girls and women: Rethinking change with time.* London: Routledge.

Johnston, C., & Freedman, H.L. (2014). *Praeger handbook of social justice and psychology*, Vols 1–3. Santa Barbara, CA: Praeger.

Kagan, C., Burton, M., Duckett, P., Lawthom, R. & Siddiquee, A. (2011). *Critical community psychology.* Chichester: Wiley-Blackwell.

Lykes, M.B., & Moane, G. (Eds) (2009). Feminist liberation psychology. Special issue. *Feminism & Psychology, 19*, 283–97.

Martín Baró, I. (1994). *Writings for a liberation psychology.* Cambridge, MA: Harvard University Press.

Moane, G. (1996). Legacies of colonialism for Irish women: Oppressive or empowering? *Irish Journal of Feminist Studies, 1*(1), 100–18.

Moane, G. (2003). Bridging the personal and the political: Practices for a liberation psychology. *American Journal of Community Psychology, 31*(1/2), 91–101.

Moane, G. (2010). Sociopolitical development and political activism: Synergies beween feminist and liberation psychology. *Psychology of Women Quarterly, 34*(4), 521–9.

Moane, G. (2011). *Gender and colonialism: A psychological analysis of oppression and liberation* (1st ed. 1999). Basingstoke: Palgrave Macmillan.

Montero, M., & Sonn, C.C. (Eds) (2009). *Psychology of liberation, theory and applications.* New York: Springer.

Murray. M. (2014). *Critical health psychology.* Basingstoke: Palgrave Macmillan.

Nelson, G., & Prilleltensky, I. (2010). *Community psychology: In pursuit of liberation and wellbeing.* Basingstoke: Palgrave Macmillan.

Orford, J. (2008) *Community psychology: Challenges, controversies and emerging consensus*. Chichester: Wiley & Sons.
Parker, I. (ed.) (1999). *Deconstructing psychotherapy*. London: Sage Publications.
Reason, P., & Bradbury, H. (2008) *The SAGE handbook of action research: Participative inquiry and practice* (2nd ed.). London: Sage Publications.
Rosado, R.Q. (2007). *Consciousness-in-action: Toward an integral psychology of liberation and transformation*. Caguas, Puerto Rico: Ile publications.
Ruth, S. (2006). *Leadership and liberation: A psychological approach*. London: Routledge.
Rutherford, A., Capdevila, R., Undurti, V. & Palmary, I. (Eds) (2011). *Handbook of international feminisms: Perspectives on psychology, women, culture, and rights*. New York: Springer.
Teo, T. (2005). *The critique of psychology: From Kant to postcolonial theory*. New York: Springer.
Ussher, J. (2014). *The madness of women: Myth and experience*. London: Routledge.
Watkins, M., & Shulman, H. (2008). *Towards psychologies of liberation*. Basingstoke: Palgrave Macmillan.
Watts, R., & Serrano Garcia, I. (Eds) (2003). Towards a community psychology of liberation. Special Issue, *American Journal of Community Psychology*, *31*: 73–203.
Wilkinson, R., & Pickett, K. (2009). *The spirit level: Why equal societies almost always do better*. London: Allen Lane.
World Health Organization (2009). *Mental health, resilience and inequalities*. Copenhagen: World Health Organization Regional Office for Europe.

INDEX

Page numbers in **bold** denote figures.

Abbott-Chapman, J. 133, 134
action research *see* participatory action research (PAR)
activists/activism 3, 4, 13–14, 18, 30, 31, 44, 45, 78, 84, 127, 176, 178, 196, 237
Adichie, C.N. 106
Afonu, D. 187–98, 229, 237
Afuape, Taiwo 9–16, 23–4, 27–34, 37–42, 64–77, 107–10, 143, 162–73, 190, 199–210, 229, 230, 231–7
Afuape, Tayo 199–210, 231, 232, 235
ageing: myth and 'counter-myths' 131–2; social construction of 128–32
ageism 129
agency 45, 93, 112, 205, 235
Aggleton, P. 116
Ailey, Baldwin, Floyd, Killens, and Mayfield (Angelou) 108–9
Ain't I a Woman? (hooks) 13
Akala 70–1, 109
Alarcon, L. 53, 58
Alarcon, R.D. 37
Aldarando, E. 225, 229
Alexander, M. 140
alienation 30, 66, 165
Allende, S. 174, 176, 179, 180
Allsopp, J. 97
alternative identity projects 91
Alternative Socialism group 215
Alzheimer's Society (AS) 134
American Committee on Africa 14

Anand, Y.P. 14
Anderson, H. 169
Anderson, J.L. 13
Andreski, P.M. 131
androgynous people 208
Angelou, M.: *Ailey, Baldwin, Floyd, Killens, and Mayfield* 108–9
anti-Semitism 201, 202, 204
apartheid 13
Argyle, M. 215, 218
Aron, L. 202
assimilation, cultural 38
Asylum Aid 90
asylum-seekers/refugees 3, 4, 151–61, 229; and domestic violence 157–9; language barrier 156; women with HIV 3, 114–26; young 2, 89–99, 235
Attride-Stirling, J. 54
Azibo, D. 27
Azikewe, N. 14

baby-boomers 129
Bakhtin, M. 91, 92, 96, 235
Bar-Tal, D. 56
Barker, M. 84
Battle, M.J. 27
Baudrillard, J. 112n5, 112n8
Bay, M. 29
Baylav, A. 156
Bazwan, Z. 71
BBC 213

Beck, P.A. 141
behaviourism 214–15
Bello, W. 175
belonging 65, 89, 91, 121, 159, 225, 231
Beloved (Morrison) 13
Bennett, A.: *The History Boys* 13
Bennett, E. 42
Bhaskar, R. 219n1
Biko, B.S. 27
Bion, W.R. 202
Bisimwa, N.A. 151–61, 229, 235, 236
Black liberation theologies 27–8
Black liberation theory 28–30
Black masculinity 12
Black and minority ethnic (BME) communities 4, 40, 65–6, 129, 152, 229; *see also* gang-affected young people
Blackley Leisure Integration Scheme (BLISS) 216
Blackness 105–6, 202
Boal, A. 172n5
Boff, I. and Boff, C. 27
Bohan, J.S. 79
Bond, S. 15, 22
boundaries 4, 164, 165; stepping out of professional 236–7
Bourdieu, P. 105, 112n7
Bowcott, O. 182
Boyarin, D. 202
Boyle, M. 44
Bradbury, H. 226
Bradley, E. 106–7
Brinton Lykes, M. 37
Brookfield, S. 134
Buckles, D.J. 182
Buddhism, socially engaged 28
Bulhan, H. 226
Bulmer, D. 40
Burck, C. 156
Burman, E. 226
Burns, J. 80
Burton, M. 41, 82, 112n4, 158, 188, 211–21, 226, 230, 231
Butler, J. 62n3, 86, 143
Byne, W. 78
Byrne, A. 40, 114–26, 229, 230, 232, 233, 236
Bytheway, B. 128

Calhoun, L.G. 89
Capdevila, R. 225
capitalism 3, 38, 130, 132
Carbado, D.W. 14
care provision: by elders 131–2; for elders 132, 133

care, self- 196
Carey, A. 215–16
Carless, D. 53
Carmichael, S. 13
carnival 92–3, 235
Castro, M. 166, 237
Catholic liberation theology 30
Cathy Come Home (TV drama) 213
Centre for Crime and Justice Studies 66
Chan, M.Y. 133
Chase, E. 97
Chevalier, J.M. 182
childcare, elders and 131–2
Children Act (1989) 89
Children of the Storm group 90
Chile 174–6
Christian liberation theologies 27–8, 30
citizenship 137
Civil Rights Movement 13, 14
Civilization and its Discontents (Freud) 200
Clayton, S. 89–99, 229, 230, 232, 235
Clennon, O. 51–63, 104–6, 230, 234, 236
closure, personal 21–2
cognitive behavioural therapy (CBT) 80, 189
Cohen, L.E. 92–3, 235
Cohen-Kettenis, P.T. 79
Cole, L. 68
collective consciousness 200–1
collective interventions 39
collective processes 231
collective self-care 196
colonisation/colonialism 37–8, 40, 91, 129, 152
Colonizer and the Colonized, The (Memmi) 37
Comaz-Diaz, l. 37
Combs, G. 165
Committee to Support South African Resistance 14
community 6, 18, 159, 230, 231, 236–7; dialogical 236; elders and 133–4
Community Care Act (1975) 136
community psychology 39, 219, 225, 228, 230
compassion 236–7
Cone, J.H. 27, 202
Connell, R.W. 56, 57
concientización (concientization) 4, 30, 32, 39, 42, 82, 179, 180, 181, 193, 200–1, 237; elders 132, 135, 136, 137; and teaching liberation psychology 164, 165, 166; transgender individuals 143; young offenders 53, 58, 59, 60, 61; *see also* critical consciousness

context 1, 17, 23, 42, 154, 157, 159–60, 188; *see also* social context
Coordinated Management of Meaning (CMM) 2, 41, **43**, 152, 154, 157, **158**, 159, 160
Costall, A. 215
counselling psychology 225, 226, 230
Cox, R. 189
creative writing 52, 55–6, 97
creativity/creative media 6, 12–13, 230, 233–4, 234–5; and gang-affected young people 67–75; and resistance 107–10; and young asylum-seekers/refugees 89–99; and young offenders 1, 51–61; *see also* creative writing; filmmaking; music technology interventions
Crenshaw, K. 115
critical consciousness 30, 115, 154, 157, 160, 164, 165, 168, 188, 195, 200, 201, 226, 232; *see also concientización* (conscientization)
critical self-reflection 196
critical thinking 164, 167, 180, 188, 189
Cronen, V. 41, 152, 154, 157
Csikszentmihalyi, M. and Csikszentmihalyi, I. 53
Cuba 214
cultural assimilation 38
cultural identity 1–2

Dabashi, H. 28
Darling, F.F. 217
Dawes, A. 225
Daymon, C. 54
De Oliveira, C. 133
de Vries, A.L. 79
de-ideologising everyday experiences 32, 96, 167, 200
decolonisation 37
deconstruction 202
defetishisation 53, 59, 61
dehumanisation 45
Deleule, D. 38
Democratic Republic of Congo (DRC) 13
Denborough, D. 167, 178
depression, transgender prisoners 142
depth psychology 228
Derrida, J. 202
developmental psychology 226
di Ceglie, D. 80
diagnosis 194
dialogical community 236
dialogue 91, 154, 169–71, 181, 233, 234; and education 164; gender non-conforming services 81, 84; as mutual interchange 168; and teaching liberation psychology 166; true 31, 154, 166, 171, 233, 234
Diener, E. 133
dignity, elders 132, 133
Dikanda, P. 71
disability 5
discrimination 40, 66, 226; gender non-conforming young people 83, 85; HIV-related 115–16, 123–4
discursive psychology 194–5, 197n11
distress, and social injustice 4
Dodds, C. 115, 116
domestic violence 157–9
dominant knowledges 29
domination 9, 34, 228
Doreleijers, T.A. 79
Douglas, K. 53
Douglass, F. 14
Drescher, J. 78
Driver, E.D. 29
Du Bois, W.E.B. 1, 28–9; *The Philadelphia Negro* 29; *The Souls of Black Folks* 29; *The World and Africa* 29
Duckett, P. 41, 212, 226
Duran, B. 54
Dyrness, W.A. 27

Eades, C. 66
ecological edge 214, 217–18
ecology 5, 217–18
Edge, I. 211, 214
edge, the inhabiting and working with 214–17, 218
education 30, 226; banking concept of 163, 164, 194; as dialogical 164; emancipatory 162–3; and oppression 163–4
Education as the Practice of Freedom (Freire) 31
efficiency, discourse of 21
Ekdawi, I. 22, 42
elders 3, 127–39, 237; Black and minority ethic 129; care of 132, 133; as care providers 131–2; and community 133–4; contexts of oppression 129–30; dignity 132, 133; end of life decisions 132; human rights 132, 133; independence 132, 133; LGBTQ 129; marginalisation of 132; memory problems 131, 134; participative action research (PAR) 136–7; peer-run groups 134; personal and collective wellbeing 33–4; political participation 130; power 132; self-fulfilment 132, 133; and social transformation 136–7; socioeconomic concerns 130; voluntary work 131, 132, 134

emancipatory education 162–3
empathy 166, 204
empowerment 3, 46, 226, 237n1
Ending Gang and Youth Violence report (2012) 64
Engels, F. 112n7
epistemology 31, 32
Epston, D. 91, 143, 163, 177
equality 40, 231
Equality Act (2010) 79
Equality Trust 132
ethical commitment to social justice 166
ethnicity 227
ethnocentrism 226
evidence-based models 189
expertise 4
externalising discourses 169

Fals Borda, O. 176, 182
false consciousness 112n7
family 59, 60
Fanon, F. 1, 28, 29–30, 178, 207
farming, family and therapy model 193–4
Farr, R. 215
Fatimilehin, I. 44
Fausto-Sterling, A. 85
femininity 85, 86
feminism 5, 40, 228
feminist liberation theologies 28
feminist psychology 228
Fender 2–3, 103–4, 107, 108, 109
Fenichel, O. 205
Ferenczi, S. 204
filmmaking 2, 67, 68–70, 72–5, 230, 234; young asylum-seekers/refugees 94–7, 98
Fine, C. 85
Fine, M. 226
fishbowl method 73, 77n3
Flores Osorio, J.M. 211, 219
Foucault, M. 21, 29, 38, 123, 233
Frankfurt School 215
fratriarchy 57–8
Fredman, G. 15, 22, 176
Freedman, D. 80
Freedman, H.L. 225
Freedman, J. 165
Freedman, V.A. 132
Freire, P. 1, 30–1, 32, 37, 66, 162, 163, 169, 172n2, 176, 215, 232; banking concept of education 163, 164, 194; *concientización* (conscientization) 39, 42, 53, 132, 164, 181, 188, 193; dialogue 30–1, 154, 168, 171, 181, 233; reflection and action 31, 166; *Education as the Practice of Freedom* 31; *Pedagogy of the Oppressed* 30, 31

Freud, S. 200–5, 206, 207, 208; *Civilization and its Discontents* 200; *Totem and Taboo* 201
Frosh, S. 112n11

Gandhi, M.K. 13–14, 28
gang-affected young people 2, 64–77, 236
Garcia, L. 174–84, 229, 230, 236
Gay, P. 201
Gaztambide, D.J. 202, 204, 206
gender 12, 85, 227; *see also* gender non-conforming young people; transgender individuals
gender binary 143–4, 235
Gender and Colonialism (Moane) 40
gender non-conforming young people 2, 78–88; and biomedical causal model 85; clinical service 79–81; and dialogue 81, 84; and discrimination 83, 85; human rights 83, 85; liberation psychology approach for 82–6; oppression of 78, 85; physical interventions 80–1, 85–6; and social action 83–4; and social context 85; 'stealth' identity 80; stigmatisation and shaming of 78, 79
Gergen, K.J. 137n1, 165
Gibbons, S. 42
Gilbert, M. 226
Gilman, S.L. 202
Giroux, H. 29
Glenn, L. 216
globalisation 38, 40
Goerres, A. 130
Goffman, E. 79
Goldblum, P. 79
Goldner, V. 85
Goodman, L.A. 226
Goodman, R.D. 225
Google 67, 68, 73, 75, 76
Gorman, W. 178
Gorski, P.C. 226
Gott, R. 176
government, influencing 159–60
Gramsci, A. 215
Grandparents plus 132
green care 193–4, 197n10
Green, D.S. 29
Greene, S. 226
grime culture 192
Grimshaw, R. 66
Guevara, E.C. 13, 171
Gurr, R. 178
Gutiérrez, G. 27

Hagan, T. 189
Haley, A.: *Roots* 10
Hall, S. 59, 215
Hamedullah: The Road Home (film) 96–7, 98
Hárdi, L. 178
Hardy, K.V. 151
Harper, D. 44–5
Harré, R. 215
Harris, A. 85
Hassan, A. 21–2
Hays, D.G. 79
health psychology 225
heart 171, 190
Heffernan, K. 178
hegemonic masculinity 1, 3, 56–8, 60, 234
helplessness 82
Herman, J.L. 178
Herzog, A.R. 133
Higgs, P. 130
Hildebrand, P. 131
Hindu liberation theology 28
Hine, R. 197n9
hip-hop music 104–5, 107, 108, 109, 192
Hip-Hop Shakespeare Company 70, 109
historical context: and elder community 129
historical memory 9, 32, 45, 58–9, 61, 62n4, 83, 91, 93, 94, 134, 158, 159, 171, 235
History Boys, The (Bennett) 13
Hitler, A. 201
HIV/AIDS 3, 114–26; HIV family 3, 121–3, 125; stigmatisation and discrimination 115–16, 123–4, 125; transgender prisoners 141
Holder, R. 156
Holland, S. 19, 39–40, 44, 66, 114, 117, 118, 160
Hollander, N.C. 205
Holloway, E.L. 189
Holloway, I. 54
Holmes, G. 190–1, 193
homophobia 57, 105, 108, 116, 129, 204
homosexuality 57, 204; biomedical explanation of 85; *see also* LGBTQ
hooks, b. 17, 22, 29, 163, 164, 165; *Ain't I a Woman?* 13
Hopkins, D.N. 27
Horgan, A. 110–12, 236
Hsieh, Y. 133
Hughes, G. 15, 16–24, 27–34, 37–42, 64–77, 89–99, 151–61, 229, 230, 231–7
human rights 40, 231; elders 132, 133; gender non-conforming young people 83, 85
hyper-masculinity 105, 108

Iantaffi, A. 84
identity 18, 89, 91, 159; cultural 1–2; elder 128; gender 85–6 (*see also* gender non-conforming young people); personal 1–2; professional, and dominant discourses 164
ideology 211; *see also* de-ideologising everyday experience
immigration, Commonwealth 129
imperialism 153
independence, elders 132, 133
individual learning programmes (ILPs) 52
individualism 153, 226
industrialisation 3, 132
inequality, social 66, 226
inferiority, sense of 82
Instagram 107
Institute for Contemporary Cultural Studies 215
Institute for Race Relations 65
institutional racism 29, 226
integrative psychology 228
Inter-American Human Rights Court 4, 174
International Journal of Human Rights, The 40
internet 67, 68
intersectionality 115
Islamic liberation theology 28

Jacobson, E. 205
Jacoby, R. 205
Jewish liberation theology 28
Jews 201, 202
Johnson, E.A. 28
Johnson, J. 128
Johnston, C. 225
Jones, R. 68, 73
Jung, C. 204
justice 40, 231; legal 46–7, 231, 233; social 82, 166, 211, 212–14, 218, 226, 227, 228, 230

Kagan, C. 41, 82, 112n4, 211–21, 226, 228, 230, 231
Kao, S. 133
Kaur, P. 93
Kee, Y. 133
Kelly, A. 70
Kelvin, P. 215
Kier, A. 19
King, M.L., Jr. 14, 27
King, S.B. 28
Király, G. 178
knowledge(s): dominant 29; and power 38; subjugated 29; true 31

Kovacova, K. 187–98, 229, 237
Kovács, E. 178
Kvifte, T. 112n9
Kyezu, N. 67

Lakatos, I. 215
Lane, H. 218
Lang, P. 155
Langer, E. 138n6
Langer, M. 205, 207
language 58; and elder identity 128
language barrier 156
Laszloffy, T.A. 151
Lawrence, S. 9
Lawthorn, R. 41, 212, 226
learning 30–1
learning communities 169
legal justice 46–7, 231, 233
Lenihan, P. 84
Levy, B. 138
LGBTQ 229; elder community 129; *see also* homosexuality; transgender individuals
liberation 33–4, 89, 165, 226, 231, 232, 233, 237; as an agenda 45, 46; cycle of 118; defined 33; social 5
liberation practices 1; core values of 41; historical development of 27–33; key players in shaping, UK and Ireland 39–41; proposed framework for 41–3; relevance today 33
liberation praxis 1, 3, 4, 166
liberation psychology 1, 27; as broad set of beliefs 46; end point of 46; as problematic concept 45
Liberation Psychology Network (libpsy) 41
liberation theologies 27–8, 30
Lima-Costa, M.F. 133
Lindner, R. 205
literacy 30
Loach, K.: *Cathy Come Home* 213
Lorde, A. 196; *Sister Outsider* 13
Louh, M.-C. 133
love 171
Lu, L. 133
Lumumba, P. 13
Lykes, M.B. 82, 226, 228

McAdam, E. 155
McCarthy, E. 227
McCarthy, I.C. 9
Macedo, D. 30
Macinko, J. 133
McIntosh, P. 195
MacKean, R. 133, 134
McLaren, P. 30

Macmillan, L. 45, 178
McPherson, S. 80
Madsen, W.C. 164, 169
Malcolm X 13
Maldonado, J. 53, 58
Mandela, N. 13, 14
Mangan, J. (Joyce) 127, 135–6, 137
Manton, K. 131
Map of Me 53–4, **61**
marginalisation, of elders 132
market, and cultural oppression 104–5
Marlo, J. 176
Marmot, M. 133
Martín Baró, I. 1, 20, 27, 31–3, 38, 39, 41, 45, 52, 66, 82, 83, 85, 87n1, 97, 112n12, 117, 127–8, 131, 153, 162, 175, 181, 188, 191, 196, 214, 219, 228, 232, 233; critical consciousness 154, 157, 165, 200–1; de-ideologising everyday experiences 32, 96; *realismo-crítico* 212; recovery of historical memory 32, 45, 64n4, 83, 91, 93, 94, 98, 134, 158, 159; utilising people's virtues 32, 135
Martin, L.G. 131, 132
Marxism 5, 215
masculinity 54, 55, 85, 86; Black 12; hegemonic 1, 3, 56–8, 60, 234; hyper- 105, 108; and prison inmates 56, 57; progressive 12
medical model 189, 194
Melluish, S. 40
Memmi, A. 207; *The Colonizer and the Colonized* 37
Memoria Chilena 175
memory, historical *see* historical memory
memory problems, elders 131, 134
Men's Advice Network (MAN) 40
Mental Capacity Act (2005) 131, 137n4
mental health services 234; limitations of 152, 153
Merriam, S.B. 133
Messerschmidt, J.W. 56
migrant women, with HIV 3, 114–16
Miller, A. 44
mind maps 53–4, **61**
mind–heart divide 4
mis-recognition 105
misogyny 105, 108, 112, 116
Moane, G. 18, 29, 30, 34, 37, 40, 66, 82, 91, 118, 225–31, 226, 228, 233, 234, 236; *Gender and Colonialism* 40
modernist scientific discourses 153
Mollinson, B. 217
monologic discourse 91

Montero, M. 31, 39, 53, 135, 136, 137, 143, 188, 219, 226, 228
Moreno, J.L. 218
Morrison, T., *Beloved* 13
Motherson, K. 215
Mudarikiri, M. 21
Muratoi, M.C. 189
Murphy, R. 71
Murray, M. 225
Murray, W.H. 24
music, hip-hop 104–5, 107, 108, 109, 192
music technology interventions 2–3, 103–4, 230; gang-affected young people 2, 70–1; young offenders 1, 51–61, 234–5

Naphtali, T. 19
narrative practice 22–3, 91, 93–7, 154, 159, 177; with transgender prisoners 143–6
narrative 're-storying' 94
National Health Service (NHS) 129, 159, 169, 189
nature 16
Ncube, N. 94
Nelson, G. 188, 199, 226, 228
neo-colonialism 38
neutrality 4, 164–5, 166
Newham Making Waves project 19, 92
Newnes, C. 189
Newton, C. 56, 57
Ngewa, S. 27
Nhat Hạhn, T. 28
Nkrumah, K. 14, 38
norms 21, 38
Nylund, D. 140–8, 230, 232, 233, 235

older generations *see* elders
oppression 9, 15–16, 31, 32, 38, 39, 40, 41, 45, 46, 82, 211, 232, 233; cultural, and the market 104–5; and education 163–4; elder 129–30; of gender non-conforming young people 78, 85; and professional discourses and identities 164–5; resistance to 10, 11, 12–14, 39, 91; and social context 115–17; socioeconomic 130
Orford, J. 19, 82, 225
Orlans, V. 226
Osorlo, F. 176
Other/otherness 203, 207
outsider witness practices 95–6, 98, 135, 138n8

Palmary, I. 225
Palmer, P. 165
Parker, I. 235, 237n1
Parker, R. 116

participation 233–4; elders 132, 133; *see also* political participation
participatory action research (PAR) 182, 192–3; elders 136–7
Partridge, K. 15
Patel, N. 15, 40, 42, 43–7, 118, 177, 189, 197, 231, 233, 234
Paton, K. 215
Pattman, R. 112n11
peace psychology 225, 230
Pearce, B. 41, 42, 152, 154, 157
Pedagogy of the Oppressed (Freire) 30, 31
Peek, C. 140, 141
Peirson, L. 188
Peña, C. 174–84, 229, 230, 232, 233, 235, 236
perfection, commercialisation of 106–7
performativity 62n3
Perry, G. 232
personal closure 21–2
personal identity 1–2
Phelan, A. 128
Philadelphia Negro, The (Du Bois) 29
Phillipson, C. 130, 132
Phipps, M. 72
Phoenix, A. 112n11
Physicians for Human Rights 178
Pickett, K. 181, 226
Pinochet, A. 174
Pinterest 107
political participation, elders 130
popular culture 1, 104
Positive East 114, 124
positivism 22, 29
poverty 5, 38, 66, 115, 213, 226, 227, 229; elder 130
power 45, 46, 62n3, 89, 229, 230, 231, 233; elder 132; and knowledge 38; modern 38, 233; relations of 82; traditional 38, 233; of trainees 189–90
prejudice 38, 226, 229
Prilleltensky, I. 132, 134, 188, 199, 226, 228
prison populations *see* transgender prisoners; young offenders
Prison Rape Elimination Act (PREA) (US) 141
privilege 38, 229, 230
professional discourses, oppressive 164–5
Project Phakama 92, 93
Prosser, J. 87
psyche 206–7, 231
psychoanalysis 5, 199–210, 235

quality of life 132, 133
Quiroga, J. 178

Rachman, A.W. 204
racism 10, 12, 17, 66, 75, 115, 116, 129, 204, 213; institutional 29, 226; structural 29, 202
radio skills 19, 20
rape, prison 141–2
rapper tag concept 2–3, 103, 107, 112n1
Raschini, S. 214
Re:Assure Women's Project 3, 114, 117–26, 236
re-membering practices 171
realismo-crítico 212
Reason, P. 226
Red Rat Collective 215
Reder, P. 176
Redress 4, 174, 182, 236
reflection 30–1, 32
reflective practice 189
refugees *see* asylum-seekers/refugees
Refusing to be a Man (Stoltenberg) 13
Reich, A. 205
Remy, J. 57
reparation 46–7, 231, 233
resilience 135
resistance 54–5, 117, 152; collective self-care as 196; and creativity 107–10; everyday acts of 188, 197; living and loving as, HIV-affected women 124–6; to change 136–7; to oppression 10, 11, 12–14, 39, 91; women and 110–12, 124–6
Reynolds, V. 196
Richards, C. 84
Rivera, E.T. 53, 58
Robeson, P.L. 13
Roen, K. 85
Romero, M.C. 127–39, 162–73, 229, 230
Roots (Haley) 10
Rosado, R.Q. 226, 228
Rosenblum, D. 142
Ruether, R.R. 28
Russell, G.M. 79
Rustin, B. 14
Ruth, S. 226
Rutherford, A. 225

Sahyoun Bowie, N. 175
Salberg, J. 202
Salusbury World group 90
Sargeant, W. 113n16
Schoeni, R.F. 131, 132
Schulman, H. 188
scientific rationalism 22
Secord, P.F. 215
Seedat, M. 19
Segal, L. 57

segregation, racist 13
self-care, collective 196
self-determination 152
self-fulfilment, elders 132, 133
self-referral 118–19
Sempik, J. 197n9
sex reassignment surgery (SRS) 141, 147n3
sexism 5, 33, 75, 226
sexual abuse, transgender prisoners 141–2
sexual orientation 28, 227; *see also* homosexuality; LGBTQ; transgender individuals
sexuality 12, 228
shaming, of gender non-conforming young people 78
Shaw, M. 27
Shulman, H. 228
Siddiquee, A. 41, 212, 226
Silvestri, A. 66
Singh, A.A. 79
Sister Outsider (Lorde) 13
Sivaraksa, S. 28
slavery 9, 10, 58
Smail, D. 19, 188
Smith, E. 177
social action 31, 32, 46, 160, 181, 237; and gender non-conforming young people 83–4
social action psychotherapy 39–40, 114, 160
social analysis 229–30
social attitudes, influencing 159–60
social context: and gender non-conforming individuals 85; and oppression 115–17
social exclusion 44, 74, 82, 116, 213, 214, 229
social inequality 66, 226
social injustice 4, 181, 226
social interventions 39
social justice 82, 166, 211, 212–14, 218, 226, 227, 228, 230
social liberation 5
social materialism, theory of 188
social media 2, 67, 107, 230
social mobility 226
social psychology 5, 215, 219, 225–6
social transformation 38, 41, 136–7, 226
socially engaged Buddhism 28
socioeconomic oppression 130; *see also* poverty
solidarity 3, 6, 15, 18, 28, 39, 45, 135, 196, 236–7
Solomon, E. 66
Sonic (db) Music Technology Project 51–61
Sonn, C.C. 39, 143, 226, 228

Souls of Black Folks, The (Du Bois) 29
South African apartheid 13
Starr, K. 202
Steensma, T.D. 79
stewardship 217–18
Stewart, A. 214
stigmatisation: of gender non-conforming young people 78, 79; HIV-related 115–16, 123–4, 125; of Jews 202; LGBTQ 129
Stoltenberg, J.: *Refusing to be a Man* 13
structural racism 29, 202
subjugated knowledges 29
suicide attempts, transgender prisoners 142
supervisory relationships 190
Swaab, H. 79
Sykes, G.M. 56
systemic therapy 22
systems theory 227
Sziklai, A. 204

Tacconelli, E. 80
Tahati, B. 70
Tavistock Child and Family Refugee Service 4, 65, 91, 151, 152, 154–9, 160
teaching liberation psychology 164; implications of 169–71; key ideas in 165–6 (conscientization 166; dialogical approach 166, 169–71; ethical commitment to social justice 166); process of 166–9 (changing the context 168–9; de-ideologising everyday reality 167; utilising trainees' values 167–8)
Tedeschi, R.G. 89
Teo, T. 226
Tew, J. 18
Theatre of the Oppressed (TO) 168, 172n5
theology, liberation 27–8, 30
theoretical psychology 226
Third World liberation theologies 27
Tibbles, A.H. 14
Tienou, T. 27
time 21
Todd, N.R. 27
token economies 213
Tolstoy, L. 13–14
Tomm, K. 165, 171
torture survivors 4, 40, 174–83
Totem and Taboo (Freud) 201
trainee clinical psychologists 4–5, 237; placement opportunities 190–1, 237; power of 189–90; research 191–5; supervisory relationships 190; taking a liberation approach as 187–98; utilising values of 167–8

transgender individuals 203, 208–9, 232, 235; native peoples 208; *see also* transgender prisoners
Transgender Law Center 146
transgender prisoners 3, 140–8; depression amongst 142; dress and grooming 146–7; gender identity classification of 146; genitalia-based classification of 140–1, 144; HIV/AIDS infections 141; hormonal therapy 141, 142, 146; liberation psychology 143–6; male to female (MTF) 141, 142, 235; narrative therapy 143–6; self-castration 142; sexual abuse of 141–2; suicide attempts 142
transphobia 143
Tree of Life methodology 94, 96, 98, 159
true dialogue 31, 154, 166, 171, 233, 234
true knowledge 31
Truth, S. 14
Tubman, H. 14
Tungana, J. 114–26, 229, 230, 232, 233, 236
Tutu, D. 27, 28

'Ubuntu' 3, 120–3
undecidability 202
Undurti, V. 225
United Nations Principles for Older Persons 132, 133
Unwin, A. 187–98, 229, 237
urban culture 1
Ussher, J. 226

Vaupel, J.W. 131
Velthius, O. 105
Venezuela 214
Vicaria de la Solidaridad 175
violence 38, 226, 228; domestic 157–9
Violent and Youth Crime Prevention Unit 64
virtues 32, 45, 76, 135, 167
voluntary work, elders 131, 132, 134
Von Freund, A. 204
vulnerability 22

Waddle, H. 140–8, 230, 232, 233, 235
Wade, A. 118, 188, 197
Waldegrave, C. 153
'walk and talk' groups 190–1
Walker, A. 130
Wallerstein, N.B. 54
Wallien, M.S.C. 79
Watkins, M. 188, 228
Watson, L.S. 79
Watts, R. 228
Watts, R.J. 33

Webster, A. 19
Weise, D. 14
wellbeing 4, 60–1, 226, 231; elders 133–4; and liberation 37–8; limitations of concept of 153; and social transformation 41; trainee 5
Wetherall, M. 199
'What's Our Story' (WOS) project 2, 66–76, 160, 233
White, C. 167
White, M. 17, 91, 93, 94, 95, 127, 135, 138n8, 143, 163, 169, 171, 172n7, 177
Wilcox, D. 197n9
Wilkinson, R. 181, 226
Williams, D.S. 28
willpower 188
Wills, W.D. 218
wisdom 135
Wolfensberger, W. 216
Wolleat, P.L. 189
women: asylum-seekers/refugees with HIV 3, 114–26; and commercialisation of perfection 106–7; and domestic violence 157–9; and resistance 110–12, 124–6

Women's Action for Mental Health (WAMH) group 39–40
women's liberation movement 33–4
Wood, R. 65, 66
working class 12
World Health Organization 226
World Professional Association of Transgender Health (WPATH) 141
World and Africa, The (Du Bois) 29
Wren, B. 78–87, 230, 232, 233

young offenders 1, 51–61, 234–5, 236
young people 229; asylum-seekers/refugees 2, 89–99, 235; gang-affected 2, 64–77, 236; green care 193–4; participatory action research with 192–3; *see also* gender non-conforming young people; young offenders
youth culture, commercialisation of 106
YouTube 67, 68–70, 71, 76

Zaretsky, E. 204
Zitz, C. 80

eBooks
from Taylor & Francis

Helping you to choose the right eBooks for your Library

Add to your library's digital collection today with Taylor & Francis eBooks. We have over 50,000 eBooks in the Humanities, Social Sciences, Behavioural Sciences, Built Environment and Law, from leading imprints, including Routledge, Focal Press and Psychology Press.

ORDER YOUR FREE INSTITUTIONAL TRIAL TODAY

Free Trials Available

We offer free trials to qualifying academic, corporate and government customers.

Choose from a range of subject packages or create your own!

Benefits for you
- Free MARC records
- COUNTER-compliant usage statistics
- Flexible purchase and pricing options
- 70% approx of our eBooks are now DRM-free.

Benefits for your user
- Off-site, anytime access via Athens or referring URL
- Print or copy pages or chapters
- Full content search
- Bookmark, highlight and annotate text
- Access to thousands of pages of quality research at the click of a button.

eCollections
Choose from 20 different subject eCollections, including:
- Asian Studies
- Economics
- Health Studies
- Law
- Middle East Studies

eFocus
We have 16 cutting-edge interdisciplinary collections, including:
- Development Studies
- The Environment
- Islam
- Korea
- Urban Studies

For more information, pricing enquiries or to order a free trial, please contact your local sales team:

UK/Rest of World: **online.sales@tandf.co.uk**
USA/Canada/Latin America: **e-reference@taylorandfrancis.com**
East/Southeast Asia: **martin.jack@tandf.com.sg**
India: **journalsales@tandfindia.com**

www.tandfebooks.com

To read:
Patel (2003) ('P: reinforcing inequalities of facilitating empowerment')

Induction

- feature proposed framework on p.4) + our model of ind. 4 within TAA
- hx & theory of Lib. Psy. + PTM collates other research paradigms supporting this view